ADENAUER TO KOHL

Adenauer to Kohl

The Development of the German Chancellorship

STEPHEN PADGETT (*editor*)

HEIDRUN ABROMEIT
FERDINAND MÜLLER-ROMMEL
WILLIAM E. PATERSON
GORDON SMITH
DAVID SOUTHERN
ROLAND STURM

HURST & COMPANY, LONDON

First published in the United Kingdom by
C. Hurst & Co. (Publishers) Ltd.,
38 King Street, London WC2E 8JT
© C. Hurst & Co. (Publishers) Ltd., 1994
Printed in Hong Kong

ISBNs
1–85065–129–9 (*cased*)
1–85065–134–5 (*paperback*)

PREFACE

This book is a study of the office of the German chancellorship as it has evolved under six post-war chancellors. Employing a dual focus, contributors adopt an analytical approach to identify the dimensions of the office and the determinants of its powers, combined with a chronological perspective to explain variations and trends in executive leadership from one incumbency to another. One of the central concerns of the book is to assess the explanatory value of the models which have been applied to executive leadership in the German context. Thus contributors examine the relevance of the 'chancellor democracy' model which has pervaded studies of the chancellorship since the early years of the Federal Republic. Deriving from the imperious incumbency of Konrad Adenauer, this model postulates a concentration of executive authority around the chancellorship. The contributors also evaluate the alternative model of 'coordination democracy', which casts the chancellor in a more managerial role, emphasising the diffusion of authority in a political system characterised by a pronounced degree of institutional pluralism. In large part, the development of the modern German chancellorship can be seen as a progressive transformation from the first to the second model.

The preparation of the book coincided with the historic events surrounding German unification. While unification has left the institutional apparatus of the Federal Republic largely unchanged, it has altered the political landscape in some significant ways. In a more heterogenous and conflictual polity, the burdens on executive leadership are multiplied. The chancellor acquires new roles, as a symbol of unity in a process of national integration which remains incomplete, and as a key figure in the redefinition of Germany's new national and international identity. A number of contributors address the question of whether the chancellorship is equipped with the political resources to enable the incumbent to fulfil these new roles. There is at present no comprehensive account of the chancellorship in the English-language literature on German politics. Indeed, the German literature is rather partial in its treatment of the subject. The present conjuncture of events amplifies the importance of such a study.

Contributors are drawn from the academic communities in both Britain and Germany. All of them figure among the leading exponents of the study of German politics, and apply their specialist expertise to key dimensions of the chancellorship. Collaboration was facilitated in large part by regular contact through the Association for the Study of German Politics, with which most of the contributors have close links. The rapid pace of political change has inevitably meant that the editor has been obliged to call upon contributors to update material during the preparation of this volume, and he would like to thank them for their forebearance in the face of these requests.

University of Essex   STEPHEN PADGETT
October 1993

CONTENTS

Contents   ix

TABLES

FIGURES

NOTES ON THE CONTRIBUTORS

HEIDRUN ABROMEIT is Professor of Government and Political Sociology at Duisburg University. Her main publications include *Staat und Wirtschaft: Zum Staatsverständnis der Wirtschaftsöffentlichkeit in der Bundesrepublik* (1981), *British Steel: An Industry between the State and the Private Sector* (1986) and *Der verkappte Einheitsstaat* (1992). She has also written widely on government–industry relations, business associations, public corporations and privatisation.

FERDINAND MÜLLER-ROMMEL is *Akademischer Rat* at the University of Lüneburg. He is editor of *Cabinets in Western Europe* (with Jean Blondel, 1988), *New Politics in Western Europe* (1989), *Small Parties in Western Europe* (with Geoffrey Pridham, 1990), *Vergleichende Politikwissenschaft* (with Dirk Berg-Schlosser, 1991: 2nd edn) and *Governing Together: Cabinet Decision Making in Western Europe* (with Jean Blondel, 1992). He is also author of *Grüne Parteien in Westeuropa* (1992).

STEPHEN PADGETT is Jean Monnet Senior Lecturer in European Politics, University of Essex. He has written widely on party politics, and on political economy and policy-making in the Federal Republic. He is co-author of *Political Parties and Elections in West Germany* (1986) and *A History of Social Democracy in Post War Europe* (1991). He is editor of *Parties and Party Systems in the New Germany* (1993) and co-editor of *Developments in German Politics* (1992). He is also co-editor of the journal *German Politics*, and chair of the Association for the Study of German Politics.

WILLIAM E. PATERSON is Salvesen Professor of European Institutions and Director of the Europa Institute, University of Edinburgh. His most recent co-authored books are *Government and the Chemical Industry in Britain and Germany* (1988), *Governing Germany* (1991) and *A History of Social Democracy in Post War Europe*. He is co-editor of *Developments in German Politics*, and of the journal *German Politics*. In addition to his extensive work on politics in Germany, he has also written widely on the European Community and comparative European politics. He is currently chairman of the University Association for Contemporary European Studies (UACES).

GORDON SMITH is Professor of Government, London School of Economics. He has written extensively on both comparative European and German politics. His publications include *Politics in*

Western Europe (1989), *Democracy in Western Germany* (1986) and (as co-editor) *Developments in German Politics* (1992). He is co-editor of two journals, *West European Politics* and *German Politics*.

DAVID SOUTHERN was formerly Lecturer in Politics at the University of Kent. He currently works as legal adviser to Lloyds Bank, and has written widely in professional journals on taxation law. His most recent academic work includes *Governing Germany* (1991) and articles on the constitutional framework of the new Germany.

ROLAND STURM is Professor of Political Science, Tübingen University. He has published a wide range of books and articles on German and European politics. Among his most recent publications are *Haushaltspolitik in westlichen Demokratien* (1989), *Grossbritannien* (1991), *Die Industriepolitik der Bundesländer und die Europäische Integration* (1991) and *Staatsverschuldung* (1992).

KEY TO ABBREVIATIONS

BDA   Bundesvereinigung der Deutschen Arbeitsgeberverbände
         (Federation of German Employers' Associations)

BDI   Bundesverband der Deutschen Industrie
         (Confederation of German Industry)

CAP   Common Agricultural Policy
         (of the European Community)

CDU   Christlich-Demokratische Union Deutschlands
         (Christian Democratic Union of Germany)

CSU   Christlich-Soziale Union
         (Christian Social Union)

DGB   Deutscher Gewerkschaftsbund
         (Federation of German Trade Unions)

ECU   European Currency Unit

E(E)C   European (Economic) Community

EMS   European Monetary System

FDP   Freie Demokratische Partei
         (Free Democratic Party)

FRG   Federal Republic of Germany

GDR   German Democratic Republic

GGO   Gemeinsame Geschäftsordnung der Bundesministerien
         (Common Standing Orders of the Federal Ministries)

NATO   North Atlantic Treaty Organisation

OPEC   Organisation of Petroleum Exporting Countries

ÖTV   Gewerkschaft Öffentliche Dienste, Transport und
         Verkehr
         (Public Service and Transport Workers' Union)

SDI   Strategic Defence Initiative

SEA   Single European Act

SPD   Sozialdemokratische Partei Deutschlands
         (Social Democratic Party of Germany)

Stasi   Ministerium für Staatssicherheit
         (Ministry for State Security in former GDR)

UN   United Nations

INTRODUCTION

CHANCELLORS AND THE CHANCELLORSHIP

Stephen Padgett

This volume contains an analysis of the anatomy of executive leadership in the German context. It is a study of the office of the chancellorship and of the six post-war incumbents of that office. The distinction between the chancellorship and the chancellors is an important one. It involves distinguishing between those characteristics of executive leadership which are institutionalised in the constitutional order or political system, and those which are attributable to individual incumbents or political circumstances. In most countries it is possible to observe marked variations in the exercise of executive leadership from one incumbent to another. This suggests that attempts to identify an enduring national pattern of executive leadership with its roots in the constitutional order should proceed with care. Generalisations deriving from an especially dominant chief executive can be particularly misleading.

Nevertheless, the parameters of executive leadership are established by its constitutional foundations. This volume therefore addresses the role of the chancellorship in the constitutional order and the relationship of the office to other governmental institutions. It explores the interplay between the constitutional and political dimensions: the manner in which politics conditions the exercise of the formal powers of the chancellorship. At the same time it contains a study of six chancellors and the evolution of the office during the course of their incumbencies. The approach adopted by each chapter reflects this dual focus. Contributors employ an analytical approach to identify the dimensions of the office and the determinants of its powers. This is combined with a chronological perspective, explaining changes in the exercise of executive power from one chancellor to another and relating these to changes in the wider political and social context.

The National Context of Executive Leadership

National context itself inevitably conditions perceptions of leadership. Leaders of powerful nations appear to be powerful simply by virtue of the global power and prestige which they represent. The

1

powers with which they are endowed within their own domain may
be more limited and constrained than their international prestige
suggests. The American president is a case in point. As leader of the
hegemonic global power, the president occupies the most powerful
office on the planet. Within his own domain, however, the 'institutional capacity' of the office is severely limited. Similarly, it is
important to distinguish the role of the chancellor as leader of the
most economically powerful nation in Europe from his role within
the German political system.

The modern German chancellorship reflects the paradox of the
Federal Republic itself. Endowed by its geopolitical position and
economic might with a formidable potential for power politics, the
Federal Republic remained bound by the constraints of its historical
legacy and, before unification, the disjunction between the Federal
Republic and the German nation.[1] A foreign policy of 'ostentatious
modesty'[2] was pursued through the medium of trans-national institutional structures, whilst the economic dynamism of the Federal
Republic was Europeanised through the EC.

In their leadership style, chancellors have been required to per-
sonify Germany's ambiguous nationhood. Chancellorial aggran-
disement in the manner of American presidents was restrained by
the imperative of diplomatic circumspection. Within these constraints, however, chancellors were not precluded from the exercise
of international statecraft. Adenauer's integration of the Federal
Republic into the Western alliance systems, Brandt's *Ostpolitik*
(Eastern policy), Schmidt's pursuit of European monetary integration and Kohl's *Einheitspolitik* (unity policy) are all indicative of
the capacity of chancellors for setting and realising their own
agendas in the international arena. Thus while German chancellors
are denied the enhanced prestige of identification with national
grandeur, they are fully equipped to play a formidable international
role. With unification, the scope for international leadership is
increased, although historical constraints remain.

Leadership opportunities are rather more restricted in the
domestic setting. A constitutional order characterised by institutional pluralism combines with the polycentrism of the political
system to produce a highly diffuse distribution of power. The dis-

---

1. See William E. Paterson, 'Gulliver Unbound: The Changing Context of Foreign
   Policy', in G. Smith, W.E. Paterson, B. Merkl and S.A. Padgett, *Developments
   in German Politics*, Basingstoke and London: Macmillan, 1992, pp. 137–44.
2. Carl Cavanagh Hodge, 'The Federal Republic and the Future of Europe: A
   Reassessment', *German Politics*, vol. 1, no. 2, August 1992, p. 224.

persal of power in the Federal Republic counteracts the centrality of the chancellor, reducing his capacity for imparting direction to government. Executive leadership in the domestic arena is managerial rather than directional. No German chancellor could have exercised the driving programmatic leadership characteristic of Margaret Thatcher. None has permanently shaped national political life in the manner of de Gaulle. Competent management is the height of chancellorial aspirations, and even this has sometimes proved elusive. Thus chancellors have often taken refuge from domestic politics in international affairs.

The Constitutional Dimension

The coordinates of executive leadership lie in the constitutional order. First, a chief executive's powers are circumscribed by the distribution of authority across the state apparatus. Among Western European countries, the principal distinction is between unitary states, where a head of government is at the apex of the constitutional order, and those states where legislative authority and administrative capacity are distributed across a federal system. The constitutional order of the Federal Republic is a blueprint for institutional pluralism. As David Southern shows in Chapter 1, the Basic Law conforms to the German tradition of the *Rechtssaat* (constitutional state) in rejecting the theory of sovereignty – that there should be some ultimate focus of authority in the system – in favour of an interlocking network of institutional counter-weights. The functions of the state are dispersed among particular areas of competence, inhibiting the concentration of power at any one point in the system. Most significantly, chancellorial power is confined by the federal system. The title *Bundeskanzler* (federal chancellor) emphasises both the scope and the limitations inherent in the role of a chief executive of a federal state. A system of cooperative federalism in which powers and competences are inseparably entwined means that the federal government must vie with *Länder* endowed with considerable autonomy. In this context the authority of the chancellor can be rather precarious.

Secondly, executive leadership is conditioned by the constitutional relationship between the executive and the legislature. In the systems of parliamentary government which predominate in Western Europe, the executive and legislative branches of government are unified. The executive is not elected separately, but derives its authority from its control over the legislature. The executive is dependent upon and responsible to parliament, yet at the same time it exercises a leadership role over the latter. The real power of the executive branch in relation to the legislature is determined by the balance between the constraints of the executive's dependency upon parliament, and its capacity for control over the legislative arena. This balance between dependency and control is contingent upon a range of political factors, notably the ability of the executive to rely on cohesive and disciplined political parties to secure its parliamentary majority.

In a system of parliamentary government, a parliamentary majority is the *sine qua non* of government. In the German system this is a constitutional requirement; a chancellor must be formally elected by Bundestag majority at the beginning of each term of office. Once he has been elected, the conditions which circumscribe the Bundestag's power to terminate a chancellor's tenure are exceptionally onerous. There is thus a constitutional presumption in favour of government stability in the Federal Republic.[3] Governments are normally able to ensure the passage of legislation through the Bundestag by virtue of the support of the government parties. The parties are not, however, merely passive by-standers in the legislative process. The highly developed Bundestag committee system gives them a role in shaping legislation. The centrality of parties in mediating between executive and legislature is reflected in the pervasive role of party *Fraktionen* in the Bundestag. Highly structured and disciplined, they exercise control over all aspects of the parliamentary procedure and agenda. Chancellors rely very heavily on *Fraktion* leaders, who often participate in cabinet meetings. Thus a chancellor's ability to manage the Bundestag depends upon his relations with his party.

The third constitutional coordinate of chief executive power lies in the sphere of inner-executive relations. In the systems of cabinet government which predominate in Western Europe, executive power is exercised collectively by a corporate government headed by a chief executive. These systems contrast sharply with presidential systems like that of the United States, in which the executive is personalised: 'The executive power shall be vested in a President . . .' (constitution of the United States, Article 2, Section 1). Within systems of corporate government, the chief executive is ascribed primacy within the collective discipline of the cabinet, whilst individual ministers exercise responsibility within their own domains. Inner-executive relations are thus formed by the inter-play between three competing principles: chief executive dominance, cabinet collegiality and ministerial autonomy. The complexity of

---

3. Gordon Smith, *Democracy in Western Germany*, 3rd edn, Aldershot: Gower, 1990, p. 57.

government defies a precise codification of inner-executive relations according to these principles, and constitutional provisions do little more than sketch a broad outline. Ultimately, it is the political environment which is decisive in establishing the parameters of executive authority. Thus countries with similar constitutional provisions display sharp variations in the exercise of executive authority. The Italian and German constitutions are strikingly similar in this respect, but the German chancellor can exercise immeasurably more power over government than his Italian counterpart can.

The constitutional provision for the conduct of government in the Federal Republic is ambiguous, with the three principles of inner-executive relations simply juxtaposed in the Basic Law. The resultant conflict between chancellor dominance, cabinet government and ministerial autonomy is a theme which runs through a number of chapters in this volume. The conclusion which emerges is that collective cabinet government is relatively weak in the German context. In practice, the key to inner-executive relations is the tension between the chancellor principle and the departmental principle. In Chapter 3 Roland Sturm argues that ministerial autonomy is reinforced by the 'sectorisation' of government. Ministers tend to act as chief executives within their own areas of policy, downgrading the executive role of the chancellor to one of coordination, or policy management. The authority of the chancellor depends upon his capacity to operationalise his constitutional responsibility for 'general policy guidelines', coordinating ministerial interests and activities, prioritising, and fashioning a sense of collective purpose. The chancellor is thus cast in the role of cabinet manager in a system of 'coordination democracy'.

The Political Dimension

Coalition government. It will already be clear that the constitution provides only the skeletal framework for the exercise of executive leadership. A fuller picture emerges from a consideration of the political dimension. A theme running throughout almost all the chapters in this volume is the effect of coalition government on the chancellorship. As a general rule, single-party majority government can be said to buttress the power of a chief executive. In the British system of government, for instance, a prime minister has almost untrammelled powers of patronage over the appointment of the cabinet, subject only to the claims of powerful groups and individuals within his or her own party. Government cohesion is strengthened by the bonds of party unity. If the party is reasonably well disciplined, a single-party government can normally rely on a parliamentary majority. A sense of purpose and direction is imparted by the party programme. As head of a coalition government, a German chancellor has none of these advantages. Although coalitions have proved stable and enduring in the Federal Republic, this form of government has inevitably curtailed the power of the chancellor.

First, the chancellor does not have free rein over the appointment of 'his' government. A significant number of cabinet appointments, including some key posts, are in the gift of the chancellor's coalition partner. By custom and practice, the junior coalition partner has acquired 'rights' to certain ministries. Thus the Foreign Ministry has been occupied by a member of the junior coalition partner since 1966, and the Economics Ministry since 1974. Coalition constraints reduce the chancellor's capacity to exercise the power of patronage as a power resource. Ministers, or aspirants to ministerial office, will be less responsive to the chancellor when they are aware that their political careers are not dependent upon his word.

Secondly, the 'colonisation' of particular ministries by the coalition partner accentuates the 'sectorisation' of the executive. Although Germany does not have an American-style spoils system, the appointment of the top echelon of civil servants is political. Typically, an incoming government makes between forty and 100 appointments. Since the power of appointment rests with the responsible minister, the chancellor is denied the opportunity to penetrate the bureaucracy in the manner of some US presidents. Instead, the staffing of ministerial departments reflects the interests and policy preferences of the party in occupancy. Ministries thus assume a distinctive political character, buttressing the principle of ministerial autonomy. Coalition politics thus reinforce the departmental principle in inner-executive relations, at the expense of both chancellor dominance and collegiality. As William Paterson shows in Chapter 5, the colonisation of the Foreign Ministry by the FDP has sometimes undermined the capacity of a chancellor to pursue his own foreign policy.

Thirdly, although coalitions in the Federal Republic have been relatively stable and enduring, they can be subject to fissiparous tendencies which undermine the internal cohesion of governments and erode chancellor authority. Underlying political differences between the coalition parties may surface in policy conflicts which the chancellor is called upon to resolve. In the case of the Christian–liberal coalition, political differences are compounded by the deep-seated acrimony between the liberals and the conservative CSU. Another source of coalition instability is the FDP's need to compensate for its junior status in the coalition by displays of self-assertion. In the arena of coalition politics, chancellors are not entirely without resources. Under certain circumstances, they have been able to use the coalition partner as a counter-weight against the more extreme elements in their own party, or to use coalition constraints as a justification for deflecting demands from within their own ranks. Generally, though, coalition politics are an impediment to chancellor-centred government. Indeed, the termination of three incumbencies – those of Adenauer, Erhard and Schmidt – was precipitated by the FDP as junior coalition partner.

Chancellor–party relations. In liberal democratic systems of government, political parties play an indispensable role in providing the connective tissue which imparts unity to the disparate parts of the whole. Their principal function is to provide coordination between the executive and legislative branches of government. In the German context they also serve to counteract the diffusion of authority across the federal system and to lend coherence to a sectorised executive. In a system characterised by a high degree of institutional pluralism, political parties play an especially crucial role: 'The real links coordinating decision-making are the organized parties . . . giving to party government and its leaders the dominant position within the organization of power.'[4] Thus a chancellor's party can be the corner-stone of executive authority, but it can also be an encumbrance. More than any other single factor, the relationship between a chancellor and his party shapes the exercise of executive leadership.

The stability of government in the Federal Republic reflects the relative stability of the two large *Volksparteien* from which all German chancellors have been drawn. In particular, the cohesion and discipline of the parliamentary parties normally assure the chancellor of support in the Bundestag. Nevertheless, no chancellor can turn his back on his party. A CDU chancellor must come to terms with the polycentric power structure of the party. He also has to mediate between the exceptionally broad spectrum of socio-economic interests contained within this archetypal *Volkspartei*. SPD chancellors, on the other hand, have to assert their autonomy from a party which has tended to regard 'its' chancellor as an instrument for the realisation of the programmatic objectives of the party.

German chancellors do not have the unconditional leadership of

4. Rudolf Wildenmann, 'The Party Government of the Federal Republic of Germany: Form and Experience', in R.S. Katz (ed.), *Visions and Realities of Party Government*, Berlin and New York: De Gruyter, 1987.

their parties enjoyed by British prime ministers. Rather, they occupy
a position of first among equals within the party élite. The office
of parliamentary party leader is constitutionally separate from that
of chancellor, and the holder of this office is an influential broker
in chancellor–party relations. Minister-presidents of the *Länder*
are powerful figures in the party and potential rivals to the chancellor. Ministerial autonomy allows politically powerful ministers to
become 'sectoral executives',[5] quasi-independent of the chancellor.
The management of this multi-faceted party élite requires considerable political skill. Moreover, parliamentary parties have become
more assertive over the life of the Federal Republic, and cannot
simply be regarded as lobby fodder.

Post-war history underlines the vulnerability of chancellors to
their parties and the speed with which party resources can turn into
wasting assets. Only one chancellor (Kiesinger) has suffered defeat
in a federal election. All other incumbencies have ended after the
chancellor lost the support of his party. To be successful, German
chancellors have had to possess the political skills of party management, along with the managerial capacity to master the executive
arena. Since Adenauer, no incumbent has combined the two sets of
skills. The two most recent incumbents, Schmidt and Kohl, are at
opposite ends of the spectrum in this respect. While the former was
endowed with a consummate capacity for executive management, he
found party management irksome. By contrast, Kohl compensates
for his uncertain handling of the executive arena with a formidable
ability to dominate party politics.

The politics of executive management. Counteracting the centrifugal forces of institutional pluralism and the polycentrism of party
politics is the Chancellor's Office (*Kanzleramt*), which Ferdinand
Müller-Rommel identifies in Chapter 4 below as the key to executive
leadership. The Chancellor's Office provides the incumbent with
resources for the coordination of, and selective political intervention in, the executive apparatus. It has no constitutional foundation, but is the legacy of a tradition reaching back to the newly
unified German Reich. In character it falls midway between an
administrative office of state and a political staff. The majority of
its personnel are civil servants, but it operates under the direction of
political appointees of the chancellor. The Office can operate as the
nerve centre of executive control, but its effectiveness as such

5. Renate Mayntz, 'Executive Leadership in Germany: Dispersion of Power or
   "Kanzlerdemokratie" ', in R. Rose and E.N. Suleiman (eds), *Presidents and
   Prime Ministers*, Washington, DC: American Enterprise Institute, 1980.

depends on the chief executive's skill in manipulating the resources it provides. In particular, success rests on the adoption of an effective organisational system with loyal and highly competent lieutenants at its key points. Thus the varying fortunes of German chancellors can be explained in terms of their management of the Chancellery.

Under Adenauer, the Chancellor's Office served as the principal instrument of control over both executive and party. His immediate successors were unable to replicate his dominance, and the Chancellery reverted to its most basic function as cabinet secretariat. The Office was enlarged and restructured under Brandt, in an attempt to create a sort of super-ministry for the realisation of the newly elected Social Democrats' reform programme. In his first term the experiment was very successful under an experienced and competent Chancellery directorate. Thereafter, under a new team led by personal aides and party managers with little administrative experience, managerial disorder prevailed. Under Schmidt, the Chancellor's Office became a finely honed instrument of executive control, with a 'clover-leaf' leadership team of three people at the head of a formal hierarchical structure. The degeneration of the Schmidt chancellorship after 1980 coincided with the break-up of this organisational system.

Under Kohl, the Chancellery has become destructured, personalised and politicised in a manner which resembles the recent evolution of the White House Office of the American president. As Sturm shows in Chapter 3, the inner circle of the Chancellery is composed of close confidants of the chancellor, often occupying posts outside the formal hierarchy of the office. They act as gate-keepers to the chancellor, exercising wide-ranging powers without holding formal positions of responsibility. Kohl's reliance on personal networks has led to a demoralisation of the permanent Chancellery staff and a breakdown in the coordinating function of the Office. This has been identified as one of the sources of a marked erosion of cabinet collectivity, which has been matched by a tendency towards a personalised executive and a drift towards presidentialisation. Critics have argued that this style of executive management intensifies the demands upon the chancellor to the point that he is unable to meet them all.

The societal context. As we have seen, the political system of the Federal Republic is marked by a highly developed form of institutionalised pluralism. In the broader context of socio-economic decision-making, a similar plurality of power centres can be observed. A broad range of quasi-institutional and extra-institutional actors has been identified within the policy process – the Bundesbank (Federal Central Bank), economic advisory councils, private banks, industrial corporations and organised interests. In the Federal Republic, organised interests are often granted a privileged status; as 'para-public institutions' they are granted a quasi-institutional role in the shaping of public policy.[6] The pervasive role of para-public institutions raises the question of whether a chancellor is a captive of their interests, merely responding to and seeking to reconcile their actions and demands, or whether he is able to impose an authoritative order upon the arena of interest politics, harnessing the organisational resources of interest groups for his own purposes.

The answer probably lies somewhere between these two alternatives. One of the distinguishing features of 'private interest government' in the German context is an organisational capacity for reconciling sectional and collective objectives which reflects the 'solidaristic' character of German civil society: 'There is in . . . Germany an organisational potential for generating interest positions and translating them into government decisions.'[7] The egotism of sectional interests is mitigated by 'a commitment to action in the national interest which transcends the interests of individuals or particular groups'.[8] The policy process corresponds closely to an 'associational order', based on the premise that 'people hold solidaristic values and communitarian identities that can contribute to social order directly and without state coordination.'[9]

In Chapter 6 Heidrun Abromeit shows how the relationship between chancellors and organised interests has differed from one chancellor to another. Interest groups have not necessarily regarded the chancellor as the central focus of their lobbying activities. Chancellors like Erhard or Brandt who were perceived by organised

6. Simon Bulmer, 'Unity, Diversity and Stability: The "Efficient Secrets" behind West German Public Policy', in S. Bulmer (ed.), *The Changing Agenda of West German Public Policy*, Aldershot: Dartmouth, 1989, pp. 13–39.
7. Christian Deubner, 'Change and Internationalisation in Industry: Towards a Sectoral Interpretation of West German Politics', *International Organisation*, vol. 38, no. 3, 1984, p. 519.
8. Wyn Grant, William E. Paterson and Colin Whitston, 'Government Industry Relations in the Chemicals Industry: An Anglo-German Comparison', in S. Wilks and M. Wright (eds), *Comparative Government–Industry Relations: Western Europe, the United States and Japan*, Oxford: Clarendon Press, 1987, p. 37.
9. Wolfgang Streeck and Philip C. Schmitter, 'Community, Market, State – and Associations? The Prospective Contribution of Interest Governance to Social Order', in W. Streeck and P.C. Schmitter (eds), *Private Interest Government: Beyond Market and State*, Beverly Hills, CA: Sage, 1985, pp. 13–16.

interests as weak or unsympathetic (or both) were simply by-passed by groups which channelled their demands through the relevant ministry. Adenauer counted among his 'advisors' leading bankers and the president of the Confederation of German Industry (BDI); Kohl is similarly connected. Social Democratic chancellors have found relations with business leaders more problematical, but after some initial coldness, Schmidt established a following among these circles. Abromeit concludes that the balance of interests is asymmetrical, with business interests predominating over those of organised labour. Organised business interests are a vital source of support. The examples of Erhard and Brandt show that no chancellor is able to survive for long without the confidence of the business community. Abromeit concludes that the price of business confidence is that the chancellor must be responsive to the demands emanating from this source; no chancellor has been able to impose his own terms upon the sphere of organised interests.

The capacity of a chancellor to counteract the polycentrism of the German political process is predicated to a large extent upon cooperation within the networks of civil society. The associational order is built upon a well-regulated and relatively homogeneous society in which sustained affluence and economic stability have reduced distributional conflict to manageable proportions. Unification presents the associational order with the most serious challenge it has faced in the history of the Federal Republic. The individualisation and atomisation of society in the new German *Länder* militate against the logic of collective action upon which the associational order rests.[10] The dense network of organisational activity comprising civil society is missing in the east of Germany. Moreover, the economic burdens of unification have created unprecedented levels of distributional conflict in the west.

Changing Styles of Executive Leadership

A distinction can be made between a chief executive acting as a 'superintendent clerk' over the nation's affairs, and one exercising inspirational or programmatic leadership. The former is merely a transient occupant of his office, discharging his constitutional functions in routine fashion and imparting little to the political life of the nation. The 'heroic' model of executive leadership consists of exploiting the scope of the office to (or beyond) its normal constitutional limits, setting the political agenda in at least some important

10. Claus Offe, 'German Reunification as a Natural Experiment', *German Politics*, vol. 1, no. 1, April 1992, pp. 1–12.

respects, and leaving behind an enduring legacy.

As we have seen, the modern German context is generally unfavourable for a heroic style of leadership. Of the six post-war chancellors, only Adenauer fulfils these latter criteria. With an authority extending far beyond the constitutional powers of the chancellorship, his pursuit of Western European integration and a security partnership with the United States shaped the Federal Republic both externally and internally. His legacy was substantial, and could justifiably be said to have established the foundations for German unification. No other incumbent has been able to sustain this form of leadership.

Adenauer's immediate successors, Erhard and Kiesinger, fall neatly into the category of the superintendent clerk. Brandt and Schmidt lie somewhere between the two models. Brandt's first term was distinguished by forceful and inspirational leadership. Although his rhetorical commitment to a more open and democratic society remained largely unrealised, it served as a lodestar to a generation. His *Ostpolitik* was a paradigm example of programmatic leadership. Yet his incumbency was marred by an incapacity for executive control when, in his second term, the emphasis shifted to economic policy. Schmidt's style was less inspirational, yet he dominated the executive by force of personality and his chancellorship became synonymous with the consolidation of '*Modell Deutschland*', an island of stability in an unstable world. Schmidt's chancellorship, however, disintegrated in his final term, and his is the only post-war incumbency to have been terminated by a no-confidence vote in the Bundestag.

Kohl's chancellorship has been characterised by a lack of purposeful direction and by loose executive management. Against the background of an otherwise undistinguished incumbency, the year of unification stands out as Kohl's *annus mirabilis*. As Paterson shows in Chapter 5, unification enabled the chancellor to colonise the domain previously reserved for Foreign Minister Genscher. In his management of the domestic consequences of unification, however, Kohl has been criticised for his failure to convey to the German people either the full historical significance of unification, or its attendant risks and burdens.[11]

Explaining Variations in Executive Leadership

How are we to account for the sharp variations in the exercise of executive leadership by the six post-war German chancellors? In part

---

11. See for instance Eberhard Jäckel, 'Interview: eine Ära Kohl's gibt es nicht', *Stern*, no. 39, p. 31.

these can be attributed to the personal and political qualities of the incumbents: Adenauer's patriarchy and manipulative skills; Brandt's idiosyncratic combination of moral authority and administrative laxity; Schmidt's consummate managerial efficiency; Kohl's innate instinct for political tactics above policy concepts. Personal attributes, however, provide no more than a partial explanation of variations in executive leadership between incumbencies. Two further explanations require examination. The first relates to political circumstances, in particular to the composition of coalitions, the shifting patterns of coalition relations and the relationship between the chancellor and his party. The second concerns changing policy agendas and their impact on executive leadership.

The political circumstances of the early years of the Federal Republic were singularly favourable for chancellor dominance. With a multi-party system in which the principal opposition party was isolated, and with the smaller parties susceptible to manipulation, Adenauer was able to dictate the terms of coalition politics. This began to change with the concentration of the party system, the consolidation of the FDP and its emergence as a key player in coalition formation. The modern 'treaty-making' style of coalition negotiations was seen for the first time in 1961. It marked the end of Adenauer's dominance, which had already been undermined by a growing restiveness on the part of the previously supine CDU.

The crucial importance of the political arena in setting the limits to chancellorial authority was graphically illustrated by the incumbencies of Adenauer's immediate successors. Little more than a 'guest' in the CDU, Erhard was unable to contend with the polycentric power structure of the party. Kiesinger's incumbency was stamped by the composition of the 'grand coalition'. The chancellor was reduced to the status of mediator between two ideologically opposed parties of broadly equal status.

During the chancellorships of Brandt and Schmidt, the impact of coalition dynamics on the office was uneven, reflecting fluctuations in these chancellors' personal relations with FDP leaders, changing policy priorities and shifts in party strategy. In Brandt's first term, coalition relations were buttressed by the chancellor's close personal relations with FDP leader Walter Scheel, and by the fact that the coalition parties were in accord over foreign policy. After 1972, however, a new emphasis on domestic reform and economic policy accentuated the latent conflicts within the Social–Liberal coalition, exposing Brandt's lack of engagement in cabinet management. Policy differences became even more pronounced during the Schmidt incumbency, although on these issues the chancellor himself was closer to the FDP than to his own party. The maintenance of coalition cohesion, and chancellor authority, was thus conditional upon Schmidt's capacity to display his autonomy from the SPD. With this capacity exhausted after 1980, and with FDP leaders planning a change of coalition partner, Schmidt's authority disintegrated.

In the absence of fundamental policy conflicts in the coalition or in his own party, Kohl might have been expected to be less fettered by political constraints than his Social Democratic predecessors had been. Denied coalition alternatives by the electoral weakness of the main opposition party, the FDP was effectively captive in the Kohl government. Moreover, with the death of his arch-critic and rival, CSU leader Strauss, and with Genscher's resignation in 1992, Kohl faced no 'internal opposition'. On the other hand, the cabinet formed after the election of 1990 was one of the weakest in the history of the Federal Republic. Without the ballast provided by experienced and prestigious ministers, the government depended heavily on the chancellor for executive leadership. Moreover, the Kohl incumbency coincided with a number of exceptionally intractable issues, particularly after unification.

This consideration brings us to the second explanation for variations in chancellor performance: the impact on the chancellorship of the changing policy agenda. The complexity of modern government and the multiplication of its functions mean that no chief executive can sustain involvement in all aspects of executive activity. Successful executive management depends upon selective intervention, concentrating attention on a few key policy areas. Adenauer and Brandt carried selective intervention further than other post-war chancellors, restricting themselves almost exclusively to external policy. In so doing, they derived considerable advantage from the autonomy which chancellors are able to exercise in foreign affairs, and from the relative freedom of this policy sector from the constraints of party and organised interests. Ultimately it was Brandt's failure to confront the growing turmoil of domestic policy which precipitated his downfall. Since then, incumbents have been denied the luxury of detachment from the inherent conflicts of the domestic policy arena.

The preoccupations of the Schmidt and Kohl incumbencies were dictated by urgent domestic policy agendas. The issues they contained were heavily laden with distributional conflict, and impinged sharply upon competing interests and priorities within the respective coalitions. Schmidt faced the fiscal and monetary dilemmas resulting from a spiral of economic instability triggered by successive OPEC oil price rises. In confronting this he inevitably came into collision with party commitments to Keynesian interventionism, employment protection and the welfare provisions of the social state. Kohl's policy agenda was shaped initially by the rhetoric with which his government had come to power. It was an 'extended agenda of policy change'[12] consisting of supply-side measures to improve the Federal Republic's competitive position in the global economic order. Kohl's agenda for 'reducing the state to its core functions' included the restructuring of tax regimes, the cutting back of pension provisions, the reform of health-care finance, and a programme of deregulation and market liberalisation. These issues impinged sharply upon the broad range of interests within the Christian–Liberal coalition. The resultant conflicts generated a morass of coalition in-fighting into which Kohl was inexorably drawn.

Identifying Trends in Executive Leadership

It has been argued above that the fluctuating quality of executive leadership apparent under six post-war chancellors can be explained by a combination of three variables: personal style, political circumstances and changing policy agendas. It is clear that the evolution of the modern German chancellorship has not taken the form of a unilinear progression. Schmidt's dominance over the executive, despite somewhat unfavourable political circumstances and a demanding policy agenda, warns against the attempt to identify a secular trend of declining chancellor authority. Nevertheless, the chapters in this volume suggest that it is possible to identify two trends which have combined to redefine the modern German chancellorship. The first relates to the nature of modern government, the second to the character of party democracy in the Federal Republic.

Executive overload is endemic to the modern state. A comprehensive account of the syndrome is inappropriate in this context, but for illustrative purposes the following will suffice: heightened interdependency between national economies, compounded by instability in the global economic and monetary order; the intensification of international competition; technological and market change; the reduced fiscal capacity of the state; and the conflict between growth and the environment. With the multiplication and intensification of pressure upon the state, the role of chief executive becomes correspondingly more problematical. The experience of almost all advanced states points to the reduced capacity of chief executives for exercising their constitutional prerogatives to steer government. In the German context the demands on executive leadership are intensified by the pronounced pluralism of the institutional order. With

12. Simon Bulmer and Peter Humphreys, 'Kohl, Corporatism and Congruence: the West German Model under Challenge', in S. Bulmer (ed.), *The Changing Agenda of West German Public Policy*, Aldershot: Dartmouth, 1989, p. 177.

the broad distribution of policy competence across a system of cooperative federalism, between departments in a sectorised executive, and among quasi-autonomous institutions like the Bundesbank, the chancellor is cast in the role of policy manager or coordinator.

Mayntz has argued that the chancellor's managerial capacity depends crucially on the support he receives from the political parties: 'More than ever, the executive needs effective support from political organizations able to function as mediators between it and the politically vocal population.'[13] Writing in the early 1980s, she identified a growing ambivalence in relations between executive and party. Parties had become, simultaneously, *more* assertive and *less* able to deliver the support required for effective executive leadership. Since then, party system stability and inner-party cohesion have declined still further. Because the two large parties are increasingly unable to maintain electoral support – as indicated by a falling *Volkspartei* share of the vote and the tendency towards electoral dealignment – they are less able to insulate the chancellor from the vicissitudes of public opinion. Moreover, with new policy agendas sharpening the latent conflicts of interest within the *Volksparteien*, parties are becoming less effective as instruments of support for government programmes.

Changing Relations between Chancellor and President

The debilitating effects of these trends upon executive leadership have been exacerbated in the harsher political environment since unification, leading to a subtle but significant change in the relationship between chancellor and president.[14] As Southern points out in Chapter 1 of this volume, the president of the Federal Republic has been restricted to a largely formal and non-political role. In no sense have the functions of the president cut across or impinged upon those of the chancellor. In view of the increasingly political interventions of President Richard von Weizsäcker, however, this interpretation may require some qualification.

Weizsäcker has undoubtedly been the most political of all the presidents of the Federal Republic, a reputation earned through a series of interventions in controversial issues. Chief of these was his contribution in the late 1980s to the emotionally charged debate over how to come to terms with the German past. During the Gorbachev

13. Mayntz, *op. cit.*, p. 187.
14. The following section relies heavily upon suggestions offered by Professor William F. Paterson, author of Chapter 5, below.

reform era he had also been one of the foremost advocates of conciliation towards the Soviet Union. In these issues, however, he had maintained a circumspect distance from partisan conflict, emphasising instead the ethical and moral dimensions of politics.

With unification, Weizsäcker's interventions became both more frequent and more immediately political. Emphasising Germany's international responsibilities, he entered the debate over the German role in the Gulf conflict, subsequently advocating constitutional change to enable German forces to participate in UN peace-keeping operations.[15] He repeatedly stated his preference for Berlin over Bonn in the debate on where the new federal capital should be located. Forceful views were also expressed over burden-sharing between the east and west of Germany, the treatment of the east's *Stasi* legacy, and the intensely political issues of asylum-seekers and citizenship. Although on some of these issues Weizsäcker's views were at variance with those of the chancellor, they were cloaked in presidential neutrality and carefully avoided direct criticism of Kohl.

Presidential neutrality was overtly breached, however, in Weizsäcker's intervention of June 1992, which was both highly political and clearly critical of the chancellor and his government. In a wide-ranging critique of national political life, Weizsäcker reflected upon the unresolved problems of unification, on the responsibilities of German foreign policy and on the flawed performance of party democracy.[16] In an indictment of the whole 'political class', he accused the parties of an obsession with power and an incapacity for handling it responsibly. Although Kohl was not mentioned by name, the chancellor's public response to Weizsäcker's critique turned the affair into a thinly veiled confrontation with the president. In a wider sense, too, the president's interventions in politics represent a challenge to the chancellor. By asserting a claim to intellectual, moral and ultimately political leadership, Weizsäcker may be seen as trespassing upon the chancellor's responsibility under Article 65 of the Basic Law for establishing the parameters of government policy.

The longer-term significance of the president's assertiveness is as yet unclear. After the end of Weizsäcker's term of office in June 1994, it may be that his successor will retreat into the presidential obscurity to which the Federal Republic is accustomed. However, as is observed by a number of authors in this volume, the challenges

15. Richard von Weizsäcker, 'Gulf War Not a Sign of Things to Come: An Interview with President Richard von Weizsäcker', *German Comments*, no. 22, 1991, pp. 6–14.
16. Richard von Weizsäcker, *Im Gespräch mit Gunter Hofmann und Werner A. Perger*, Frankfurt am Main: Eichborn Verlag, 1992; for a summary of Weizsäcker's argument see *Die Zeit*, 19 June 1992.

of post-unification Germany call for a wider repertoire of leadership styles than those associated with the chancellorship in the past. On the domestic front, the task of national integration accentuates the inspirational dimension of leadership. In the international arena, Germany's new status requires a far-reaching redefinition of its role, calling for directional leadership. These leadership qualities are not encompassed within the 'superintendent clerk' model of the chancellorship. A higher-profile presidency may be an answer to the perceived shortcomings of executive leadership, although it is hard to see how this could be reconciled with the political neutrality of the office.

From 'Chancellor Democracy' to 'Coordination Democracy'?

Perceptions of the German chancellorship were indelibly marked by its first incumbent. Adenauer's dominance over both the executive and indeed the wider political system led to the characterisation of the early Federal Republic as a 'chancellor democracy' – a deviant form of parliamentary democracy in which the chief executive's powers were untrammelled by the usual constraints. Although this concept was derived from the experience of the first incumbent, there was a widespread feeling that Adenauer's imprint was permanently stamped upon the office and that, provided they possessed the requisite political acumen, his successors would inherit this legacy from him. In this conception, the primacy of the chancellor was seen as either embedded in the constitutional order of the Federal Republic,[17] or intrinsic to the party system.[18] In retrospect it is clear that chancellor democracy was a transient phase in the evolution of the Federal Republic, arising out of the first incumbent's capacity to exploit the inchoate character of the new state.

Subsequently, the concept of chancellor democracy lost its persuasiveness as Adenauer's successors found it impossible to sustain his dominance. It was not until the 1980s, however, that an alternative concept began to emerge. The redefinition of the chancellorship in terms of its coordination function was derived from an analysis of institutional pluralism. This emphasised the limits on the chancellor's constitutional competence for establishing policy guidelines, stressing the role of the chief executive as policy manager. Coordination democracy also reflects the trends towards executive

17. Wilhelm Hennis, *Richtlinienkompetenz und Regierungstechnik*, Tübingen: J.C.B. Mohr, 1964.
18. Arnold Heidenheimer, 'Der starke Regierungschef und das Parteiensystem. Der Kanzlereffekt in der Bundesrepublik', *Politische Vierteljahresschrift*, vol. 2, Sept. 1961, pp. 251–2.

overload and the weakening of party system cohesion which have been identified above. In the face of an extended policy agenda laden with increasingly intractable issues and less able to rely on the connective tissue of party democracy, the coordination function of the chancellorship becomes increasingly important.

As Sturm argues in Chapter 3, the distinction between chancellor democracy and coordination democracy may be little more than a semantic issue. In practice, the 'guidelines' function which lies at the core of the chancellor democracy model is hard to separate from the 'coordination' function upon which the alternative model is based. How does a chancellor perform his role as coordinator other than by establishing guidelines to impart coherence to the disparate parts of government? From this perspective, the redefinition of the chancellorship in terms of coordination democracy simply implies that the institutional and political latitude of executive leadership is considerably narrower than the chancellor democracy model implies.

Attention has already been drawn to the dangers of generalising from the experience of a single incumbency. It is worth noting in this respect that the concept of coordination democracy dates from the Kohl chancellorship.[19] As has been seen, the Kohl incumbency has been characterised by a rather loose style of executive leadership and a failure to establish directional guidelines for government. Is there a risk, then, of repeating the error of taking the personal style of the incumbent for a secular trend in the evolution of the office of the chancellorship? Doubtless there is such a risk, but most of the chapters in this volume suggest that the reduced scope of executive leadership is more than simply a reflection of the present chancellor's individual style. It reflects change in the institutional dynamics and political system of the Federal Republic, the origins of which can be traced back to Kohl's predecessors. The evolution from chancellor democracy to coordination democracy may therefore be said to provide the broad framework for understanding the evolution of the modern German chancellorship.

19. See, for instance, Karlheinz Niclauss, *Kanzlerdemokratie; Bonner Regierungspraxis von Konrad Adenauer bis Helmut Kohl*, Stuttgart: Kohlhammer, 1988; Jost Küpper, *Die Kanzlerdemokratie*, Frankfurt am Main: Peter Lang, 1985; Thomas Ellwein and Joachim-Jens Hesse, *Der Regierungssystem der Bundesrepublik Deutschland*, Opladen: Westdeutscher Verlag, 1987; Peter Haungs, 'Kanzlerdemokratie in der Bundesrepublik Deutschlands. Adenauers Nachfolger', *Aus Politik und Zeitgeschichte*, 1–2, 1989; Wolfgang Jäger, 'Von der Kanzlerdemokratie zur Koordinationsdemokratie', *Zeitschrift für Politik*, vol. 35, 1988; Axel Murswieck, 'Die Bundesrepublik Deutschland–Kanzlerdemokratie Koordinationsdemokratie oder was sonst', in H.-H. Hartwich and G. Mewer (eds), *Regieren in der Bundesrepublik. I: Konzeptionelle Grundlagen und Perspektiven der Forschung*, Opladen: Westdeutscher Verlag, 1984; Rolf Zundel, 'Ein Kanzler wie ein Eichenschrank', *Die Zeit*, 6 January 1989, p. 3.

1

THE CHANCELLOR AND THE CONSTITUTION

David Southern

Savigny observes that

law has a double life, firstly as part of the whole national life, secondly as a special science in the hands of the jurists. . . . we call the connection of law with the general national life the political aspect, the separate academic life of law the technical aspect.[1]

The Federal Constitutional Court in its decision of 23 October 1952 banning the neo-Nazi *Sozialistische Reichspartei* (SRP) interpreted the constitution so as to provide a whole framework for the conduct of politics. It explained that the free democratic basic order constitutes 'a system of government under the rule of law'.[2] The chancellor functions as part of this system, and it is with this political aspect of law, as it defines and conditions the office of the federal chancellor, that this chapter is concerned.

The federal designation has a double-edged significance. On the one hand, he is chancellor *of* the Federation, transcending party and provincial partisanship and particularism. On the other hand, he is chancellor *in* a federation, and this significantly constrains his role. The essence of the constitutional position of the chancellor is that the application of the majority principle remains restricted in favour of the consensus principle. The chancellor cannot rely on majority support the absence of a broader consensus. The need for consensus arises in part from the existence of regional governments and the institutions of federalism. Federalism is related to the subsidiarity principle, now enshrined in Article 3(b) of the Maastricht Treaty.

Historical Evolution

Whilst the task of political science is to grasp new political phenomena as they arise, not to regard them as the linear outcome of

1. Friedrich von Savigny, *Vom Beruf unserer Zeit für Gesetzgebung und Rechtswissenschaft*, Tübingen: J.C.B. Mohr, 1814, p. 12.
2. *Entscheidungen des Bundesverfassungsgerichts*, vol. 2, pp. 1ff. at p. 12 (hereafter cited as *B Verf GE*).

earlier changes, some historical introduction is required to show the derivation of the characteristic institutions and vocabulary of German constitutionalism.

The position of the chancellor as the pre-eminent royal official became established in the eighteenth century, the period in which the substitution of bureaucratic conditions of governmental administration for non-bureaucratic ones began to erode rule by monarchical prerogative. The common denominator of bureaucratisation is that the earlier involvement of public employment with family prerogative, and the identification of office with property, were superseded by the emergence of the nation-state in which public officials administer a 'service-rendering organisation for the protection of rights and the enforcement of duties'.[3]

The term 'chancellor' first entered the vocabulary of German constitutionalism with the constitution of the North German Federation of 16 April 1867. This was the federation constructed by Bismarck following the conclusion of the Austro–Prussian war of 1866. Article 11 of the 1867 constitution provided that 'the praesidium of the Federation is vested in the Crown of Prussia'. Article 15 stated that 'The presidency in the Bundesrat and the conduct of business is vested in the Federal Chancellor (*Bundeskanzler*), who is appointed by the praesidium.'[4]

In the debates on the 1867 constitution, the constitutive assembly adopted Benningsen's proposal that the validity of all acts of the federal praesidium (that is, the king of Prussia) should be dependent upon the counter-signature of the federal chancellor. Thereby a minister was identified for the *Reichstag* who could be held politically responsible for government acts. As Erich Eyck commented: 'From this moment on there existed in fact a "Reich government", however much Bismarck might seek to deny this when he wished to oppose the development of the constitution.'[5] Under the Deputy Law of 1878, the Kaiser could on the recommendation of the chancellor appoint a vice-chancellor, who had the right of countersignature and was answerable to the *Reichstag* in place of the chancellor.

The 1867 federation paved the way for the Reich of 1871. The chancellor alone constituted the federal government, and was appointed by the king of Prussia. As early as 1869, the demand was made by members of the *Reichstag* for a central government

3. Ernest Barker, *The Development of Public Services in Western Europe 1660–1930*, Oxford University Press, 1944, p. 6.
4. E.R. Huber, *Documente zur Deutschen Verfassungsgeschichte*, 3rd edn, Stuttgart: Kohlhammer, 1986, vol. II, p. 272.
5. Erich Eyck, *Bismarck*, 3 vols, Zurich: Eugen Rentsch, 1943, vol. II, p. 337.

accountable to parliament.[6] Such proposals achieved only a limited resonance in nineteenth-century Germany.[7] The two articles from the 1867 constitution became Articles 11 and 15 of the 1871 constitution. Bismarck described the position of the chancellor in a letter to Kaiser Wilhelm I of 15 January 1878, in these terms:

> Under Article 17 . . . the Reich Chancellor is given according to the Constitution the position as the only Reich minister, responsible to the Emperor and the Reich, and thereby is assigned the responsible conduct of all Reich business, which lies in the imperial governmental power of Your Majesty, regardless of the office to which these matters belong.[8]

The formal symbol of the chancellor's overall responsibility for the formulation and coordination of policy was what Bismarck's rules of procedure for Reich offices of 1878 called his 'guidelines competence' (*Richtlinienkompetenz*). The Weimar constitution of 1919 gave constitutional status to three principles of government: the guidelines competence, the Reich cabinet, and the principle of parliamentary control over the executive. It also established a double executive of president and chancellor, without making one preeminent over the other or reconciling this arrangement with the overall principle of parliamentary responsibility. The degradation of parliamentary life in the Weimar Republic prevented the chancellor from realising his constitutionally ascribed role and encouraged the false antithesis between 'strong' government independent of parliament, and 'weak' government dependent upon parliamentary support. The ideology and language of the opponents of parliamentary institutions helped Hitler legitimise his power. He transformed the offices of chancellor and president into that of *Führer* (leader), and made that post the instrument of permanent revolution. When after 1945 Germany returned to a normal course of development, the institutions and language of earlier German constitutional tradition were revived, though in a completely different political context.

The Framework of Government

According to Article 2 (1) of the Currency Union Treaty of 18 May 1990, between West and East Germany, Germany is a free, demo-

---

6. Fr. v. Hotzendorff and E. Benzold, *Materialen der Deutschen Reichs-Verfassung*, Berlin: Carl Hebel, 1872-3, vol. 3/2, pp. 1132-95.
7. See sources cited in Erich Hahn, 'Ministerial Responsibility in Prussia 1848-63', *Central European History*, vol. X, 1977, pp. 3-27.
8. Huber, *op. cit.*, p. 406.

cratic, federal, *rechtsstaatlich* system with social welfare provision. In short, Germany is a federation, based on a consensus and corresponding to the model of a *Rechtsstaat*. The office of chancellor has to be considered in this context. The changes wrought by the unification of West and East Germany on 3 October 1990 significantly altered but did not fundamentally change this framework.

In 1945 the area of Germany extending up to the western Oder–Neisse rivers was divided into four zones of occupation – American, British and French in the west and Russian in the east – while the areas of Prussia lying east of this line were effectively transferred to Poland and Russia.[9] By mid-1948, with the onset of the Cold War, the three Western powers had decided that it was now impossible to construct a common political framework for Germany. Their zones had already been merged for the purposes of economic administration. In all four zones German administration had been built up from the bottom. The highest German-run level of authority was located in the federal states (*Länder*), which had been revived or reconstructed in all four zones in 1945-7. On 1 July 1948 the Western powers invited the minister–presidents of the *Länder* in their zones to draft a constitution for a new West German state.

While the *Land* chief ministers had little choice but to comply with this proposal, great pains were taken to ensure that the constitution was, superficially at least, only of a provisional order. Hence, instead of the more weighty term 'constitution' (*Verfassung*), the less demanding term 'Basic Law' (*Grundgesetz*) was adopted. It was drafted by an assembly of *Land* parliamentarians, ratified by the *Land* parliaments and came into force on 23 May 1949. The Russians reacted by turning their occupation zone into a 'people's democracy', in which political power was increasingly organised on Marxist-Leninist lines. Because of the circumstances in which the West German constitution was enacted, the *Länder* came to play a far more influential role in the political process than had been intended or envisaged.

The Basic Law follows the Weimar constitution of 1919 in important respects, but to a significant extent it is also a conscious rejection of those elements of the Weimar system which were regarded as having contributed to the instability of the first German republic. How far formal political arrangements contribute to good government is a question which can never be resolved to anyone's perfect satisfaction. In the case of the Basic Law, what is more important than its detailed provisions is that, because of the immediate

---

9. R.C. Raack, 'Stalin Fixes the Oder–Neisse Line', *J. of Contemporary History*, no. 25, 1990, pp. 467–88.

political situation in 1948-9, it was brought into being in a climate of political consensus which ensured its substantive political legitimation. This in turn promoted the consolidation and continuation of that consensus. The stability of the Federal Republic has derived to a significant extent from the formal and normative provisions of the Basic Law.

The Rejection of Sovereignty

An important element in this consensus, and one of the essential normative elements of the Basic Law, is the idea that public authority must be based on some legal grant of powers. The law itself must rest upon certain ethical values. Thus Article 1 (3) requires the organs of government to observe certain basic rights; Article 20 (1) states that the Federal Republic is a 'democratic and social federation'; Article 28 (1) provides that the constitutional order in the *Länder* must conform with 'the principles of the republican, democratic and social *Rechtsstaat* in the sense of this Basic Law'. From these fragmentary statements can be derived distinguishing characteristics of the style and content of the German political order.

These features set the German system apart from the classic Westminster model. Anglo-Saxon political theory has traditionally regarded a written constitution as an attempt to limit something which by its very nature is legally illimitable. A constitution is something which makes a system of government what it is; successfully realised in practice, a constitution creates its own reality. To argue whether the state precedes law, or law the state, is an idle question. As Gierke observes: 'We shall no longer ask whether the state is prior to law, or law is prior to the state. We shall regard them both as inherent functions of the common life which is inseparable from the idea of man.'[10] The democratic structure gives the legal system its distinctive institutions and practices, and the one cannot be regarded in isolation from the other.

German theorists have consistently rejected the doctrine of sovereignty. Paul Laband, the pre-eminent commentator on the constitution of 1871, wrote: 'Sovereignty in the sense of a supreme, ultimate power, not legally subordinated in any respect to an external will, does *not* belong to the essential characteristics of the state.'[11] The idea of the *Rechtstaat* was inconsistent with the doctrine of parlia-

10. Otto von Gierke, *Natural Law and the Theory of Society*, transl. E. Barker, Cambridge University Press, 1958, p. 224.
11. Paul Laband, *Deutsches Reichsstaatsrecht*, 7th edn, Tübingen: J.C.B. Mohr, 1919, p. 20.

mentary sovereignty. German constitutional theory preferred to stress what Thoma called 'the pluralistic differentiation of state authority'.[12] In other words, the state was seen as embodied in a number of organs and institutions, each with a measure of autonomy and without clear relationships of superiority and subordination *inter se*. The function of public law was to prevent institutional anarchy. The theory of sovereignty was rejected in favour of an interlocking system of institutional counter-weights. As Schmitt puts it:

It is a criterion of the Rechtstaat that it delimits all state functions into particular areas of responsibility and regulates the state omnipotence into a system of competences, so that nowhere at any point can the abundance of state power appear without restriction in direct concentration.[13]

After 1945 democratic politicians and theorists sought to find universally accepted values upon which to build the new political order in Germany. The revival of natural law was – as in the Weimar period – associated with a movement for a more liberal and elastic judicial technique (*la libre recherche scientifique*) than had been orthodox in most European countries. It was also bound up with controversies concerning the nature and limits of the power of the state. The belief in the creative role of the judiciary was twinned with the belief that law had an ethical foundation. The direct institutional product of this synthesis was the establishment of the Federal Constitutional Court in 1951. More generally, the constitution consistently blocks majority wills, so that the chancellor finds he is bound to the procedural and substantive norms of the system of which his office forms a part.

This means that a chancellor has sometimes found that his hands are tied, as in the case of the Gulf conflict of 1990–1. Urged by President Bush to send German troops to join the coalition of forces opposed to Iraq, Kohl was bound to decline on the grounds that the Basic Law (Article 87a [2]) explicitly forbade the deployment of German forces outside the NATO area, except when used for national defence, A protracted constitutional debate followed, over whether 'defence' included the duty of mutual assistance under the United Nations Charter, or whether control of the armed forces could be made over to UN authority under Article 24 (1) of the Basic

---

12. Gerhard Anschütz and Richard Thoma, *Handbuch des Deutschen Staatsrechts*, 2 vols, Tübingen: J.C.B. Mohr, 1930, vol. I, p. 609.
13. Carl Schmitt, 'Die Diktatur des Reichspräsidenten nach Art. 48', *Veröffentlichungen der Vereinigung der Deutschen Staatsrechtslehrer*, new series, no. 7, 1924, p. 84.

Law, which provides for rights of sovereignty to be transferred to
international authorities. The indecisive outcome of this debate, and
the generally negative view of public opinion over participation, left
Kohl unable to commit German troops to combat in the Gulf. Moreover, his determination to amend the constitutional prohibition on
'out-of-area' operations ran up against the requirement that amendments to the Basic Law need a two-thirds majority in both Bundestag and Bundesrat.

The Chancellor and Parliament

The core provisions of the Basic Law in relation to executive power
are found in Articles 62–9, regulating the relationship between
chancellor and parliament. The central idea of these provisions is
simultaneously to strengthen parliament against the chancellor and
the chancellor against parliament. The powers of parliament are
restricted in favour of executive stability, while the powers of the
executive over parliament are curtailed to prevent dictatorship.
Stalemate is prevented primarily because the identity of chancellor
and governing parties limits the range of possible divergence. The
Federal Constitutional Court authoritatively adjudicates on disputes over how the system should operate. Moreover, there is a pervasive consensus over the constitutional balance between chancellor
and Bundestag.

Once a Bundestag has been elected and a chancellor appointed,
each enjoys a degree of immunity from the other until the termination of the legislative period. Since each is essential to the other,
political leadership is effectively shared. Although the chancellor
represents the government as a whole in the Bundestag, his appear-
ances there are comparatively infrequent. There is no equivalent of
prime minister's questions at Westminster; the chancellor's appear-
ances in the plenum of the Bundestag are restricted to making statements in the name of the government, and giving speeches in debates
on general government policy.

One of the first and most important tasks of the newly-elected
Bundestag is to elect the chancellor upon the nomination of the
president according to Article 63 (1) of the Basic Law. The nominee
must obtain an absolute majority of Bundestag votes. If he is not
elected, the Bundestag has fourteen days in which to elect another
candidate by an absolute majority under Article 63 (3). Failing this,
the president can, within seven days, either appoint a candidate who
has achieved a *relative* majority, or dissolve the Bundestag under
Article 63 (4). This latter procedure thus represents one of the rare
circumstances in which the president can exercise a political discre-

tion and in which the Bundestag can be dissolved prematurely.

The president has no discretion over whom to nominate as chancellor. He must simply name the candidate of the party which (usually by virtue of a coalition agreement) commands the broadest parliamentary support. In 1959, under pressure to step down as chancellor, Adenauer considered becoming president. His thinking was based on the assumption that he would then be able to use the powers of the office to block the nomination of Erhard as his successor to the chancellorship. When he found that the presidency carried no such power, he promptly withdrew his candidacy for the office.[14] The fallback provisions for electing a chancellor have never been used in practice, since at the convening of every new Bundestag from 1949 onwards the candidate proposed by the president has always received the requisite majority at the first vote. The narrowest majority was that obtained by Adenauer in 1949, when he had a majority of one vote.[15]

Each Bundestag election since 1949 has been a 'chancellor election' (*Kanzlerwahl*), in that the parties have entered the election as two rival groups, each with its own chancellor candidate. All that the president and parliament have had to do in those circumstances is to ratify the decision of the electorate. The selection of chancellor-candidates is carried out by the national leadership of the political parties. Likewise, if the chancellor resigns during the term of the legislature, it is the leaders of the majority in government who effectively decide who his successor shall be. Thus the last word in the election of the chancellor lies with the parties, not the electorate. The only way in which chancellors in office can be removed against their will is by the constructive vote of no confidence procedure, set out in Article 67, which stands in a close systematic relationship with Article 63. The essential significance of the events of 1982 – when the constructive vote of no confidence was carried for the first and only time since 1949 – was that they established that change of government can be carried through by parliament alone, and does not under the constitution require the endorsement of the electorate.

The Constructive Vote of No Confidence

From the responsibility of government to parliament derives the responsibility of parliament *for* government. It is the function of Article 67 to put this duty into practice. Under Article 54 of the Weimar constitution, the chancellor and the Reich ministers were

---

14. K. Adenauer, *Erinnerungen, 1955–1959*, Hamburg: Fischer, 1969, pp. 47–52.
15. K. Adenauer, *Erinnerungen, 1945–1953*, Hamburg: Fischer, 1967, p. 222.

required to have the confidence of the Reichstag, and to resign if this confidence was withdrawn. This permitted 'destructive' votes of no confidence, whereby a government could be removed from office without regard to the consequences or to the question of who should succeed it. As Reich president, Ebert observed to the leaders of the SPD on 23 November 1923, after they had caused the defeat of Chancellor Stresemann's government: 'Your reasons for overthrowing the chancellor will be forgotten in six weeks, but you will continue to suffer the consequences of your folly ten years hence.'[16] In fact, Weimar governments generally broke up because of internal party divisions, and only two chancellors were removed by hostile votes in the Reichstag. Article 67 was the result not of specific weaknesses of the Weimar system, but rather of the generalised fear of parliamentary instability which haunted the Parliamentary Council when drafting the Basic Law.

Under Article 67, the Bundestag can only remove a chancellor from office if it passes a motion by an absolute majority to elect his successor. The president is then obliged to dismiss the incumbent and appoint the new chancellor. This is the 'constructive' vote of no confidence procedure. Article 67 also provides the constitutional basis for a 'loyal' opposition, in that it presents the opposition parties with a means of taking over the government if they can muster sufficient votes in parliament. Article 67 forbids the introduction of motions of no confidence in individual ministers. The general purpose of the provision is to prevent 'the arising of a vacuum in governmental authority'.[17] It does not prevent parliament from passing motions critical of the government. Such resolutions, however, unless they satisfy Article 67, have no legal force.

Under Article 59 (2) every federal government is dependent for the implementation of its policies on new laws, grants of parliamentary approval and authorisation of expenditure. A minority government surviving under the protection of Article 67 would be able to accomplish little in practice. Hence the contribution of the constructive vote of no confidence procedure to governmental stability is only limited. In a parliamentary system of government, stable government cannot be secured in the long run by constitutional provisions but only by reliable and disciplined parliamentary majorities, the pre-condition for which is a stable party system.

Since 1949 the constructive vote of no confidence has only been introduced on two occasions. In 1969 an SPD/FDP government was elected with a small majority, headed by Willy Brandt. During his

16. Gustav Stresemann, *Vermächtnis*, 3 vols, Berlin, 1932–3, vol. I, p. 245.
17. K. Sattler, *Deutsche öffentliche Verwaltung*, 1967, p. 767.

first term a number of government deputies switched to the opposition, because of his policy of *Ostpolitik*. On 24 April 1972 the CDU/CSU introduced a motion expressing no confidence in Brandt and proposing Rainer Barzel (leader of the CDU/CSU parliamentary group in the Bundestag) as his successor. Of a Bundestag membership of 496, 247 voted for the motion and 10 against, and 3 abstained. The motion thus failed to achieve the requisite absolute majority of 249. The second occasion followed the 1980 Bundestag election, whereby the SPD/FDP was returned to power with a clear majority. By the autumn of 1982 a rift had developed between the two parties; the FDP resolved to switch sides and to form a government with the CDU/CSU. On 1 October 1982 the Bundestag passed a constructive vote of no confidence in Chancellor Schmidt and appointed Helmut Kohl (CDU) chancellor in his place. The CDU/CSU and FDP voted for the motion (256 votes), the SPD and dissenting FDP members against.

In practice, therefore, the constructive vote of no confidence procedure has afforded a means by which the opposition can force a change of government in advance of a general election. On both occasions when the constructive vote of no confidence was employed, it was followed by an engineered dissolution of the Bundestag before its term had expired. The consideration of Article 67 leads logically to Article 39 (which fixes the term of the lower house at four years) and Article 68 (which affords the principal means by which the Bundestag can be dissolved prematurely).

Dissolving the Bundestag: the Chancellor Constrained

The vital feature of Article 39 is that it denies parliament a power of self-dissolution. A Bundestag is elected for four years; a fresh election must take place within the last three months of its term; the term expires automatically at the end of four years; the new Bundestag must assemble within thirty days of the election, but not before the expiry of the previous Bundestag's term. The denial of the power to dissolve the Bundestag protects parliament from the chancellor. The denial of the right of self-dissolution is the logical corollary of Article 67. Without it, a parliament unable to topple the chancellor by a constructive vote of no confidence could side-step this restriction by dissolving itself. A premature dissolution is only possible in two circumstances. One has already been mentioned; namely, if a candidate for the chancellorship can only obtain a relative majority, the president can under Article 63 either appoint him or dissolve parliament. This has never happened in practice. The other possibility of terminating a parliament before its term expires is afforded by Article 68. This has been used twice – in 1972 and 1983 – but under special circumstances. Article 68 (1) provides that, if a chancellor seeks a vote of confidence and is unable to obtain an absolute majority of votes in his favour, the president *can* (*kann*) 'at the request of the chancellor' dissolve parliament.

In April 1972, the day after Brandt had narrowly survived a constructive vote of no confidence proposed by the opposition CDU, his government's budget failed to pass the Bundestag by virtue of a tied vote. Having struggled through the next five months, Brandt subsequently adopted the expedient of seeking and contriving to lose a confidence vote under Article 68 (1). The chancellor then obtained a dissolution of the Bundestag through President Heinemann. Since the confidence vote had only been lost (by 233 votes to 248) through the abstention of government ministers, it was clear that the condition for a premature dissolution had been contrived. On the other hand the failure to carry the budget vote earlier in the year showed that the government had genuinely lost its majority.[18]

After the successful constructive vote of no confidence in October 1982, the new government under Chancellor Kohl wished to see a dissolution to enable the electorate to give retrospective sanction to the change of government. Such a course was regarded as a political, though not a constitutional, necessity. Following the precedent of 1972, the government introduced a vote of confidence under Article 68. The vote was lost by 218 votes to eight, the government parties having abstained, and the chancellor duly advised President Carstens to dissolve the Bundestag. After consulting party leaders, all of whom favoured an election, the president delivered his assent. Maintaining constitutional niceties, he elaborated his reasoning. First, he argued, what was important was the fact that the confidence vote had been lost; the circumstances of the result were of secondary importance. Secondly, he went on, the FDP had voted for the constructive vote of no confidence only on condition that it would be followed by new elections. Thus Chancellor Kohl did not have a true majority, but was chancellor only 'subject to a proviso'.

On this occasion, four dissenting members of the Bundestag succeeded in bringing a case to the Constitutional Court. The Court was thus called upon to decide whether or not the contrived dissolution was an authentic application of Article 68. In its judgement, the Court expressed its disapproval of the sham which had been employed to secure the dissolution. The expedient was clearly

18. M. Müller, 'Das Konstruktive Misstrauensvotum', *Zeitschrift für Parlamentsfragen* (hereafter *Z Parl.*), vol. 3, 1972, p. 275; Busch, 'Die Parlamentsauflösung', *Z Parl*, vol. 4, 1973, p. 212.

intended to circumvent Article 39. On the other hand, it had to try to make sense of the existing situation. It was held, therefore, that there was no general power to dissolve the Bundestag in mid-term, and that Article 68 could not be used to engineer a dissolution where the Basic Law did not provide for it. Under the circumstances, however, this particular dissolution was valid.[19] The judgement confirmed the prevailing opinion that the president could decide at his discretion whether or not to accede to a chancellor's request for a dissolution. But the ruling laid down criteria for the exercise of this discretion which will considerably restrict it in future.

If a chancellor who has genuinely lost a confidence vote does not wish to take the dissolution option, he can fall back on the 'legislative emergency' provision of Article 81. Under this procedure, if the Bundestag rejects a law which the government designates as urgent the president can, at the request of the government and with the consent of the Bundestag, proclaim a 'legislative emergency', lasting for six months. During this period, legislation can be passed without the agreement of the Bundestag, but subject to the consent of the Bundesrat. This provision has not been employed in practice.

The general effect of Articles 39, 67 and 68 is, first, that parliament can change the chancellor and government without the need for new elections. Secondly, a contrived dissolution for the purposes of securing a popular endorsement for a mid-term change of government is constitutional, as long as the new government has a secure majority. Thirdly, a chancellor who loses his majority must in practice either resign or seek a vote of confidence. Finally, a chancellor cannot choose when to dissolve parliament.

Chancellor and Government: an Ambiguous Relationship

The federal government consists of the chancellor and the federal ministers (Article 62). Together they constitute the cabinet. In addition there are parliamentary state secretaries, introduced in 1967 by statute rather than by virtue of the Basic Law.[20] Parliamentary state secretaries are members of the Bundestag who serve as assistants to ministers and have a limited capacity to deputise for them. The general rule is that the parliamentary state secretary cannot be given independent discretions to exercise. Under Paragraph 8 of the Law on Parliamentary State Secretaries, the president can confer on

19. *B Verf GE*, vol. 62, p. 1.
20. Law on the Legal Position of Parliamentary State Secretaries: *Bundesgestzblatt* (hereafter cited as *BGBl*), 1967, vol. I, p. 396; Law of 24 July 1974 *BGBl*, 1974, vol. I, p. 1538.

them the title of 'state minister'. There are usually one or two state ministers, representing a halfway-house between ministers and parliamentary state secretaries.

Within government, the chancellor occupies a special position. As explained above, the incumbent alone is elected and subject to dismissal by the Bundestag. Federal ministers stand or fall with the chancellor. In consequence of the chancellor's rights of nomination to and dismissal from ministerial office, and of the fact that their appointments are coterminous, government ministers are largely dependent upon him. The pre-eminence of the chancellor is realised through his sole responsibility to the Bundestag, and in the so-called 'guidelines competence'.

Article 65 of the Basic Law derives from Article 56 of the Weimar constitution. It defines the responsibilities exercised respectively by the chancellor, individual ministers and the government as a collective body. It forms the central reference point for the constitutional role of the chancellor and therefore requires examination in some detail:

The chancellor determines and bears responsibility for the guidelines of policy. Within these guidelines each federal minister conducts his department independently and under his own responsibility. The federal cabinet decides on differences of opinion between ministers. The chancellor conducts the business of government in accordance with the standing orders adopted by it and approved by the federal president.

This Article is generally held to establish three principles: the chancellor principle (*Kanzlerprinzip*), the departmental principle (*Ressortprinzip*) and the cabinet principle (*Kabinettsprinzip*). These principles are embodied in rules of procedure (introduced by Bismarck in 1878). These standing orders constitute a form of subordinate legislation within the administration. Their effect is to formalise cabinet procedure to an unusual extent.[21]

The term 'guidelines competence' remains undefined. Essentially it means a framework of policy determined by the chancellor, within which the cabinet works. The chancellor's constitutional capacity to determine policy parameters in this way is considerably restricted by the political requirements of the parliamentary system and coalition government. Following the 1990 election, for instance, the FDP made it a condition of its participation in government that the five eastern German *Länder* should be designated a low-tax area in line with their strategy for investment and economic development here.

21. The current rules of procedure (*Geschäftsordnung*, or *Gesch O*) were enacted on 11 May 1951, as revised at 23 January 1970; *Gemeinsames Ministerialblatt*, vol. X, 1970, p. 50.

Coalition agreements of this sort receive a sort of constitutional sanction through Article 21 of the Basic Law, which ascribes to the parties the function of contributing to the formation of the political will of the people.[22] The very generality of the 'guidelines' principle counteracts the effect which the chancellor's exclusive responsibility for their formulation would otherwise produce. Their concrete expression and actual implementation leave a wide margin of political discretion to individual ministers.

Although it possesses legal force, the determination of guidelines by the chancellor does not have to assume any particular form. They can be embodied in statements of the chancellor before the Bundestag or in cabinet meetings or in verbal or written communications to individual ministers. Public statements of ministers must be in accordance with the guidelines (Standing Orders, para. 12). The chancellor has an extensive right of information in respect of other ministries (Standing Orders, paras 3 and 4) in order to ensure that his policy guidelines are being observed. The chancellor alone has a single role (formulating and implementing policy guidelines), but can be represented by any other minister appointed for this purpose.

The effective realisation of the chancellor's guidelines is also achieved through various institutions which derive implicitly from Article 65, although they are not explicitly mentioned in the Basic Law. These include the Federal Chancellor's Office (see Chapter 4), the Press and Information Office of the federal government, and various cabinet committees.[23] The Chancellor's Office functions, *inter alia*, as a general staff supporting the chancellor in the exercise of the guidelines competence. Its principal role is the coordination of the entire range of government policy. The senior state secretary in the Chancellor's Office is a key political figure, at times second only in influence to the chancellor.

Ministers occupy a double role. On the one hand they are members of the collective cabinet; on the other, they are official heads of government departments. In this latter role ministers are assigned constitutional autonomy over the affairs of their department. There is some potential for conflict between the principle of ministerial autonomy and the chancellor's guidelines competence (see Chapter 3). In practice, the separation of functions between cabinet member and departmental head is not strictly observed.

At various points in the Basic Law, decision-making power is given to the cabinet rather than to the chancellor. For example, the

22. *B Verf GE*, vol. 20, p. 98.
23. W. Hennis, *Richtlinienkompetenz unter Regierungstechnik*, Munich: Piper, 1964, p. 18.

cabinet has the right to introduce bills (Article 76 [1]) and to issue subordinate legislation (Articles 80 [1], 84 [2], 85 [2], 86). It is empowered to supervise and give directions to the *Länder* (Articles 35 [3], 84 [3] and [5], 85 [4] 91 [3]). Government Standing Orders make provision for collective cabinet responsibility. It can thus be seen that the structure of the German executive rests on a rather ill-defined combination of chancellor predominance in the government as a whole, ministerial predominance within the domain of coordinate and equal departments, and a coordinating function exercised by chancellor and cabinet collectively.

Ministerial Appointments

The freedom of chancellors to appoint ministers of their choice is substantially restricted by the needs to share out office among the coalition of parties which invariably form the federal government, and to respect personal and maintain political balance within the government party. The restrictions on the chancellor are part and parcel of the constitution as *de facto* limitations.

The constraints on a chancellor's power to determine the composition of the cabinet extends even to key posts. This is graphically illustrated by the events which followed the resignation in May 1992 of the Foreign Minister and vice-chancellor, Hans-Dietrich Genscher of the FDP. Under the terms of the coalition agreement, the post of foreign minister – after the chancellor, the most important figure in the cabinet – belonged to the FDP, and the leadership nominated the construction minister, Irmgard Schwätzer, to the post. In defiance of the party leadership, however, the parliamentary group of the FDP overturned this decision, nominating the justice minister, Klaus Kinkel, as Foreign Minister and the Economics Minister, Jürgen Möllemann, as vice-chancellor. Kinkel was a newcomer to politics and not even a member of the Bundestag. The chancellor had no influence over these fundamental decisions on the composition of his government, but was simply obliged to implement the decisions of his coalition partner.

The chancellor's proposals for the appointment or removal of ministers are subject to presidential approval to ensure procedural correctness. A president has no powers to question a proposal on personal or political grounds, though some have occasionally attempted to exercise such influence. A minister may resign at any time. The request is directed to the chancellor and effected formally by the president.

Closely connected with the selection of federal ministers is the power of the chancellor to determine the number, structure and responsibilities of ministries. This is the 'power of organisation' (*Organisationsgewalt*). This competence is implied though not expressly conferred by the constitution.[24] It enables the chancellor to appoint ministers without portfolio, in order to achieve party balance.

The Chancellor and the Federal System

Article 65 does not contain any principle applicable to the Federation–*Land* relationship.[25] However, the federal system places considerable political power in the hands of the *Land* governments and the Bundesrat. To some degree, the federal system thereby unburdens the chancellor and leaves him free to concentrate on high politics. However, in practice things are not so simple. *Land* elections are seen as tests of the national political standing of the parties and so of the chancellor. In addition, the chancellor needs to ensure that the government's legislative programme is not held up in the Bundesrat, which has an independent power of veto. Moreover, federal government is responsible for the resolution of disputes between *Land* authorities, and between Bonn and the *Länder*. The diffusion of authority across the federal system inevitably means that chancellors are drawn into political issues arising in the *Länder*. To promote the interchange of knowledge and views between the federal and *Land* governments, broad networks of formal and informal arrangements have been developed. The most important of these is the standing conference of the heads of government, which consists of the chancellor and minister-presidents of the *Länder*.

In its dealings with the *Länder* the federal government is constrained both by the constitutionally entrenched position which the *Länder* enjoy and by the doctrine of 'federal comity' (*Bundestreue*) – the obligation not to press the interests of the *Länder* or the claim for greater centralisation beyond a certain point. The impact of this doctrine was illustrated in the 'Television Case' of 1961, though this was an extreme and untypical case of behaviour by the federal government.[26] Under the Basic Law cultural and educational matters, including broadcasting, belong in the sphere of responsibility of the *Länder*. Adenauer, dealing direct with commercial interest groups, had promised them a second, commercial television channel. The Bundesrat, representing the *Land* governments, refused to pass the

24. E. Böckenförde, *Die Organisationsgewalt im Bereich der Regierung*, Tübingen: J.C.B. Mohr, 1964, p. 120.
25. *B Verf GE*, vol. 1, p. 310.
26. *B Verf GE*, vol. 12, p. 205.

necessary legislation. In 1961 Adenauer, deciding to press ahead regardless, and after informing the CDU-and CSU-controlled *Länder* but not those governed by the SPD, set in hand the administrative arrangements for a commercial second television channel by establishing a private company, in which the federal government held one share. The SPD-controlled *Länder* challenged the federal government's actions in the Federal Constitutional Court, which severely criticised the government's conduct of the negotiations and treatment of the *Länder* as breaches of 'federal comity'.

Disputes between federal government and the *Länder* are less common than those between one group of *Länder* and another, with the federal government playing an intermediary role as broker. The revision in 1985 of the system of financial equalisation among the *Länder* was a case in point. Six *Länder* opposed to the reform, but lacking the majority in the Bundesrat to enable them to block the measure, successfully took their case to the Federal Constitutional Court. The Court ruled that the financial system of federalism was not to be regarded as having substantial discretionary elements, but was a system of strict rules, binding on all concerned.[27] Thus the federal system both occasions and reinforces the formal constitutional restrictions to which the chancellor is subject.

The Chancellor and the Parties

The federal system gives the opposition a much stronger position than that derived from its role in the *Bundestag*. Disputes between federal government and the *Länder* are always in some measure party-political. It was no accident that the *Länder* which invoked the Constitutional Court in the Television Case were those governed by the opposition SPD. The opposition in the Bundestag is represented in the Bundesrat by virtue of its government role in the *Länder*. The powerful position of the Bundesrat in the legislative process means that the constitution simply does not allow the chancellor to achieve his political aims through his command of a Bundestag majority.

The prevalence of coalition government is another constraint upon the chancellor's power. Governments are only formed after a period of intense party wrangling. The resultant coalition agreement inevitably cuts across the chancellor's guidelines competence. The parties of both coalition and opposition are an essential part of the system of parliamentary government as established by the con-

27. *B Verf GE*, vol. 72, p. 330; M. Kilian, 'Das System des Länderfinanzausgleichs und die Finanzierung der neuen Bundeslander', *Juristen Zeitung*, no. 46, 1991, 425–31.

stitution. Indeed, the chancellor fills his office as a representative of a party.[28]

Coalition negotiations and inner-party debate can be seen as the real centres of decision-making, determining the balance between government and parliament. Cabinet decisions and parliamentary resolutions often represent little more than the implementation of agreements concluded at the inter-party and intra-party levels. Over time, coalition negotiations have become increasingly formalised and the resultant agreements much more detailed. In common with previous practice, the coalition agreement concluded between the CDU/CSU and the FDP in 1982 covered only the fundamental issues. By contrast, the agreement concluded by the same parties in 1991 consisted of a detailed document of some eighty pages, covering virtually all aspects of government policy. Parallel to this development, the routine 'coalition discussions' of a government in office were formalised in 1991 in a coalition committee (*Koalitionsrunde*), convened on a regular basis with agendas and minutes. The institutionalisation of coalition discussions has had a significant effect upon cabinet procedures and those of the parliamentary groups of the governing parties. The formulation of major decisions in the coalition committee pre-empts the cabinet and anticipates the decisions of Bundestag committees.

In a system of government with no formal locus of authority, the recognition of invisible lines of division between distinct institutions and functions is of crucial importance. The blurring of distinctions between party and government, politician and minister, is difficult to reconcile with the constitutional system. Moreover, it serves to obscure responsibilities and to restrict parliamentary influence. The principle set out in Article 21 of the Basic Law that the parties should participate in the formation of the political will of the people is a marker not only of the extent, but also of the limits of the role of the coalition parties.

The Vice-Chancellor

Article 69 of the Basic Law provides that the chancellor shall appoint a federal minister as his deputy. This deputy is unofficially called the 'vice-chancellor', following the 1878 practice. In political terms the second position in the government is always that of the foreign minister. Until 1955 Adenauer acted as his own foreign minister, and the post only came into existence formally in 1955, when West Germany attained sovereign status. From 1949 to 1957 the

28. *B Verf GE*, vol. 2, p. 15.

vice-chancellor, who traditionally sits on the chancellor's right in
cabinet meetings, was an FDP minister without portfolio, Franz
Blücher. From 1957 to 1963 Ludwig Erhard was vice-chancellor and
Economics Minister. During Erhard's chancellorship (1963-6) the
title was conferred on the FDP president, Erich Mende, who was
a minister without portfolio. From 1966 to June 1992 the functions
of Foreign Minister and vice-chancellor were united in one person,
who was also the leader of the junior coalition partner, the FDP.
With the resignation of Hans-Dietrich Genscher, however, the post
of Foreign Minister was separated from the title of vice-chancellor.
This raised a delicate question of protocol: who would sit on
the chancellor's right? Kohl followed the tradition of 1966-92,
rather than that of 1949-66. The Foreign Minister took the place
on the chancellor's right, while the vice-chancellor sat opposite
the chancellor.

Consensus

The term 'consensus' – a quality so conspicuously absent at earlier
stages of German development – is difficult to escape from in discussions of modern Germany. A system of tacit understandings is
part of the reality of the constitutional process, as much as its express
provisions are. Consensus means the recognition of the necessity not
to push political differences beyond a certain point and, when that
point is reached, to agree on a common position. Thus the exercise
of political power, rather than articulating a government/opposi-
tion dichotomy, embodies an inter-party accord. This is fostered by
the constitutional provisions which make the government dependent
upon support from the opposition and *Land* governments. It is also
found in German management and administration where, rather
than dependence on hierarchical authority to reach and impose decisions, reliance is placed on exhaustive discussion to achieve an
agreed strategy which then becomes the property of all concerned.
This characteristic also favours the long-term institutional values of
local autonomy, judicial detachment and administrative integrity.

The notion of consensus underlies the governing assumption of
the Basic Law that a state cannot fulfil its function of integrating the
wishes and interests of the people without a minimum level of agreement on fundamental values. The contentious part of social life, the
regulation of which arouses conflicts of interest and values, must be
counter-balanced by an accord on the foundations of society. What
the consensualism of the Basic Law essentially postulates is a form
of objective pluralism – the attempt to provide an authoritative
framework within which to preserve individual freedoms whilst
reconciling conflicting social and political objectives. As such it was

an attempt to redress a tradition in which individual freedom and political democracy were often seen not as complementary but as incommensurables, between which a trade-off had to be made and a balance struck.

In common with other West European countries, post-war Germany has experienced a decline of normative values, engendered by a sustained period of affluence and the relaxation of the Cold War. The resultant 'value relativism' has been manifested since the late 1960s in the emergence of extremist parties (albeit marginal to the party system), the persistence of an undercurrent of political violence against the leaders of German society and the rise of a 'New Politics' orientation towards post-materialism. The weakening of the forces of political integration in society has made consensual solutions more difficult to reach. These tendencies are further exacerbated by the social tensions resulting from unification and the formidable task of integrating the two parts of the new Germany. Overcoming the social and economic disparities between east and west without departing from the consensus model may require qualities of political leadership very different from those to which the Federal Republic has become accustomed.[29]

The Impact of the Constitution on the Chancellor

Chancellors would be less than human if they did not at times resent the constraints imposed by the panoply of the constitutional order. As Ernest Newman said of Wagner, he 'never objected to criticism, except when it was unfavourable to him'.[30] The openness and malleability of the Basic Law in the opening decade of the Federal Republic gave Adenauer a freedom of movement which distinguished his situation sharply from that of his successors. Indeed, in an important sense he created the constitutional system within which subsequent chancellors had to work. As the constitution stabilised and assumed firmer contours, Adenauer's room for manoeuvre diminished. Some of the errors of judgement in his closing years as chancellor – the presidential non-candidacy, the broadcasting dispute, the *Spiegel* affair (see Chapter 3, note 33) – may be attributed to his failure to appreciate the changed context in which he operated.[31] The apparent lack of respect for the constitution

29. Gordon Smith, 'The Resources of a German Chancellor', *West European Politics*, no. 14, 1991. pp. 48–61 at p. 59.
30. Ernest Newman, *The Life of Richard Wagner*, vol. 1: *1813–1848*, London: Cassell, 1933, p. 446.
31. See Jost Kupper, *Die Kanzlerdemokratie*, Frankfurt am Main: Peter Lang, 1985, pp. 65–71.

which he displayed undermined his political authority.

Consciously or unconsciously, Adenauer adopted a strategy of 'lonely decisions', embodying in the office of the chancellor a presidential executive similar to that of de Gaulle. The leadership instrument of his chancellorship was the Office of the Federal Chancellor and its official head, Hans Globke. The Standing Orders of the federal government (Para. 7 [1]) assigned to this post a double function: 'The State Secretary of the Office of the Federal Chancellor is simultaneously responsible for the business of the Federal government.' Thus the ministry was drawn into the conflicting pulls of the chancellor principle and the cabinet principle. As the instrument of the chancellor, it acquired under Adenauer its characteristic functions of providing information and advice, and implementing decisions.

Besides leaving Adenauer space to put his personal imprint on the new constitutional structure, the Basic Law in the early years of the Federal Republic took second place to the Occupation Statute. This reserved important policy areas to the occupation powers: foreign policy, control over the Ruhr industry, disarmament, foreign trade, refugees, war crimes. In practice, the Allies only made very limited use of these powers, leaving a political vacuum which Adenauer could fill. The pre-sovereign state of the Federal Republic increased the power of the chancellor.

Erhard sought to move to a more collegiate style of government, but in the face of Adenauer's continued influence over the CDU outside the Bundestag found that he lacked the control of party necessary to make cabinet government coherent. In the 'Grand Coalition' period from 1966 to 1969 the chancellor's guidelines competence was largely delegated to an inter-party coalition committee. This period marked the start of attempts to modify and modernise the institutions of chancellor democracy. When he became chancellor in 1969, Brandt placed great reliance on the proposals of the cabinet committee for the reform of the federal government, formulated during the previous government.[32] In accordance with this plan the cabinet was reduced in size from nineteen to fourteen members. The coalition agreement between the SPD and FDP established the foundations of the foreign policy – the *Ostpolitik* – with which the social–liberal government was principally identified in the period 1969–72. Just as Adenauer made his own foreign policy, so the *Ostpolitik* enabled Brandt to usurp foreign policy from the Foreign

32. Hartmut H. Brauswetter, *Kanzlerprinzip, Ressortprinzip und Kabinettsprinzip in der ersten Regierung Brandt 1969–1972*, Bonn: Eichholz Verlag, 1976, p. 70.

Ministry. In domestic matters – co-determination and abortion law reform – Brandt was constrained by the requirements of coalition government to conform to the FDP line. On the central issue of the *Ostpolitik*, however, he was not constrained by the constitutional obligation to work for reunification, because in the earlier judgement dealing with the Saarland Treaty the Constitutional Court had ruled that governments must determine for themselves the means by which this goal was to be pursued.[33]

Perhaps because he restricted himself to a managerial role, Brandt's successor, Helmut Schmidt, rarely encountered constitutional restraints. In some important policy areas, however, such as the expansion of nuclear energy, he encountered legal obstacles to programmes which he regarded as important to the country on pragmatic grounds.

Kohl came to power in a constitutional *coup d'état* – the constructive vote of no confidence of 1 October 1982 – and thereafter put the constitution under strain by engineering a premature dissolution of the Bundestag. Having overcome these obstacles, he was then criticised for adopting too relaxed a style of government and letting slip the reins of the guidelines competence. Unification, however, transformed his chancellorship. From the start Kohl pressed for full unification on the basis of the accession of the whole of East Germany to the Federal Republic under Article 23, and for sovereignty for the unified Germany. Against the odds he secured all these objectives, the critical point being the gaining of Soviet agreement in May 1990. The unification treaties effected constitutional amendments and so required two-thirds majorities in the Bundestag and Bundesrat. Kohl accordingly could only carry through his policy by securing the agreement of the opposition SPD, and this constraint influenced the form which his policy took. Likewise, the Federal Constitutional Court determined the form of the electoral law for the first all-German election since 1945, which was held on 2 December 1990.[34]

Conclusion

When considering the effect of the constitution on chancellors since 1949, the outstanding feature is the great elasticity of Article 65. The chancellor has both a political position and a constitutional position, and when under pressure in one area can switch his weight to the other. At the beginning of this chapter, a distinction was made

33. *B Verf GE*, vol. 4, p. 174.
34. *B Verf GE*, vol. 82, p. 322.

between the 'setting' *in* which government is conducted and the 'apparatus' *with* which it is conducted. Law provides both the setting (Savigny's political aspect of law) and the apparatus (the technical aspect). It is this dual aspect of law which makes the relationship between law and politics so difficult to characterise. The Basic Law furnishes both the formal environment within which the chancellor works and the means by which the political struggle is carried on.

Government arrangements institutionalise the means for maximising some values and for minimising others. In the 1920s Kelsen, together with liberal commentators on the constitution such as Anschütz, argued that democracy was an organisational framework for reaching decisions without recourse to any universally accepted values. By ruling out of order all relative problems of political and social power, this approach paved the way for 'decisionism', the demand for action instead of deliberation, decision instead of evaluation, the acceptance of all political decisions whatever their source or content because of the power structure behind them.[35]

The system of government established and developed under the Basic Law constitutes the deliberate rejection of the view that everything is at the disposition of the popular will and its instruments. The state of West Germany was originally based on a deep pessimism about the political effects of politics. While the earlier history of Germany explained this fear, the subsequent history of the Federal Republic did not justify it. The legal apparatus of the constitution was given the function of interpreting and maintaining a certain type of political rule. Chancellors have had to ask themselves how to come to terms with the mandate not only of the electorate but also of the Basic Law. The appeal to ultimate values can appear authoritarian and generate extremes of both radicalism and conservatism. Happily, the chancellors of the Federal Republic have been quietly competent, steady, not particularly inspiring figures who have, notwithstanding occasional grumbles, accepted the system for what it is and used the opportunities which it affords in the manner best designed to further their policies.

The post-war constitutional system, while intended to impose fixed elements, has also shown itself capable of flexible evolution, most comprehensively by the ability to adapt West German institutions to incorporate the new German *Länder* which were formerly part of East Germany. A constitutional system of government is not

35. D.B. Southern, 'German Legal Ideas in the Nineteenth and Twentieth Centuries', *Liverpool Law Review*, vol. X, 1988, pp. 63–83; see also Stefan Korroth, 'Erschütterungen des staatsrechtlichen Positivismus im ausgehenden Kaiserreich', *Archiv des öffentlichen Rechts*, no. 117, 1992, pp. 212–38.

a kind of automatic pilot which runs by itself. Its effectiveness in practice largely depends on the wit and wisdom of those entrusted with its operation. Nevertheless, the stability of the Federal Republic and its political and economic success, over which the chancellors have presided, are derived in significant measure from the values and structure of the Basic Law.

2

THE CHANCELLOR AND HIS PARTY

Stephen Padgett

The chancellor's relationship with his party is the key to his ability to turn his constitutional powers into political authority. The experience of all incumbents suggests that effective executive leadership depends upon chancellor dominance over the party arena, or at least the capacity to exercise autonomy from party constraints. The dependency of chief executives on party support is a feature of all parliamentary systems of government, but it is accentuated in the German case by three features of the political system. First, the ambivalence of inner-executive relations under Article 65 of the Basic Law means that the chancellor's capacity to exercise the guidelines competence is dependent on party backing. Secondly, in a system characterised by a high degree of institutional pluralism, the chancellor's party plays a crucial unifying role. Thirdly, coalition government multiplies and intensifies the demands on a chief executive. Control over the chancellor's own party is a pre-requisite of effective coalition management.

Chancellors have at their disposal some very effective instruments of party management. A chancellor has a prerogative to lead the party, although the two roles are not always combined as they are in Britain. The party chairmanship gives the chancellor access to the resources of the national party organisation. Since most chancellors have risen to prominence through the party, they generally have a personal power base in the organisation. Moreover, discipline in the *Bundestagsfraktionen* (parliamentary groups) of both major parties is strong, orchestrated by parliamentary leaders who normally serve as loyal lieutenants of the chancellor. *Fraktion* leaders have extensive powers of patronage which can be deployed to counter tendencies towards factional mobilisation. Finally, government and party are unified by the presence of government ministers in the executive organs of the party.

Despite all these advantages, however, chancellors cannot merely rely on the support of their parties. They must cultivate it actively, and often strenuously, whilst at the same time asserting their autonomy as head of government. No chancellor has been able to treat his party simply as a personal instrument. Adenauer came

44

closest to exercising unconditional dominance, but some accounts of his incumbency have stressed the constraints on him in regard to domestic policy.[1] Like all Christian Democratic chancellors, he had to come to terms with the polycentric power structure of the party, and to mediate between the exceptionally broad spectrum of socio-economic interests contained within this archetypal *Volkspartei*. Social Democratic chancellors, on the other hand, have had to assert their autonomy from a party which has tended to regard 'its' chancellor as an instrument for the realisation of the programmatic objectives of the party.

In the 1970s, Edinger developed two models of chancellor–party relations. The first variant represented the chancellor as the autonomous and authoritative head of an executive-centred élite coalition, who dominated his party and considered it his instrument. In the second, the chancellor acted as chief of government only in the formal sense. In reality he was no more than chairman of a team of more or less equal party leaders. Thus party élites inside and outside the legislature may play a much greater role in fashioning government policy.[2] In fact Edinger's model turned out to be of limited value, since the first variant only really applied to the Adenauer incumbency. His successors have all acted more or less in accordance with the second model. Nevertheless his contribution was part of a trend which located the determinants of chancellorial power decisively in the arena of chancellor–party relations: 'The real power of a Chancellor depends largely on the support he gets from his party and the parliamentary party group.'[3]

The dependency of executive leadership on party support suggests that *chancellor* democracy is heavily conditioned by *party* democracy. Thus the development of the German chancellorship is closely bound up with the evolution of the *Volksparteien* from which all post-war chancellors have been drawn. Since the early 1970s, both *Volksparteien* have experienced a loss of internal cohesion, reflecting patterns of social change. In particular, social and electoral fragmentation has weakened the foundation of party stability and cohesion. Party system change on these lines has gone some way towards redefining the relationship between chancellor and party, and with it the character of the chancellorship itself.

1. See Peter H. Merkl, 'Equilibrium, Structure of Interests and Leadership: Adenauer's Survival as Chancellor', *American Political Science Review*, vol. 56, no. 3, Sept. 1962, pp. 634–50.
2. Lewis Edinger, *Politics in Germany*, Boston: Little, Brown, 1977, p. 189.
3. Renate Mayntz, 'Executive Leadership in Germany: Dispersion of Power or "Kanzlerdemokratie"', in R. Rose and E.N. Suleiman (eds), *Presidents and Prime Ministers*, Washington, DC: American Enterprise Institute, 1980.

The Subordination of Party to Chancellor: the Adenauer Era, 1949–1959

Adenauer's dominance over the CDU was the inevitable product of the party's infancy and the circumstances of its inception. Christian Democracy was a post-war movement inspired by the belief that Christian values contained the potential for the political and moral regeneration of Germany. This belief gave the movement a veneer of unity, but beneath the surface lay a diversity of conflicting political tendencies and personalities. Organisationally, the movement arose out of regional and local initiatives, each with its own distinctive social and political identity. Those who chaired the *Land* parties spoke on behalf of the social interests which they represented. Their political views were thus sharply divergent, and Adenauer was able to exploit their differences with a strategy of divide and rule. Adenauer's initial dominance stemmed from his success in consolidating the heterogenous political groupings out of which the movement had emerged, outmanoeuvring and marginalising his rivals in the process.

Regional diversity retarded the organisational development of the CDU at federal level. When federal party organs were belatedly brought into being in the early 1950s, they were deprived of political weight by regional party barons who maintained a jealous hold over their own authority. Adenauer skilfully exploited the organisational immaturity of the CDU. The absence of formal procedures of decision-making enabled him to manipulate the party, convening *ad hoc* meetings whose composition he engineered to ensure that his view would prevail. By the time he assumed the chancellorship in 1949, he was already well on the way to control over his party. His dominance was reflected in the composition of his first cabinet: 'Adenauer evidently did not feel it necessary to take into the cabinet many party leaders representing factions other than his.'[4]

Once in power, Adenauer's ability to subordinate the party was increased by his possession of the resources of the state apparatus. Indeed, the offices of state and party were almost indistinguishable. Adenauer himself combined the offices of chancellor and party chairman. The CDU executive was too large a body to be effective, and party management was conducted from the Chancellor's Office. Its chief, Hans Globke, acted as the chancellor's personal agent in the CDU although he had no formal party post.[5] Adenauer was

4. Arnold J. Heidenheimer, *Adenauer and the CDU: The Rise of the Leader and the Integration of the Party*, The Hague: Martinus Nijhoff, 1960, p. 186.
5. Hans-Peter Schwarz, *Die Ära Adenauer. Epochenwechsel, 1957–1963* Stuttgart/ Wiesbaden: Deutsche Verlagsanstalt (hereafter DVA)/F.A. Brockhaus, 1983, pp. 20–1.

thus able to remain aloof from the party apparatus.

Adenauer's disdain reflected the weakness of the party organisation. The CDU was little more than a machine for re-electing the chancellor – a *Kanzlerwählerverein*. Even this function was downgraded by the plebiscitary character of German democracy in these years, and by the direct and personal appeal which Adenauer projected to the electorate. Between elections, local branches of the party were often dormant. Membership of the CDU, which in the immediate post-war years had stood at 400,000, declined by the middle 1950s to little more than half that figure. In fact the CDU in the Adenauer era could hardly be described as a *mass* party. Duverger has described an élitist type of political party which 'does not aim at recruiting the largest possible membership, but at enlisting the support of prominent individuals.'[6] The CDU corresponded to this model. Its membership was passive and the policy function of the party was minimal. The party organisation was thus 'destined to remain hopelessly in the shadow of the government.'[7]

The chancellor's relationship with the CDU *Bundestagsfraktion* was rather more complex, and requires careful assessment. On the one hand, the party's electoral success brought into the Bundestag a large number of politically inexperienced deputies who were ill equipped to challenge the chancellor on policy issues. Moreover, as Bundestag elections assumed the character of personal votes for the chancellor, CDU deputies knew that they owed their election to Adenauer's prestige. They were also aware that they were dependent upon his patronage for career advancement. These factors made it easy for Adenauer to subordinate the *Bundestagsfraktion*, especially in foreign policy. A sharp polarisation between the CDU/CSU and the Social Democracts in this policy area meant that he could rely on the unquestioning support of his party, simply informing the Bundestag of his policy decisions without feeling the need to explain or justify. As Heidenheimer has pointed out, foreign policy was the agent of party cohesion: 'It was on questions related to foreign policy that the CDU developed its own version of party discipline.'[8]

Whilst foreign policy transcended factional differences and was less encumbered by considerations of party politics, the domestic policy process revolved around the interplay of group interests

6. Maurice Duverger, *Political Parties: Their Organisation and Activity in the Modern State*, 2nd edn, New York/London: Wiley/Methuen, 1964. p. 64.
7. Heidenheimer (1960), *op. cit.*, p. 206.
8. *Ibid.*, p. 211.

within the party. A multiplicity of social groups competed for position and influence, each with its own organisational identity in an elaborate system of party committees representing business and industry, organised labour, the self-employed middle class, and farmers. Divergent social tendencies were compounded by confessional rivalries between Catholics and Protestants. Cohesion and stability were fostered by a shared interest in party unity, a common allegiance to Christian Democratic values, and by a mutual recognition of the right of all inner-party groups to be heard. Nevertheless, this configuration of competing interests contained the potential for policy conflict. To be successful, the chancellor had to be able to balance factional claims for influence in the party and in government.

The *Bundestagsfraktion* served as a sort of clearing house for the competing interests in Adenauer's CDU. *Fraktion* discipline was maintained through compromise: 'The structural incapacity of the CDU for policy agreement meant that time and again it was compelled to take the middle line.'[9] Adenauer's role was one of mediation, a role he played with consummate skill, pragmatically placing party unity before policy commitments. The result of the chancellor's tactical flexibility, however, was an underlying inertia in domestic politics. During the 1950s this weakness was masked by foreign policy achievements and by the economic miracle. As the chancellor's foreign policy lost its gloss in the last four years of his incumbency, his domestic policy shortcomings became more apparent.

These considerations should not be allowed to detract from Adenauer's dominance over his party. They merely indicate that he had to contend with the same tendencies towards polycentrism which have faced his successors. In one important respect the social fragmentation of the CDU actually served to enhance Adenauer's power over the party, since it prevented the emergence of a concerted challenge to his leadership. His political dexterity enabled him to exploit the structure of the party, playing off competing power centres against one another. This strategy was central in his approach to the succession question which dominated the later years of his chancellorship.

9. Schwarz, *op. cit.*, p. 156.

The Succession Struggle

The succession struggle of 1959–63 provides valuable insights into the relationship between a CDU chancellor and the party. It was played out against the background of mounting disquiet over the chancellor's autocratic style of leadership, and a groundswell of opinion in favour of an 'unfreezing' of government policy and internal party affairs. Adenauer, however, was able to defy the challenge by drawing on the strength of his support in the party at large and by exploiting the internal fragmentation of the CDU, which greatly reduced its capacity to take decisive action.

The challenge was inspired by a number of factors. The most significant of these was a sense of frustration at the rigidity of the chancellor's foreign policy. Adenauer's absolute power in this domain, combined with the entrenchment of his policy positions, convinced party élites of the necessity of a change of leadership. Personal factors also played a part in the formation of the 'internal opposition'. The semi-permanent tenure granted to the chancellor's loyal subordinates in the cabinet thwarted the ambitions of those outside this circle. Finally, there was a growing assertiveness in the CDU, born of the recognition that its subordination to the chancellor was damaging to the party's prestige.

The first opportunity to force the succession issue was the CDU nomination of a candidate for the federal presidency in 1959. Initially Adenauer agreed to accept the nomination on the understanding that as president he would retain control over foreign policy, and that he would have a voice in the nomination of his successor. This pact between Adenauer and the CDU élite became impossible to sustain, however, in the face of widespread allegations of constitutional impropriety. Moreover, chancellor and party were irreconcilably divided over the succession. The heir apparent, Ludwig Erhard, was anathema to Adenauer, while the chancellor's own candidate was unacceptable to the CDU.

There followed a protracted struggle between chancellor and party. Recognising that he could not dictate the terms of his succession, Adenauer now sought to evade the presidential nomination; for its part, the CDU tried to corner him into acceptance. In the parliamentary party, support for Erhard was overwhelming. Having opened up the succession question, the party was increasingly confident of success, and this confidence was echoed in the press, where the end of the Adenauer era was widely heralded. This judgement was premature and sprang from a misreading of the power relationship between chancellor and party. Ultimately, Adenauer simply withdrew his presidential nomination, declared his intention of retaining the chancellorship and challenged the parliamentary party to deploy the only instrument at its disposal: a no confidence vote in the Bundestag. Having stood in the shadow of the chancellor for a decade, the CDU was incapable of taking such drastic action.

The second unsuccessful challenge took place after the election of 1961 which deprived Adenauer of the absolute parliamentary majority he had won in the previous election. On this occasion, the challenge was spearheaded by the Free Democratic Party (FDP), with the backing of the chancellor's opponents within his own party. The Liberals' immediate rejection of an Adenauer-led coalition was to serve as a catalyst for an 'internal revolution' within the CDU, out of which a Christian–Liberal coalition would be formed under Erhard.

In countering this threat, Adenauer was able to exploit the competitive relationship between the diverse political forces within the CDU itself. The labour wing of the party feared the prospect of a coalition with the business-oriented FDP under Erhard, the arch-advocate of economic liberalism. An alliance with this section of the party served as the foundation of Adenauer's strategy. After he had secured the support of this group, the chancellor issued a thinly veiled signal of his willingness to form a grand coalition with the SPD, a move calculated to arouse the anxiety of business interests. The strategy had the desired effect; the Bundesverband der Deutschen Industrie (BDI – Confederation of German Industry) threw its support behind Adenauer, putting pressure on the FDP not to drive him into the arms of the Social Democrats.[10] Erhard then withdrew his candidacy for the chancellorship and the FDP capitulated, albeit after an undertaking from Adenauer that he would step down before the end of the legislative period.

A number of reasons have been put forward to account for the inability of Adenauer's opponents to oust him. First, and perhaps most significantly, was his continued ability to invoke the 'chancellor effect' in the CDU.[11] At the Karlsruhe party congress of 1960, against the background of the succession question and with an undercurrent of conflict between the chancellor and his economics minister never far beneath the surface, Adenauer's re-election as party chairman was almost unopposed. Even after the second suc-

---

10. See Daniel Koerfer, *Kampf ums Kanzleramt. Erhard und Adenauer*, Stuttgart: DVA, 1988, pp. 555–609; Schwarz, *op. cit.*, pp. 228–39.
11. Arnold J. Heidenheimer, 'Der starke Regierungschef und das Parteiensystem; der Kanzlereffekt in der Bundesrepublik', *Politische Vierteljahresschrift*, vol. 2, 1961, pp. 251–2.

cession struggle the 1962 party congress re-elected him by 391 out of 461 votes.[12] Support in the party at large was a key resource in countering opposition within the *Bundestagsfraktion*. A second significant factor was the reluctance of his opponents to be identified with the overthrow of so venerable a figure.[13] A pervasive sense of diffidence, born of standing so long in the old man's shadow, appears to have prevented Erhard from acting decisively at key stages in the succession struggles.

A third explanation for Adenauer's ability to triumph in 1961 focuses on his role as the integrating force holding together the complex system of competing interests within the CDU. The succession question meant renegotiating power relations within the CDU/CSU. 'Beneath the surface party groups began to jockey restlessly for an eventual redistribution of intra-party power.'[14] Adenauer's ability to exploit this syndrome was very apparent in 1961. Ultimately then, inner-party power politics took precedence over the succession question.[15]

Although Adenauer was able to withstand the challenges from within the CDU, his final years in office witnessed a decline in his authority over the party and with it the erosion of chancellor democracy.[16] His government was divided over major issues of domestic and foreign policy, with differences openly articulated by Erhard and the foreign minister, Gerhard Schröder. Moreover, the election of 1961 had seen the CDU share of the vote reduced from 50.2 per cent to 45.3 per cent. It was impossible to avoid the conclusion that the total subordination of party to chancellor had exacted its price in a loss of vitality in the CDU. Reasoning along these lines, *Land* party leaders took the initiative in creating a new post of general secretary,[17] a first step in the CDU's transition to a mass organisation party.

It was the *Bundestagsfraktion* and party executive which compelled Adenauer to step down in 1963 after Erhard had finally issued the call. It was a measure of the party's impotence that it acted only after the government had been compromised by the *Spiegel* affair (see Chapter 3, note 33), and when the chancellor's agreement with the FDP was shortly due to expire. Nevertheless, the manner of

12. Koerfer, *op. cit.*, pp. 433, 654.
13. Schwarz, *op. cit.*, p. 228.
14. Heidenheimer (1960), *op. cit.*, p. 222.
15. Merkl, *op. cit.*, pp. 637–42.
16. Thomas Ellwein, *Das Regierungssystem der Bundesrepublik Deutschland*, Opladen: Westdeutscher Verlag, 1977, p. 317.
17. Koerfer, *op. cit.*, pp. 625–8.

Adenauer's withdrawal underlines the fact that chancellors are sustained in power by the consent of their party. While Adenauer was able to prolong his tenure of office by tactical manoeuvre, even he was ultimately subject to party fiat.

In retrospect, it is clear that the dominance of chancellor over party in the Adenauer era was a product of historial circumstances. The chief of these was the immaturity of the CDU, together with the malleability of the institutions and procedures of government in a newly formed state. Skilfully exploiting these circumstances, Adenauer dominated both party and state, effectively fusing them into a single power complex which sustained what Heidenheimer termed a feudal style of leadership. No subsequent chancellor has been able to replicate Adenauer's dominance over his party, least of all his immediate successor.

Erhard: a 'Guest' in the CDU

Ludwig Erhard had the misfortune to come to power at a time when political and economic circumstances were placing increasing strains on the delicate balance of forces within the CDU/CSU. A changing international environment called for adjustments in the Federal Republic's foreign policy, and the consensus which had served as the foundation of party unity began to break up in conflict between Gaullists and Atlanticists (see Chapter 5). In domestic policy, a slowdown in economic growth led to conflicts between budgetary priorities which served to intensify the mobilisation of group interests within the party, strengthening its centrifugal tendencies and accentuating its polycentric character.[18]

Lacking his predecessor's tactical skills, Erhard was entirely unsuited to this style of leadership. He was not by nature a politician; he lacked the politician's innate conception of power and how to use it. Moreover, his relationship with the party was a distant one. Indeed, he has been described as a 'guest' in the CDU.[19] Erhard's estrangement from the party and his lack of appreciation of the realities of power were both exemplified in his willingness to allow Adenauer to remain as party chairman. Erhard's eventual succession to the chairmanship in 1966 took place against the background of strong opposition on the part of the *Bundestagsfraktion*, and only served to erode still further his credibility in the party. As chan-

---

18. Klaus Hildebrand, *Von Erhard zur Grossen Koalition; 1963-1969*, Stuttgart/Wiesbaden: DVA/F.A. Brockhaus, 1984, p. 58.
19. David Conradt, *The German Polity*, Harlow/New York: Longman, 1982, p. 158.

cellor, Adenauer had publicly and frequently derided his economics minister, and he continued to do so after Erhard became chancellor, in concert with Franz Josef Strauss, leader of the CSU. Free of cabinet responsibility, but backed by the strong and loyal CSU *Fraktion* in the Bundestag, Strauss was ideally placed to engage in intrigue against the chancellor in the furtherance of his own ambitions. Adenauer and Strauss both played the role of *Nebenkanzler* (shadow chancellor) to Erhard, the one reluctant to give up the office, the other coveting it. In addition, Erhard had powerful enemies amongst CDU ministers in the *Länder*. They were able to use the Bundesrat as a forum for opposition to the chancellor. Personal enmity against Erhard was interwoven here with conflict over economic relations between Bonn and the *Länder*.

Erhard's potential allies in the party élite were of limited support to the chancellor. Bundestag president Eugen Gerstenmaier was an elder statesman of some standing, and had been one of Erhard's backers in the succession struggle. However, foreign policy differences distanced Gerstenmaier from the chancellor and he was insufficiently engaged in internal party life for his support to be of great value. Within the cabinet, Foreign Minister Schröder was the dominant figure, but he too lacked a strong power base in the party. As newly installed *Fraktion* chairman, Rainer Barzel was rapidly acquiring a reputation for competent leadership, and he supported the chancellor as well as he could in the circumstances. However, Erhard's failure to recognise the importance of having support in the Bundestag meant that relations between the two were often strained. Moreover, Barzel's ambition prevented him from identifying himself too closely with a chancellor with an uncertain future, a factor which became decisive in 1966. Thus Erhard's distance from the party was compounded by his inability to rely, as Adenauer had at crucial times, on loyal lieutenants in key party positions.

Erhard's ineptitude in the arena of inner-party power politics was not simply a personal failing. It was also a function of the analysis of West German society which he had evolved and expounded in the last years of the Adenauer chancellorship. It involved a critique of the egoism and power of organised group interests, and the tendency of government to engage in horse-trading between these at the expense of a consistent economic policy and the pursuit of the general interest. Erhard had developed a vision of the '*Formierte Gesellschaft*' – a fully formed society in which group interests would be subordinated to wider societal objectives.[20] The vision

---

20. Koerfer, *op. cit.*, p. 460; Hildebrand, *op. cit.*, pp. 160–70.

would have been an ambitious one for any government leader. It was particularly ill chosen for a CDU chancellor, given the entrenchment of social interests within the party. Unsurprisingly, the idea of the *Formierte Gesellschaft* failed to make any impact in the CDU. Erhard enunciated the concept as part of his government statement of November 1965, but without the backing of the party it was impossible to translate this vague and abstract concept into a definite programme.

Far from addressing the mounting disarray in the CDU, Erhard merely distanced himself from the party, making a direct appeal to the electorate by projecting the image of a *Volkskanzler* (people's chancellor). For a time he was able to draw on the political capital which he had built up as a successful economics minister, and in the Bundestag elections of 1965 the CDU/CSU succeeded in reversing the electoral decline of the early 1960s. Electoral success, however, did nothing to enhance Erhard's authority in the party. Ultimately the reliance which the chancellor placed on plebiscitary democracy was to contribute to his downfall. The CDU's losses in the North Rhine/Westphalia Landtag elections of July 1966 were a particularly serious blow in view of Erhard's unfortunate declaration that the vote would represent a judgement on his government. The final crisis came three months later, precipitated by the FDP's defection from the coalition. The underlying cause, though, was the chancellor's loss of authority over his own party, signalled by the unanimous rejection of the federal budget by the Bundesrat – in which the CDU/CSU had a majority.

Under Erhard's incumbency, then, *Kanzlerdemokratie* was transformed into *Kanzleranarchie* as the chancellor's passivity gave full play to the multiple political and personal conflicts within the CDU/CSU. The Erhard experience shows very clearly that constitutional powers and the resources of the government apparatus are not in themselves sufficient to sustain a chancellor, underlining the importance of a consolidated party power base.

Kiesinger and the Politics of Inter-Party Accommodation

The Kiesinger chancellorship was structurally conditioned by the composition of his government. A Grand Coalition between two parties broadly equal in status and representing opposing ideological tendencies left very little scope for the exercise of the chancellor's right to set guidelines (*Richtlinienkompetenz*) for government policy. The terms of the coalition were clearly articulated by SPD Vice-Chancellor and Foreign Minister Willy Brandt:

'There can be guidelines only in relation to the ground rules of the coalition.'[21] For his part, Kiesinger accepted the constraints, which meant that he was no more than the first among equals within the government. Thus the Kiesinger chancellorship corresponds closely to Edinger's second model of chancellor–party relations, in which party élites both inside and outside the legislature participate in the formulation of government policy.

Like most German chancellors, Kiesinger's career had included high office in *Land* government. After a successful parliamentary career in Bonn, albeit one unadorned with ministerial office, he was minister-president of Baden-Württemberg during its emergence as the model state of the Federal Republic. Here he acquired an almost monarchical status as *Landesvater* (state patriarch). From this position he was able to intervene effectively in federal politics, especially foreign policy. Thus he was well versed in Bonn politics without being tainted by the rivalries and intrigue which characterised the federal CDU at the end of the Adenauer era. In short, he was ideally placed to rescue party and government from the sense of crisis which had pervaded both since the end of the Adenauer era.

The government's overwhelming parliamentary majority inevitably altered the relationship between executive and legislature. In the absence of adversarial rivalry between government and opposition, the Bundestag assumed a more independent role, with the coalition parties markedly more assertive in relation to the government. SPD *Fraktion* chairman Helmut Schmidt's assertion that the government was bound to carry out parliament's wishes was exaggerated, and was met by Kiesinger's rejoinder that if that was the case, the Bundestag would have to find a new chancellor.[22] Nevertheless, the Bundestag was able to participate in the formulation of government policy, as underlined by the frequent presence in the cabinet of Schmidt and Rainer Barzel, the chairmen of the parliamentary *Fraktionen* of the coalition parties. A close working relationship between the two *Fraktion* chairmen was an essential element in the management of coalition relations. This was bound to reduce the centrality of the chancellor's role.

Kiesinger's principal function as head of a Grand Coalition was that of mediation, not an easy role to play under the circumstances. Emerging from the shadow of Adenauer, but still lacking organisational independence, the CDU/CSU was in some disarray. Accustomed to coalition dominance, it was unused to intra-coalition

21. Hildebrand, *op. cit.*, p. 269.
22. *Ibid.*, p. 271.

bargaining with a partner of equal strength. After its prolonged exile in opposition, and represented in the government by forceful and able ministers like Brandt and Schiller, the SPD could not be restricted to a passive supporting role. The depiction of the chancellor as 'a walking mediation committee' (a term coined by government press secretary Conrad Ahlers) may appear to denote weakness; in fact, Kiesinger's success in persuading his party to come to terms with the new configuration of forces within the government is indicative of considerable political resourcefulness.

The chancellor's main instrument of mediation and conflict resolution was the inter-party élite discussion group first convened in August 1967 at Kressbron on Lake Constance. Composed of government ministers and leading party figures from both coalition parties,[23] the *Kressbronner Kreis* (Kressbron circle) was regularised in weekly working lunches which served to establish common ground between the parties and acted as a sort of clearing house for coalition conflicts. Although it was very successful as such, this informal coalition committee functioned almost like a 'shadow government' encroaching significantly on the chancellor's responsibility for establishing policy guidelines. Additionally, there was a significant increase in the exercise of ministerial autonomy in the Grand Coalition.

Although the Grand Coalition was successful in a number of respects, it was essentially a provisional arrangement, a stage in the transition from Christian Democratic to Social Democratic government. In this sense, the Kiesinger incumbency was little more than an inter-regnum. This was reflected in the chancellor's relationship with his party. Although he was elected party chairman in 1967, Kiesinger never assumed a leadership role in the CDU. During this period, the party itself was embarking on a transformation from the chancellor party it had been under Adenauer, to a party with a modern organisational apparatus geared to electoral mobilisation.[24] Lacking both charisma and the skills of party political

23. The standing membership of the *Kressbronner Kreis* was as follows: Kiesinger (chancellor and CDU chairman), Brandt (vice-chancellor, foreign minister and SPD chairman); Barzel and Schmidt (*Fraktion* chairmen CDU and SPD); Bruno Heck (minister for family affairs and CDU general secretary); Franz Josef Strauss (CSU chairman and finance minister); Richard Stücklen (parliamentary group chairman CSU and parliamentary state secretary in the Chancellor's Office); Karl Theodor zu Guttenberg (CSU member of the Bundestag); Herbert Wehner (SPD deputy chairman and minister for inner-German affairs): Alex Möller (deputy chairman SPD *Fraktion*); Gerhard Jahn (SPD member of Bundestag and parliamentary state secretary, Foreign Ministry).
24. Ute Schmidt, 'Die Christlich Demokratische Union Deutschlands', in Richard Stöss (ed.), *Parteien Handbuch. Die Parteien der Bundesrepublik Deutschland, 1945–80*, vol, 1, Opladen: Westdeutscher Verlag, 1983, p. 511.

manoeuvre, Kiesinger was ill equipped to lead the party through that transition.

Brandt as Instrument of the Party?

It has already been observed that the authority of German chancellors can be greatly enhanced by their simultaneous occupancy of the chairmanship of their party. The Adenauer chancellorship is a case in point; the party chairmanship and chancellorship were entwined in a single power complex. Willy Brandt also combined the two offices. Instead of merging the two roles, however, Brandt consciously sought to maintain a distinction between them. As chancellor he repeatedly emphasised his autonomy from the SPD and his independence from party interests. As party chairman, on the other hand, he identified intimately with the party, upheld the legitimacy of internal party debate and continued to play the role of reconciler within the SPD. Ultimately this role differentiation proved very difficult to sustain.

It is impossible to understand Brandt's relationship with his party during his time as chancellor without reference to his background in the SPD. Unlike his predecessors, Brandt's life and career before becoming chancellor had been intimately entwined with his party. Brought up within the pervasive culture of pre-war German social democracy, Brandt entered the party at the age of sixteen. A brief flirtation with leftist socialism was followed by exile in Norway during the twelve years of the Third Reich. On his return to Germany in 1945, he became a key figure in the regeneration and renewal of the SPD. His early career was in Berlin, where his election as mayor in 1957 made him a focus of international attention. Simultaneously rising in the Bonn party hierarchy, he became party chairman in 1962 and fought two unsuccessful elections as the SPD's candidate for chancellor, serving as vice-chancellor and Foreign Minister in the Grand Coalition before becoming chancellor in 1969.

Brandt's career was synonymous with the transformation of the SPD from the working-class socialist party of the early 1950s into a socially diverse *Volkspartei*, combining the reforming ideals of the Social Democratic tradition with a pragmatic orientation towards government power. Brandt himself epitomised the synthesis between idealism and pragmatism. However, it was a difficult balance to maintain, particularly in the context of the changing social composition of the SPD in the late 1960s and early 1970s.

The 1960s had seen a steady rise in party membership – the so-called '*Genosse* trend'. From 1969 to 1972 the trend accelerated exponentially, with an increase of 175,000 members. In 1972 alone recruitment reached 153,000, giving a net increase of over 100,000.

58   *Stephen Padgett*

By 1973 over two-thirds of SPD members had joined the party within the previous decade. The *Genosse* trend was accompanied by fundamental changes in the age and class structure of the SPD. The new membership was predominantly young, educated and middle class. Over half of the new recruits were under thirty years old. One-third were white-collar workers and almost one-fifth were students or in vocational training. In contrast to the passivity of the traditional manual worker membership, the new SPD generation was articulate, highly motivated and active, demanding a participatory role within the party.

Politically, the new SPD generation was indelibly marked by the association with the Extra-Parliamentary Opposition (APO), an amorphous student movement loosely based on the values of libertarian socialism and a radical critique of post-war German society. Initially SPD leaders had been highly critical of the demagogic and often violent character of the movement, and had tried to distance the party from it. With the failure of this strategy, SPD leaders now concluded that the party must attempt to embrace the critical youth of the APO movement. Although their overtures were at first greeted with some scepticism,[25] the integration strategy was ultimately very successful. The key figure in its success was Brandt.[26] Sympathetic to many of the objectives, though not the methods of the APO movement, Brandt engaged in a political dialogue with its adherents. The promise of 'democratisation' he held out in the campaign for the 1969 election was an echo of their own aspirations.

The consequences of the integration strategy proved very difficult to manage in the longer term. Change in the social and political composition of the party had a profound impact upon internal party life. Social diversity bred political conflict and the demand for participation was hard to reconcile with the élite-dominated structure of the party. The legacy was an intensification of factional mobilisation[27] and a sharp upturn in programmatic activity as the new generation of party members attempted to turn their demands into party policy. These tendencies made it doubly difficult for Brandt to combine the exercise of chancellorial power with the party chairman's role of conciliation and integration.

The demands behind the APO movement were an extreme expression of more broadly based aspirations towards a relaxation of the

25. Stefan Gorol, 'Zwischen Integration und Abgrenzung: SPD und Studentische Protestbewegung', *Die neue Gesellschaft/Frankfurter Heft*, no. 7, 1988, p. 606.
26. Arnulf Baring, *Machtwechsel. Die Ära Brandt-Scheel*, Stuttgart: DVA, 1982, pp. 90–3.
27. Klaus von Beyme (ed.), *Die Grossen Regierungs-erklärungen der deutschen Kanzler von Adenauer bis Schmidt*, Munich: Carl Hanser, 1979, p. 281.

political and cultural constraints of post-war West German society. Brandt's success in the election of 1969 sprang from his ability to encapsulate the prevailing spirit of the time in slogans like 'We are creating the modern Germany' and 'Dare more democracy', and in his statement upon becoming chancellor that 'We are not at the end of our democracy, we are only just beginning.' The rhetoric of 'the Social Democratic revolution' and the 'myth of a new *Stunde Null*' (zero hour or new beginning)[28] found a resonance in the SPD during Brandt's first term as chancellor (1969–72). Thereafter, however, the expectations which this rhetoric had created became an increasingly heavy burden on the chancellor.

Despite the SPD's tradition of inner-party democracy, Brandt was effectively insulated from direct pressures from below by the hierarchical structure of the party.[29] The praesidium – in practice the supreme party organ – was almost exclusively composed of members of the federal and *Land* governments. Although the left was represented on the party executive, it remained an insignificant minority. In the *Bundestagsfraktion* the presence of the left increased after the election of 1972. Discipline was maintained, however, by the astute management of *Fraktion* chairman Herbert Wehner. Factional mobilisation on the left was more an exercise to secure posts than an attempt to create an ideological caucus. Challenges to chancellor and government were restricted to the party congress. The Hannover congress of 1973, for example, expressed dissatisfaction over the slow pace and limited scope of the government's promised reform programme.[30]

Brandt's response to these challenges was twofold. On the one hand he reiterated his frequently stated position that as chancellor his primary responsibility was to the electorate and that he and his government had to maintain their independence from the party. Congress resolutions could influence the government but they were in no sense binding upon it.[31] Government programmes were indicative of the autonomy of the chancellor from his party, reflecting a Social–Liberal consensus much more clearly than party commitments did. On the other hand Brandt recognised the legitimacy of policy formulation and debate within the party. Participation in

28. Karl Dietrich Bracher, Wolfgang Jäger and Werner Link, *Republik im Wandel 1969–74: die Ära Brandt*, Stuttgart: DVA, 1986, p. 439.
29. Stephen Padgett and Tony Burkett, *Parties and Elections in West Germany: The Search for a New Stability*, London: Hurst, 1986, pp. 67–72.
30. Gerhard Braunthal, *The West German Social Democrats 1969–1982: Profile of a Party in Power*, Boulder, CO.: Westview Press, 1983, p. 67.
31. Gerard Braunthal, 'The Policy Function of the German Social Democratic Party, *Comparative Politics*, vol. XIX, no. 2, Jan. 1977, p. 142.

programmatic activity, he hoped, would integrate the radical elements into the party mainstream. Thus, while maintaining his autonomy as chancellor Brandt sought neither to dominate nor to distance himself from his party.

A temperamental bias towards the politics of conciliation rather than power politics was also evident in the chancellor's relations with his cabinet. Brandt's cabinets contained some powerful personalities with political profiles which rivalled that of the chancellor. Karl Schiller and Helmut Schmidt were able to draw on their reputations from the grand coalition to sustain semi-independent cabinet roles. Cabinet cohesion also suffered from the resignation of Finance Minister Alex Möller in 1971, followed a year later by that of Schiller, who had taken over the Finance Ministry in addition to that of Economics. On each occasion, the chancellor's responses were hesitant and indecisive. Generally, Brandt failed to impose his authority on the cabinet, eschewing the path of 'lonely decisions' in favour of dialogue and building consensus. When the latter broke down in deadlock he would often retreat into a private world of introspective depression.

Brandt's first term was sustained largely by the spectacular success of his *Ostpolitik*, which received an overwhelmingly positive response in the party and served to offset disappointments over the slow pace of domestic reform. The chancellor also benefited from the partisanship aroused by the acute political polarisation which accompanied the first change of party government in the history of the Federal Republic. The year 1972, however, marked the highwater mark of the Brandt chancellorship. Its subsequent decline was manifested on a number of fronts. First, Brandt progressively lost control over the executive arena. A slackening growth rate, rising inflation and a mounting budget deficit narrowed the government's room for manoeuvre, leading to a virtual paralysis of policy. It was clear that a managerial rather than a visionary approach to government was now required. In the face of cabinet conflict, Brandt's remoteness from decision-making became more pronounced, and Schmidt increasingly assumed responsibility for the conduct of government. Secondly, Brandt's capacity for integrating different sections of the party was also weakening. Attacks on the government from the SPD's youth wing intensified, and there were calls on the right for disciplinary measures. An internal report of 1973 pointed to the danger of the party disintegrating into sectarianism.[32]

---

32. Douglas Webber, 'German Social Democracy in the Economic Crisis: Unemployment and the Politics of Labour Market Policy in the Federal Republic of Germany from 1974 to 1982', unpubl. thesis, University of Essex, 1984, p. 28.

Thirdly, Brandt's relations with previously loyal trade union leaders deteriorated under the pressure of the government's counter-inflation policies. There followed a wave of strikes, unprecedented in the Federal Republic, culminating in a strike of public sector employees in the spring of 1974. Brandt's failure to act positively to discipline the unions further eroded his authority.

The crisis also revealed a fatal loss of confidence in Brandt amongst the upper echelons of the party. Schmidt and Wehner had doubted Brandt's leadership from the outset. It had been Wehner's view that Brandt was the ideal candidate for chancellor, but that he lacked the qualities of an effective head of government. He was 'insufficiently diligent, far too easy going, never in bed on time'.[33] Schmidt was also sceptical of Brandt's stability and managerial competence, and from September 1973 onwards the two mounted a campaign of public criticism designed to undermine the chancellor. Brandt staggered on for a further two months, due largely to Wehner's reservations about Schmidt: Wehner recoiled, briefly, from Schmidt's aggressive ambition, fearing that as chancellor he might destroy the delicate equilibrium of the SPD. Brandt's fall was precipitated by the disclosure that the Chancellor's Office had been penetrated by an East German spy. Although Brandt was not personally compromised by the affair his will for political survival was by now exhausted. More significantly, although neither Wehner nor Schmidt demanded his resignation, they did not offer him their support, or attempt to dissuade him from that course.

Brandt's receptiveness to the radical youth wing of the SPD, his tolerance for inner-party debate and his relaxed style of government leadership were frequently interpreted as signs of weakness. An alternative interpretation is given by Klaus Harpprecht in terms of the role which Brandt occupied within the SPD and which he continued to play as chancellor:

What characterises Brandt is not that he is hesitant to make decisions, but the careful, economical use of his leadership authority. Precisely because he is the uncontested symbol of party unity he is careful not to dissipate his authority. . . . Brandt is a man who wields power subtly, not out of weakness but out of the realisation that that kind of power is more enduring.[34]

A further explanation of Brandt's style of leadership can be found in his temperament and intellectual leanings. His philosophical pluralism is plain in his speech on being awarded the Nobel Peace Prize in 1971:

33. Baring, *op. cit.*, p. 173.
34. Klaus Harpprecht, *Willy Brandt: Portrait and Self Portrait*, Los Angeles: Nash, 1974, p. 213.

I say to my young friends and to others who want to hear it: there are several truths, not merely the one which excludes all others. That is why I believe in diversity and hence in doubt. It is productive. It questions existing things.[35]

No other chancellor of the Federal Republic has had the same sort of symbiotic relationship with his party that Brandt enjoyed with the SPD. Indeed the closeness of the relationship has led some to portray him as a deviant from the normal style of chancellor government, as the instrument of his party and the executor of its political will.[36] This stereotype has been challenged on the grounds that even in domestic policy the programmes of the Brandt governments were those of the SPD–FDP coalition rather than those of the chancellor's party. Moreover, this view of Brandt fails to make the distinction between his dual roles. As chancellor, he asserted his autonomy from the party and received the full backing of the *Bundestagsfraktion*; as party chairman he was tolerant of discussion and programmatic debates.[37]

This second model of chancellor–party relations under Brandt comes closest to the reality, although it requires one important qualification. Brandt repeatedly made the distinction between his two roles, but he was not entirely successful in putting it into practice. The assertion of chancellor autonomy did not free him from his ties to the SPD. As chancellor, Brandt was never able to forget that he was a Social Democrat. Thus, while he was never the prisoner of his party, neither was he ever fully its master.

Uneasy Coexistence: Schmidt and the SPD

Helmut Schmidt went some way towards recreating the Adenauer model of the chancellorship. Styling himself 'managing director' of the Federal Republic, Schmidt deployed the instruments of chancellorial power much more energetically than Brandt had done. For a time he successfully asserted his autonomy from the SPD, although the culture and composition of the party meant that he was unable to dominate it in the imperious manner of Adenauer. The relationship can best be described as one of mutual resignation to uneasy coexistence; 'I am not wholly satisfied with my party, nor it with me. . . . But I can find no better party and it has no substitute for

35. Cited in Jonathan Carr, *Helmut Schmidt, Helmsman of Germany*, London: Weidenfeld and Nicolson, 1985, p. 56.
36. Mayntz, p. 169.
37. William E. Paterson, 'The Chancellor and his Party: Political Leadership in the Federal Republic', *West European Politics*, vol. 4, no. 2, 1981, pp. 3–17.

me. So we must get along with one another.'[38] Schmidt identified himself much more closely with the coalition than with the SPD.

The formidable authority which Schmidt commanded at the height of his chancellorship hardly rested at all on a power base in the party. It stemmed rather from his control over the executive arena itself, and particularly from the Chancellor's Office, which realised its full potential under his tutelage (see Chapter 4). Schmidt's authority also derived from his personal standing in the electorate, which was always higher than that of his party. The decline of his authority after 1980, however, originated in the erosion of his ability to maintain his autonomy from the SPD. Remoteness now became estrangement, and his subsequent fall underlines the principle that no chancellor can govern effectively without at least the passive support of his party.

Schmidt's remoteness from the SPD is an unbroken strand running through his career. Politically inactive throughout his youth during the Third Reich, Schmidt joined the SPD at the age of twenty-seven at the end of the war, out of a conviction that Social Democracy offered the best vehicle for national reconstruction. His rapid rise through state politics and government in Hamburg owed more to his managerial capacity than to an affinity with the cultural and ideological life of the party. In the Bundestag, where he became *Fraktion* leader in 1967, he took up positions, on defence and over the SPD's entry into the Grand Coalition with the CDU, which were deeply unpopular with sections of the party. At the Economics and Finance Ministries, Schmidt had courted the wrath of the left by his emphasis on economic discipline and his strictures against those in the SPD who wanted to turn the state into a 'supermarket' for costly reforms.

Schmidt's chancellorship is associated above all with crisis management – a rational, pragmatic and largely supra-partisan approach to steering the economy through an international recession. It was a style of government which maintained the greatest possible flexibility of response, steering clear of any long-term objectives which might impede that flexibility. It entailed a general restriction on the growth of public expenditure, and the exercise of monetary caution, with the government acting in tandem with the Bundesbank. Fiscal discipline was periodically punctuated by spending programmes designed to stimulate growth and employment, but judiciously calculated to minimise their inflationary consequences. Combined with the underlying resilience of the West German economy, these measures were successful by 1978 in

38. Schmidt (1975), cited in Carr, *op. cit.*, p. 101.

restoring monetary stability and sustaining a modest rate of growth while other European economies were experiencing decline.

Crisis management in the economy had a counterpart in internal and external security. A wave of terrorist violence culminated in 1977 in the killing of banker Jürgen Ponto and the kidnap of industrial leader Hanns-Martin Schleyer. The kidnap episode coincided with the hijack of a Lufthansa jet by Arab terrorists. Although it resulted in Schleyer's killing, Schmidt's refusal to deal with the German terrorists, together with the operation which he ordered to free the hijack hostages at Mogadishu in Somalia, greatly increased his public stature. This was further enhanced by his conduct of global economic and political relations, especially in the context of the European Community and NATO, which established him as an international statesman of the first rank.

These accomplishments, and the acclaim which they brought, elevated Schmidt to the height of his authority, yet they also brought him into conflict with the SPD. Economic crisis management meant the virtual abandonment of the commitments and values associated with the Social Democratic tradition. Moreover, changes to the criminal law enacted during the terrorist crisis, and in response to the emotionally charged public debate which followed, were seen by many in the SPD as an attack on civil liberties. Finally, his advocacy of the modernisation of NATO weaponry was sustained in the face of criticism from the peace movement within the party. Schmidt's response was to reiterate the principle of chancellor autonomy which Brandt had asserted. He did not, however, combine this principle with Brandt's tolerance for inner-party debate.

By 1974, the influence of the left in the federal party had begun to recede. The disintegration into sectarianism of the SPD youth movement JUSOS had enabled the party leadership to expel its most militant leaders. The left occupied no more than about a quarter of seats in the party executive, which was in any case a fairly ineffectual body. In the *Bundestagsfraktion* the left was represented by around thirty or forty deputies, but no more than a handful of these were prepared to take their opposition to the point of withdrawing support from the government. Thus, in the early years of his chancellorship Schmidt was able to dismiss criticism from this quarter with a disdain which approached arrogance.

Matters began to change after the elections of 1976, in which the coalition's Bundestag majority was reduced to ten. The management of the *Fraktion* became more difficult, and on a number of occasions *Fraktion* chairman Wehner was hard pressed to provide the government with a majority. Although outright dissent was confined to a handful of deputies, there was a larger number who were not prepared to give unconditional support to the government, and the chancellor or his ministers were sometimes obliged to justify their policies to the *Fraktion*. Moreover, it was sometimes necessary to defer proposals for which Wehner could not guarantee a majority.

Control over the party congress also became more problematic. Although officially the congress was the sovereign policy-making organ, the reality had been quite different.[39] The infrequency of its meetings meant that it usually deliberated issues which the party's leading organs had already settled. The executive had a large measure of control over the agenda and was usually able to secure support for the policy of the leadership, especially since the procedures for the selection of delegates tended to ensure that party functionaries predominated and they were usually predisposed towards compliance. SPD chancellors, moreover, were normally able to invoke their electoral mandate, national responsibilities and prestige to restrain the congress from passing resolutions that were at odds with government policy.

Under the Schmidt chancellorship, however, this model began to break down, with sizeable minorities of the congress opposed to government positions. The chief of these issues was the nuclear energy programme, which the chancellor had stepped up in response to the oil price crisis. The conflict which this aroused ran through the SPD, penetrating the party executive and threatening to provoke a confrontation between party opinion and chancellor prerogative.[40] The 1977 and 1979 party congresses took place against this background. While asserting his autonomy from congress decisions, Schmidt was nevertheless obliged to undertake an exercise in persuasion and conciliation. On each occasion he won majorities only through compromise resolutions which left his government's energy options open, but made gestures towards the anti-nuclear position.

Thus, even when Schmidt was at the height of his prestige there was a tension between chancellor and party. The containment of this tension was due above all to Brandt's role as party chairman. Employing a subtle balance of loyalty to the government and identification with the party, Brandt acted as intermediary between the two, absorbing much of the pressure exerted by the SPD. The balance was hard to sustain, however, and Brandt incurred sharp criticism from *Fraktion* leader Wehner for his 'counter-productive'

39. Jürgen Dittberner, 'Die Parteitäge von CDU und SPD', in J. Dittberner and R. Ebbighausen (eds), *Parteiensystem in der Legitimationskrise*, Opladen: Westdeutscher Verlag, 1973, pp. 105–8.
40. Paterson, *op. cit.*, p. 12.

efforts to integrate the left into the SPD mainstream, and for the flexible line which he took with dissent in the party. Schmidt also became impatient with Brandt and in 1979 attempted to stiffen the party leadership by installing a trusted aide from the Chancellor's Office, Hans-Jürgen Wischnewski, as party vice-chairman. Nevertheless, the triumvirate of Schmidt, Brandt and Wehner operated effectively for the first five years of the former's chancellorship.[41] Whilst the SPD was not 'the chancellor's party', Schmidt was able, for the most part, to retain his autonomy in the face of the critical currents which it contained.

After the election of 1980, however, the latent tension between chancellor and party progressively assumed crisis proportions. With the second oil price shock in 1978 the already slender margins of economic manoeuvre were narrowed still further, and the conflict between crisis management and the basic values of Social Democracy became harder to reconcile. In the presentation of his budget for 1981, Schmidt's Finance Minister Hans Matthöfer argued that the state was no longer in a position to maintain full employment, that its capacity to influence economic development had to be more modestly assessed and that it was not state spending but entrepreneurial vitality which was decisive for economic success.[42] This statement was an explicit renunciation of the values on which modern post-war Social Democracy had been constructed. Support in the party for the policy which it represented was particularly difficult to sustain in the context of an unemployment level of 1.25 million by the summer of 1981. Against this background, there was a steady erosion of the good terms between Schmidt and the trade unions which had previously served to consolidate SPD support for the government. At the party congress of April 1982 in Munich, more than fifty resolutions on the economy were debated, most of them critical of government policy and many advocating radical solutions to the economic crisis.[43]

On defence and security issues, which focused on the upgrading of NATO weapon systems and the deployment in the Federal Republic of intermediate-range nuclear missiles, it became increasingly difficult to find a policy formula which could command a majority in the SPD without tying the hands of Schmidt and his defence minister, Hans Apel. A growing section of the party wanted to reject the NATO plan outright, which would have brought party policy and government commitments into direct conflict. A number

41. *Die Zeit*, 22 December 1978.
42. Webber (1984), *op. cit.*, pp. 99–100.
43. *Protokoll. SPD Parteitag*, Munich, April 1982, pp. 933–1111.

of regional party congresses in 1981 passed resolutions sharply critical of government policy, and in a Bundestag debate in May that year ten SPD deputies either voted against the government or abstained. At the Munich congress of the federal SPD, a full-scale confrontation between chancellor and party was only averted by a compromise resolution in which the peace politics of the SPD was given full expression, while the issue of missile deployment was postponed.[44]

The Munich congress was a watershed for the SPD, underlining the fact that on the major issues of policy the government no longer commanded a majority in the party. It also made clear how deep was the gulf which by now ran through the party's functionary corps, membership and electorate. A substantial post-materialist enclave, identified with the new left, sought to reorientate the SPD towards the new politics issues of environmental protection and the peace movement. Although these ideas were represented by few in the upper echelons of the party, lower down the hierachy they were gaining the ascendancy. The traditionalists on the right, on the other hand, who saw the SPD as a party of and for industrial society, continued to adhere to the orthodoxies of economic stability and reaffirmed the commitment to security through nuclear deterrence, were no longer sufficiently strong to guarantee Schmidt the backing of the party. These fundamental conflicts of perspective had been apparent in the party since the early 1970s, but they were intensified by the policy agenda at the beginning of the 1980s, and by the rise of the new left to positions of responsibility within the SPD. Party management became correspondingly more difficult, reflected in the deteriorating relationship between Schmidt, Brandt and Wehner. Much of the strain was also taken by party bosses in the *Länder*, resulting in the resignation of a number of SPD majors and *Land* leaders.

The erosion of the chancellor's control over the SPD steadily undermined the government. In particular it had serious repercussions on coalition relations. Schmidt had often identified with the coalition rather than with the SPD. His close affinity with the FDP on many issues had been an important factor in holding the coalition together. Forced to make concessions to his own party, Schmidt had found it increasingly difficult to bridge the widening policy gap between the SPD and its coalition partner. On most policy issues, the FDP now stood closer to the CDU than to the Social Democrats. Thus, whilst it was the FDP which precipitated Schmidt's downfall in the constructive vote of no confidence of October 1982,

44. *Ibid.*, pp. 907–11.

the underlying reason for the premature collapse of the government was the chancellor's loss of authority over his own party.

The fragmentation of the SPD reflected wider societal changes in the Federal Republic which weakened the internal consensus of both of the *Volksparteien*. The progressive disintegration of historic social formations, the increasing complexity of the policy agenda, and a more highly educated, informed and vocal electorate imposed multiple pressures upon the parties. At the same time, the demands upon modern government, and the corresponding increase in the scope and complexity of its functions, intensified the reliance of the executive branch upon the parties. Social and political change along these lines served to redefine the relationship between chancellor and party, and with it the character of the chancellorship itself. The redefinition of the modern German chancellorship is reflected very clearly in the incumbency of Helmut Schmidt.

The Apotheosis of Party Management in the Kohl Chancellorship

The experience of the Kohl chancellorship underlines the lessons of the Schmidt era, pointing to what appears to be an intrinsic condition of the modern German chancellorship. A steady erosion in the capacity of the *Volksparteien* to mobilise voters means that no chancellor is long able to escape from the shadow of electoral vulnerability or from the mesh of party politics. Although the SPD has been worst afflicted by this syndrome, the CDU has not been immune from its effects. Under these conditions, the skills of party management have become an essential part of a chancellor's armoury.

Since first becoming chancellor in 1982, Kohl has scaled the heights and plumbed the depths of chancellorial power. His desire to emulate Adenauer's style of leadership proved impossible to realise in the more complex political environment of the late twentieth century. An incumbency which rarely aspired to much more than survival reached a low point in 1988–9, with seething unrest in the CDU over the chancellor's erratic exercise of personalised power. Kohl recovered to enjoy an *annus mirabilis* in the unification year of 1990, when his stature invited comparison with that of Adenauer. However, forced to wrestle with the intractable difficulties of welding the new Germany together as the harsh realities of unification asserted themselves the following year, Kohl was once more condemned to the state of siege to which he had been subjected previously. His capacity for survival stemmed in no small part from his adroit political touch and mastery of the internal life of his party.

Kohl's style of chancellorship was very heavily conditioned by his background in the CDU. His power base was in the extra-parliamentary party, where he progressed from chairman of the *Junge Union* (the party's youth wing) to minister-president of his home state, Rhineland Palatinate, becoming party chairman in 1973. In this role he orchestrated the organisational overhaul and programmatic renewal of a party which had been in considerable disarray following its loss of government office in 1969.[45] Narrowly defeated as chancellor candidate in 1976, he consolidated his hold on the pivotal power points in the CDU by becoming chairman of the *Bundestagsfraktion*.

The main characteristic of Kohl's leadership in the CDU was conciliation and integration. Avoiding potentially divisive policy issues whenever possible, he sought to balance the claims of the CDU's progressive social wing with those of the conservative right. Kohl himself avoided identification with either group. Tactical flexibility was also the key to his management of the difficult relationship between the CDU and its quasi-autonomous Bavarian sister party, the CSU. By allowing CSU chief Franz Josef Strauss to lead the Union parties' vain challenge for the chancellorship in 1980, Kohl effectively drew the sting from this figurehead of the right and was subsequently able to resist Strauss's claims for a leading cabinet post. In short, by assiduously building alliances, marginalising rivals and cultivating loyalty at all levels of the party Kohl laid the foundations for later in his career.

A leadership style geared to party management, however, was imperfectly adapted to the management of the executive. The Kohl government came to power in 1982 against the background of an emotionally charged debate over the economic and social foundations of the Federal Republic. Christian–Liberal rhetoric had proclaimed a historic turning point (*Wende*) in all aspects of national life. The *Wende* 'signalled the intention of reducing the role of the state in the economy and society . . . and bring[ing] about a "renaissance" in the market economy'.[46] This policy agenda raised fundamental questions of structural economic change, precipitating conflict between the forces of economic liberalism in the CDU and the Christian social traditions of the party. The government was

45. Padgett and Burkett, *op. cit.*, pp. 113–14.
46. Douglas Webber, 'Kohl's *Wendepolitik* after a Decade', *German Politics*, vol. 1, no. 2, Aug. 1992, pp. 149–80.

thus subjected to a barrage of competing party pressures which compounded the conflicting demands emanating from the CSU and FDP within the coalition. The resultant conflicts came to a head during Kohl's second term of office (1987–90).

In the face of this conflict, Kohl adopted a highly personalised form of leadership in which the formal channels of decision-making in both government and party were circumvented in favour of a kitchen cabinet and Kohl's own political network (see Chapter 3). The result was administrative disorder in which policy was highly susceptible to the pull of competing demands from inside and outside the party. Ministers found themselves over-ruled and undermined, and party organs were informed of rather than consulted about policy. Decisions which emerged in response to political pressures were often inconsistent and disjointed, especially since Kohl's adroitness at political manoeuvring was not matched by his capacity for administrative control.

Perceptions of executive mismanagement had an adverse effect on chancellor–party relations, which reached a nadir early in 1988. At an acrimonious meeting with the chancellor, the party's top leadership body, the praesidium, demanded that it should be consulted before the unveiling of new legislative proposals. Similarly, the *Bundestagsfraktion* became more assertive, with deputies openly questioning Kohl's leadership and *Fraktion* leader Alfred Dregger struggling to impose party discipline. Perhaps most damaging of all in view of Kohl's long-standing reliance upon a power base in the party at large, there was mounting disquiet over the conduct of government amongst the grass roots of the CDU, leading to large-scale resignations and critical resolutions from regional party congresses.[47]

Disquiet in the party reflected the weakening electoral performance of the CDU/CSU. In the election of January 1987 its share of the vote fell from 48.8 to 44.3 per cent, despite the relatively strong performance of the economy during Kohl's first term. This was followed by a series of severe setbacks in *Land* elections. Between May 1987 and January 1989 the CDU suffered heavy losses in the chancellor's home state of Rhineland Palatinate (6.8 per cent), Bremen (9.9 per cent), Schleswig-Holstein (6.4 per cent in September 1987, 9.3 per cent in May 1988) and Berlin (8.7 per cent).

Electoral decline precipitated a divisive debate over the best strategic direction for the CDU to take. One proposed alternative was to mobilise a conservative majority based on the CDU's tradi-

47. *Der Spiegel*, 11 July 1988.

tional Christian-bourgeois milieu. The other favoured a reorientation towards the political centre, and an electoral appeal to a wider Christian–Liberal alliance.[48] The debate brought the chancellor into sharp conflict with the party general secretary, Heiner Geissler. Occupying a pivotal position between Kohl and the party, Geissler might have been expected to bring the party into line behind the chancellor. Temperamentally and politically, however, there was a wide gulf between the two, which Geissler did nothing to disguise. Progressively distancing himself from Kohl, Geissler aligned himself with the chancellor's critics. Similarly, CDU minister-presidents and *Land* party chairmen kept their distance from Kohl. Chief of these was Baden-Württemberg premier Lothar Späth, who fought a state election in March 1988 with a campaign that contrasted the success of his own government with the parlous state of affairs in Bonn. Späth's open criticism of Kohl and his relative success in the state election served to identify him as the leading contender for the chancellorship in the event of Kohl's political demise – a scenario which was the subject of increasing speculation.

Kohl's ability to reassert his authority over the CDU sprang from his formidable capacity for party management, and in particular from his close relationship with the party base. In part also his reassertion of control stemmed from the organisational structure of the party. Although the CDU had constructed a powerful central party apparatus in the 1970s, the legacy of earlier organisational weaknesses remained. Formal organisational links between CDU headquarters and the regional, district and local levels of the party were still largely informal, mediated by the party chairman. Kohl was well equipped to exploit this role. His unassuming geniality enabled him to relate instantaneously to the myriad ranks of local and district notables. Through commonplace human gestures of recognition, and the bestowal of small personal favours during fifteen years as party chairman, Kohl had accumulated an enormous fund of goodwill on which he was able to draw when under pressure from Geissler and Späth.

Here lies Kohl's strength, which he believes sets him head and shoulders above all the challengers from within his own ranks. He likes to boast that in contrast to. . . . Geissler, he is much more intimately in touch with the

---

48. William M. Chandler, 'The Christian Democrats and the Challenge of Unity', in Stephen Padgett (ed.), *Parties and Party Systems in the New Germany*, Aldershot: Dartmouth, 1993, p. 143; see also K. Naumann, 'Die Normalisierung der Republik und die Zukunft der Koalition', *Blätter für deutsche und internationale Politik*, vol. 10, 1987, pp. 167–71.

inner life of the party and that he is on close personal terms with many more party dignatories.[49]

This residual loyalty sustained Kohl through the crisis of his chancellorship and discouraged his rivals from mounting a challenge at the decisive moment.

Kohl's re-mastery of the CDU represented a formidable display of power politics. In a cabinet reshuffle in April 1988, potential critics such as Theo Waigel of the CSU were given responsibilities to bind them to the government. The refusal of arch-critic Geissler to accept the offer of a government role which would have meant vacating his strategic party post served to reduce his standing in the CDU. Geissler's credibility was eroded still further as Kohl manoeuvred the blame for electoral failure on to his shoulders. The *coup de grâce* came in September 1989, shortly before the party congress, when Kohl unceremoniously ditched Geissler as general secretary. Most significantly of all, after eighteen months of speculation, the congress produced no challenge to Kohl either as chancellor or as party chairman. Decisively signalling the restoration of the chancellor's authority over the CDU, the congress rebuffed the foremost of Kohl's rivals. Späth's failure to secure re-election as party vice-chairman and the loss of his place on the praesidium underlined the advantage which CDU chancellors derive from their incumbency of the office of party chairman.

Kohl and the Decline of Party Democracy

Although the unification process was driven for the most part by forces beyond political control, it provided a stage for displays of chancellorial finesse which recalled the Adenauer era. Kohl's centrality in the political process derived from his pivotal role in the international negotiations surrounding unification. The chancellor assumed the role of international statesman, largely free of party constraints. Moreover, internal party differences were temporarily forgotten in the emotional euphoria of unification. Most significantly of all, the identification of the CDU with national unity restored its electoral momentum. An improved showing in the 1990 elections reduced the intensity of the debate over the party's strategic orientation and identity.[50]

This apparent restoration of chancellor dominance proved illusory, however, as the acute economic and social pressures of post-

49. *Der Spiegel*, 24 March 1988.
50. Chandler, *op. cit.*, pp. 137–8.

unification Germany brought an unprecedented burden to bear upon all aspects of executive leadership. At the same time it placed immense strain upon intra-party cohesion and inter-party coopera-tion. Thus, whilst multiplying the pressures on the chancellor, unifi-cation weakened still further the supportive infrastructure of a party system already under stress.[51] The failure of the parties to take pur-poseful political action to address the growing crisis of economic performance and social conflict in post-unification Germany led to the deepening of the alienation from party politics which was already evident in the 1980s. This was forcefully articulated by the federal president, Richard von Weizsäcker, in his indictment of 'the political class' for its self-serving pursuit of power.[52] Although Weizsäcker's critique of party democracy was not directed specifi-cally at the governing parties, it served to strengthen perceptions that the government was lacking in political and moral leadership.

The prevailing mood of scepticism towards party democracy was reflected at the electoral level in a deepening of the long-term decline in voter participation, a very sharp decline in CDU support and the rise of the radical right. These trends culminated in the Baden-Württemberg *Land* elections of April 1992, where CDU support fell by 9.4 percentage points and the *Republikaner* gained 10.9 per cent of the vote.[53] The fact that the party's electoral performance continued to slide after the 'false dawn' of 1990 precipitated a sense of crisis which inevitably undermined the chancellor's authority. A pervasive sense of lassitude and drift in the CDU was reflected in the weakening of party discipline in the Bundestag, where *Fraktion* chairman Wolfgang Schäuble struggled at times to secure government majorities. In the extra-parliamentary party, moves to establish conservative discussion groups pointed to an increase in the intensity of ideological mobilisation.[54]

Mobilisation also occurred at the regional level, with the CDU in the new *Länder* adopting quasi-autonomous organisational struc-tures to articulate specifically east German interests.[55] The CDU is

51. Gordon Smith, 'Dimensions of Change in the German Party System' in S.A. Padgett (ed.), *Parties and Party Systems in the New Germany, op. cit.,* pp. 87–101.
52. Richard von Weizsäcker, *Im Gespräch mit Gunter Hofmann und Werner A. Perger*, Frankfurt am Main: Eichborn Verlag, 1992.
53. Dieter Roth, 'Volksparteien in Crisis? The Electoral Success of the Extreme Right in Context – The Case of Baden Württemberg', *German Politics*, vol. 2, no. 1, April 1993, pp. 1–20.
54. *Süddeutsche Zeitung*, 14 July 1992.
55. Clay Clemens, 'Disquiet on the Eastern Front; The Christian Democratic Union in Germany's New Länder', *German Politics*, vol. 2, no. 2, Aug. 1993, pp. 217–18.

a microcosm of the conflicts of values and priorities which divide post-unification Germany. In the east, the party combines the values of social solidarity with advocacy of state intervention in economic reconstruction, displaying a marked scepticism towards the concepts of the social-market economy and *Westpolitik*, the pillars of Christian Democracy in the old Federal Republic. The 'separatism' of the CDU in the east was evident in *Land* parliaments, where advocacy of regional interests often took precedence over party discipline and support for federal government policies. In the CDU *Bundestagsfraktion*, eastern deputies formed a caucus under the leadership of the Mecklenburg-Vorpommern party chairman and federal transport minister, Günther Krause. Against the warnings of *Fraktion* leader Schäuble, the group adopted the CSU's practice of convening prior to meetings of the CDU/CSU *Fraktion* to determine their own policy positions. Ideologically and organisationally, then, unification has exacerbated the polycentrism of Kohl's party.[56]

Disunity in his own party has left the chancellor more than ever subject to the fissiparous tendencies in the coalition. Kohl's dependence on the FDP was underlined by the appointments of foreign and economics ministers following the respective resignations of Hans-Dietrich Genscher and Jürgen Möllemann. With both ministries falling within the conventional purlieu of the Liberals, Kohl was powerless to intervene in the succession, despite the disarray in the FDP and the absence of outstanding liberal contenders for either post.

Moreover, without a majority in the Bundesrat, the chancellor was dependent on the opposition Social Democrats for measures requiring its approval. Social Democratic consent in both parliamentary chambers was also required for constitutional amendments to place restrictions on Germany's very open provisions on political asylum, and to enable German forces to be deployed outside the NATO area. In addition, opposition endorsement was a prerequisite for the success of the chancellor's 'solidarity pact', combining social solidarity and economic stabilisation, concluded in March 1993. Thus, on a range of key issues the chancellor has been dependent upon the formation of a broad cross-party consensus. Kohl has faced a balancing act between two competing pressures. On the one hand the stability of his government depends on integrating his own party and buttressing its electoral performance. On the other, the chancellor's ability to enact important

56. *Ibid.*, p. 219.

legislative measures on the basis of cross-party accord demands a leadership style which transcends party politics.

The government's heavy reliance on cross-party accord with the opposition has fuelled suggestions of a Grand Coalition between the CDU/CSU and the SPD. Speculation about this option can be traced largely to the social wing of the CDU, and to those in the east who advocate a more interventionist approach to economic reconstruction. It was also, reportedly, an option to which *Fraktion* leader Schäuble was not averse. Kohl is said to have threatened to sack Schäuble for adding to the speculation.[57] For the chancellor, the latent threat of a Grand Coalition is a particularly potent one, as it would probably signal the end of his incumbency.

Kohl's capacity for survival, however, is not yet exhausted. Greatly assisted by the electoral weakness and internal disunity of the SPD, he has been able to manoeuvre the opposition into acquiescence on issues where he requires its support. In his own party, there are few who believe that a change of chancellor would provide an escape from the difficulties in which government and party are entrapped. The imperious manner in which Kohl disposed of his rivals in 1989 has had a salutary effect upon potential challengers. The leading candidate for the succession, Defence Minister Volker Rühe, has sometimes appeared to distance himself from the chancellor. However, his rise in the party suffered a setback at the Düsseldorf conference of October 1992, when he failed to secure election as party vice-chairman. Rühe is young enough to hold his fire until circumstances are more propitious. Under present economic and political conditions, the chancellorship bears some resemblance to a poisoned chalice.

Chancellor Democracy and Party Democracy

This chapter has demonstrated the dependency of chancellors upon the supportive infrastructure of their parties. Alternative sources of authority – national prestige, the power resources of the executive apparatus, or electoral success – have enabled some chancellors to transcend party ties for a time, but no chancellor has been able to sustain this form of leadership. Ultimately, party support is the key to the chancellor's authority over the executive (the capacity to establish government guidelines), and to that command over the parliamentary arena which is the *sine qua non* of effective government. To some extent this could be said of all countries where

57. *Frankfurter Rundschau*, 11 Sept. 1992.

collective cabinet government is located within a parliamentary system. In the German context, however, a chief executive's reliance on party is exacerbated by the 'sectorisation' of the executive (see Chapter 3) and by the prevalence of coalition government. It follows from this that executive leadership is heavily conditioned by chancellor–party relations and by the cohesion and discipline of the chancellor's own party.

In the introduction to this volume, the distinction was made between variations in executive leadership resulting from differences of personal style, and those resulting from structural changes in the institutional and political context in which the chancellorship is located. No aspect of the German chancellorship illustrates the importance of this distinction more clearly than the party dimension. This chapter has shown that the personal styles and strategies of party management have varied widely from one incumbent to another. Adenauer's successors were unable to replicate his dominance over the CDU, with Erhard isolated from the party and Kiesinger reliant on inter-party accommodation in the Grand Coalition. The close identification between Brandt and the SPD was in sharp contrast with Schmidt's remoteness, his assertion of chancellorial autonomy and his reliance on others to ensure party discipline. Kohl's relations with his party are characterised by adroit tactical manoeuvre, underpinned by an intimacy with the internal life of the CDU.

This chapter has also identified long-term trends in party democracy which have had a more significant impact on the German chancellorship than have variations in personal style. First, there has been a long-term decline in the capacity of the *Volksparteien* for electoral mobilisation. This is manifested in the fact that the *Volkspartei* share of the vote in Bundestag elections fell from 91.2 per cent to 77.3 per cent between 1976 and 1990, and in the pronounced volatility in Landtag elections. The decline in votes for the parties, and thereby in the basis for stable government majorities, leaves the chancellor vulnerable to shifting currents of public opinion.

Secondly, both major parties have suffered a loss of internal cohesion and discipline, which have been identified above as prerequisites of successful executive leadership. The fragmentation of the SPD between the old and the new left, evident in both the social composition and the value system of the party, was a crucial factor in undermining the Schmidt chancellorship. Since then this tendency has intensified, leading one observer to characterise internal party life as 'loosely coupled anarchy'.[58] The capacity of the SPD to pro-

---

58. Peter Losche and Franz Walter, *Die SPD: Klassenpartei, Volkspartei, Quotenpartei. Zur Entwicklung der Sozialdemokratie von Weimar bis zur deutschen Vereinigung*, Darmstadt: Wissenschaftliche Buchgesellschaft, 1992, pp. 380–4.

vide the supportive infrastructure needed for effective executive leadership is now seriously in question. Although the 'decomposition' of the CDU has been less pronounced, a widening gulf is evident between its traditional Christian-bourgeois milieu and a more centrist constituency based on the politics of the 'middle way'. The tension between the 'social solidarity' orientation of its labour wing and the neo-liberalism of party-related business interests has also increased. Combined with the polycentric distribution of power in the CDU, these conflicts have crucially undermined the foundations of internal party cohesion.

Both these tendencies – the fall in electoral support for the *Volksparteien* and the erosion of their internal cohesion – are accentuated in post-unification Germany. De-structured by the successive social revolutions of national socialism and communism, and lacking 'organic bonds' with political parties, the electorate in the east is inherently volatile. Moreover, value differences and distributional conflicts between east and west have added another fracture to the existing 'fault lines' within the *Volksparteien*. Unification has both intensified the pressures on executive leadership and reduced still further the capacity of the parties to provide essential support.

The implications for executive leadership of the long-term decline in party performance are far-reaching. First, the chancellor must devote increasing attention to the management of his party, deflecting him from his role as chief executive. Secondly, entrapped in conflicting inner-party interests and values, the chancellor is inhibited from formulating over-arching national interests and policy guidelines. Thirdly, electoral vulnerability leaves the chancellor susceptible to the vicissitudes of public opinion and the clamour of populist demands. In a variety of ways, then, the transformation from chancellor democracy to coordination democracy is inextricably bound up with the decline of party democracy.

3

THE CHANCELLOR AND
THE EXECUTIVE

Roland Sturm

The Dynamics of Inner-Executive Relations

The framework of executive leadership adopted on the establishment of the Federal Republic was largely determined by a critical assessment of the Weimar Republic. The Weimar experience, a mixture of unstable government and presidential omnipotence, was reflected in the Federal Republic's constitutional provisions serving to strengthen parliament and to anchor the executive in parliamentary majorities. The powers of the *'Ersatz Kaiser'* (substitute emperor), the president, were reduced to symbolic dimensions.

Rather than the executive of the Federal Republic being legitimised by direct elections, it was to be a truly representative executive, with the president elected by a Federal Assembly and the chancellor by the Bundestag. Thus neither office was endowed with the semblance of superior legitimacy conferred by the people through direct elections.

The Basic Law formally structures the executive by vesting powers in the chancellor, the cabinet and individual ministers. Article 65 gives the chancellor the right to control the policies and direction of government by formulating a framework of guidelines (the chancellor's *Richtlinienkompetenz*). This concept should be viewed in connection with the chancellor's organisational powers to appoint and dismiss ministers under Article 64, which includes the right to establish new federal ministries and to change the jurisdiction of existing ones. Formally, all government decisions are made in the cabinet. Ministers are bound by cabinet decisions and should not oppose them publicly or propose a new policy project without prior consultation with the chancellor.[1] Differences of opinion between ministers are to be resolved in cabinet (*Kabinettsprinzip*). The cabinet, however, is not allowed to intervene in the day-to-day business of individual ministries. Article 65 assigns responsibility for the

1. See on this topic, with examples from the Weimar Republic to Helmut Kohl, Theodor Eschenburg, 'Kanzler, Kabinett und Koalitionen. Eine kleine Chronik der Richtlinienkompetenz der Regierungschefs', *Die Zeit*, 8 April 1988, p. 9.

functioning of ministries to the minister in charge. If the chancellor disagrees with the way a ministry is led, he can dismiss the minister, but he cannot issue binding directions with regard to the running of the department (*Ressortprinzip*).

The constitutional framework for executive leadership does not provide answers to two important questions. First, how do the realities of party competition impact upon political balance in the executive? In the history of the Federal Republic this question has been resolved by the development of two stable characteristics of the political system: coalition government, and the control of the Bundestag *Fraktionen* (parliamentary party groups) through the executive and in the last resort through the chancellor himself. This phenomenon has a parallel in prime ministerial government in the British context. Secondly, what is the relative importance of the respective powers of the chancellor, the cabinet and the individual minister?

There is no definitive answer to this question. Chancellors have two choices. One is to emphasise their role as political leaders by controlling cabinet decision-making, using general policy guidelines for all or at least the most important fields of government. This automatically makes the chancellor not only the central but the dominating figure in the executive. The term coined for this style of government is *Kanzlerdemokratie*.[2] In the opposite model, *Koordinationsdemokratie*, the chancellor intervenes in a cautious and selective manner, depending less on his power to issue guidelines than on building consensus. In this scenario the chancellor sees himself mainly as a coordinator of policies formulated by his ministers and collectively endorsed by cabinet.

For historical reasons the coordination model has often been regarded as synonymous with inefficient government. The yardstick for this judgement is Konrad Adenauer's interpretation of the role and power potential of the federal chancellorship. Critics who refer to Adenauer as a model for the modern chancellorship, however, tend to forget the exceptional circumstances under which he took office.[3] In particular, Adenauer formed his first government before his party had established a national organisational structure. This gave the chancellor, who was also leader of his party, the opportunity to use the resources of his office to shape the decision-making apparatus of his party (see Chapter 2). In the early Adenauer

---

2. For an annotated bibliography see Heinz-Josef Sprengkamp, *Regierungszentralen in Deutschland. Bibliographie mit Annotierungen*, Speyer: Hochschule für Verwaltungswissenschaften, 1989 (= Speyerer Forschungsberichte 84).
3. Karlheinz Niclauss, *Kanzlerdemokratie. Bonner Regierungspraxis von Konrad Adenauer bis Helmut Kohl*, Stuttgart: Kohlhammer, 1988, p. 40.

years, his party lacked the resources and independent initiative to challenge the general policy guidelines set by the chancellor. The same was true for the smaller parties which were necessary for Adenauer to form a parliamentary majority; they were kept under control through the chancellor's deployment of his powers of patronage and great tactical skills. Adenauer's position was strengthened further by the unique conditions of post-war Germany. There was no Foreign Office in Germany until 1951, and no Ministry of Defence till 1955. Foreign and defence questions were decided by the chancellor. For instance, Adenauer secured West German integration into the community of Western democracies almost single-handedly.[4]

In the tradition of Konrad Adenauer successful political leadership in German politics has been defined as the predominance of the federal chancellor over his cabinet colleagues. As we shall see, at first sight this interpretation may still appear valid as a characterisation of the relationship between chancellor and executive. However, there are two misinterpretations that must be avoided in an analytical approach to this problem. On the one hand *Kanzler-demokratie* may relate to a notion which encompasses much more than cabinet government. Niclauss,[5] for example, has written a political history of the Federal Republic in these terms. This is much too wide a perspective for our purposes. On the other hand, the narrow preoccupation with the personality of specific chancellors that is to be found in journalistic accounts[6] is far too limited. The focus here is on chancellor, cabinet and the upper echelons of the civil service, and on their inter-relationship within the institutional and political logic of decision-making.

The Structure of the Executive

From a West European perspective, German cabinets have been about average in size.[7] They have seldom had more than twenty members (see Table 3.1). In this respect they have been similar to British cabinets, which since 1900 have been made up of around

4. See Josef Foschepoth (ed.), *Adenauer und die deutsche Frage*, 2nd edn, Göttingen: Vandenhoeck and Ruprecht, 1990.
5. Niclauss (1988), *op. cit.*
6. Recent examples are Hans Halter, 'Überlebensgross Herr Kohl', *Der Spiegel*, 9 April 1990, pp. 34–40; Paul Pucher, 'Der Wellenbrecher. Wie Helmut Kohl sich als Bundeskanzler durchsetzt', *Die politische Meinung* no. 249, 1990, pp. 59–62.
7. See Jean Blondel, 'Introduction: Western European Cabinets in Comparative Perspective', in Jean Blondel and Ferdinand Müller-Rommel (eds), *Cabinets in Western Europe*, Basingstoke: Macmillan 1988 (pp. 1–16), p. 9.

Table 3.1.   CABINET GOVERNMENT
FROM ADENAUER TO KOHL

Chancellor (party)	Size of cabinet (at the time of its formation or reshuffle)	Share of cabinet seats in hands of leading coalition partner (%)*	Share of Bundestag coalition seats in hands of leading coalition partner (%)*
Adenauer I (CDU) (1949–53)	14	42.9 (64.3)	55.7 (67.0)
Adenauer II (CDU) (1953–7)	19	42.1 (57.9)	57.4 (72.5)
(1955)	21	47.6 (61.9)	62.9 (78.9)
(1956)	16	56.3 (75.1)	71.4 (89.3)
Adenauer III (CDU) (1957–61)	18	66.7 (88.9)	76.3 (94.3)
(1960)	17	76.5 (100.0)	81.6 (100.0)
Adenauer IV (CDU) (1961–3)	21	57.1 (76.1)	63.2 (78.9)
Erhard I (CDU) (1963–5)	21	57.1 (76.1)	63.2 (78.9)
Erhard II (CDU) (1965–6)	22	59.1 (81.8)	67.1 (83.4)
Kiesinger (CDU) (1966–9)	21	42.9 (57.2)	43.2 (53.5)
Brandt I (SPD) (1969–72)	16	75.0	88.4
Brandt II (SPD) (1972–4)	18	72.2	85.2
Schmidt I (SPD) (1974–6)	16	75.0	85.2
Schmidt II (SPD) (1976–80)	16	75.0	84.8
Schmidt III (SPD) (1980–2)	17	76.5	80.9
Kohl I (CDU) (1982–3)	17	52.9 (76.4)	63.6 (81.5)
Kohl II (CDU) (1983–7)	17	52.9 (82.3)	69.7 (88.0)
(1984)	18	55.6 (83.4)	70.1 (87.7)
(1986)	19	57.9 (84.2)	70.1 (87.7)
Kohl III (CDU) (1987–9)	19	57.9 (79.0)	65.6 (83.0)
(1989–90)	20	55.0 (80.0)	65.6 (83.0)

Table 3.1 *(contd)*

Chancellor (party)	Size of cabinet (at the time of its formation or reshuffle)	Share of cabinet seats in hands of leading coalition partner (%)*	Share of Bundestag coalition seats in hands of leading coalition partner (%)*
Kohl IV (CDU)			
(1991–2)	19	52.6 (73.7)	67.8 (80.2)
(1992–3)	19	52.6 (73.7)	67.8 (80.2)
(Since 1993)	19	52.6 (73.7)	67.8 (80.2)

* Shown in brackets: percentages of CDU + CSU in the case of CDU-led governments.

Sources: Datenhandbuch zur Geschichte des Deutschen Bundestages 1949 bis 1982, Bonn: Deutscher Bundestag, 1983, pp. 366ff.; *Datenhandbuch zur Geschichte des Deutschen Bundestages 1980 bis 1987*, Baden-Baden: Nomos 1988, p. 334: Antje Vorbeck, 'Regierungbildung 1990–91: Koalitions-und Personalentscheidungen im Spiegel der Presse', *Zeitschrift für Parlamentsfragen*, no. 22, 1991, p. 388.

eighteen ministers.[8] As would be expected, the strongest party in government reserves the chancellorship for itself, whereas the vice-chancellorship has (with the exception of the vice-chancellorship of Ludwig Erhard of the CDU under Konrad Adenauer of the CDU between 1957 and 1963) always been given to the major coalition partner.

Under all German chancellors two considerations have determined the way cabinets are structured. One is the need to provide the personnel to head government departments. The other is the need to strike a political balance to satisfy the expectations of the coalition partner and to balance the factions within the chancellor's own party. With regard to the latter, there are some unwritten rules which have been respected by every chancellor. The minister of agriculture, for example, has to come from the farmers' lobby (see Chapter 6), whereas the job of employment minister goes to a union representative. A justice minister should be trained in law, while a minister responsible for the family and the young should not be a bachelor. As a general rule defence ministers should have served in the armed forces, although Helmut Schmidt (who appointed Hans Apel in 1978) and Helmut Kohl (who appointed Rupert Scholz in 1988) have both taken the risk of ignoring this convention. To some extent ministers tend to be regarded as experts in their fields. This

8. See Richard Rose, *Ministers and Ministries*, Oxford: Clarendon Press, 1987, p. 35.

is one factor which has limited the practice of rotating ministers between departments.

The logic of coalition-building has so far always resulted in the junior coalition partner being over-represented in the cabinet in relation to its parliamentary strength (see Table 3.1). Only once has the Federal Republic experienced a sustained period of British-style one-party government. This occured under Adenauer between September 1960 and October 1961, when those ministers who were members of the coalition partner, the German Party (*Deutsche Partei*, DP), joined the CDU. German chancellors have seldom inflated the size of the cabinet to form coalitions, although Christian Democratic chancellors have been more inclined to pacify competing political interests by creating new ministries than their Social Democratic counterparts. Only the former have had cabinets with more than twenty members. To a certain extent, larger cabinets are indicative of a chancellor's weakness.

To consolidate his first coalition between the CDU/CSU, FDP and DP in 1949, Adenauer had to enlarge his cabinet to include fourteen ministers, although the original intention was for a cabinet of eight.[9] He also had to form a larger cabinet at the end of his political career after his authority over both the coalition partner and his own party had begun to decline. That he became chancellor again in 1961 was only because of major concessions to the FDP, the most important of which was that he would remain in office only till 1963.

Erhard inherited Adenauer's 'over-sized' cabinet. His style of consensus government, and the increasing difficulty of maintaining the Christian–Liberal coalition, did not allow him to reduce the size of his cabinet significantly, even after he had won the general election of 1965. It is almost self-evident that Kiesinger, who succeeded Erhard in 1966, had no choice but to preside over a larger than usual cabinet. His Grand Coalition was based on the cooperation of two partners, the CDU/CSU and the SPD, who were of comparable strength and who both wanted their top personnel to hold office. In government for the first time in the history of the Federal Republic, the SPD was not willing to forgo maximum representation in the cabinet through modesty. A twenty-member cabinet came into being after Kohl's cabinet reshuffle of 1989. Here again it was above all the chancellor's relative weakness which forced him to make compromises in this matter.

9. See Niclauss (1988), *op. cit.*, p. 25, and Jost Küpper, *Die Kanzlerdemokratie*, Frankfurt am Main: Peter Lang, 1985, p. 75.

Not only do cabinet appointments have to be distributed between competing political interests, but the posts of *Parlamentarische Staatssekretäre* (parliamentary state secretaries) also have to be allocated on a similar basis. These junior ministerial offices were created in 1967 by the Grand Coalition, when they were given the formal task of handling ministerial relations with parliament and the general public. At first only the largest ministries had these junior ministers. Now every ministry has at least one, many have two and the Chancellor's Office has occasionally even had three (see Table 3.2). In 1967 the total number of *Parlamentarische Staatssekretäre* was seven; in 1990 this had increased to twenty-seven. A typical example of the room for political manoeuvre offered by these non-cabinet but still sought-after posts was the way in which Helmut Kohl used them in 1983 to strengthen the representation of the German north in a cabinet which had a strong southern bias.[10]

When the first all-German government was formed in early 1991, the number of parliamentary state secretaries rose to a record thirty-four. As previously, these posts were used to accommodate the demands of coalition partners and regional interests, but now two new considerations came into play as well. New posts were created to increase the representation of women in the cabinet and to meet East German expectations that they would be adequately represented in the government of the new Germany. This increase in the number of parliamentary state secretaries was, however, reversed in 1993. In response to public perceptions of waste in government, and against the background of the debate over the state deficit, the number of these positions was cut back to twenty-six. Nevertheless, this figure remained high in comparison to cabinet size in earlier governments of the Federal Republic.

The extent of government reorganisation (see Table 3.2) has been comparable to changes experienced in Britain.[11] Seldom has it been the case that ministries have been created for purely party political reasons. However, there have been isolated examples of this – as with Hans Klein (CSU), who lost his portfolio for the Third World in 1989 and was moved by Kohl to the position of press secretary which, exceptionally, was given ministerial status. There have been relatively few cases of merging or dividing ministries. When this has occurred it has usually been for pragmatic reasons, as in the creation of the so-called Super-ministry of Economics and Finance, equivalent to the British Treasury. This reflected the SPD's intention

---

10. See Thomas Ellwein and Joachim Jens Hesse, *Das Regierungssystem der Bundesrepublik Deutschland*, Opladen: Westdeutscher Verlag, 1987, p. 303.
11. See Rose, *op. cit.*, p. 46.

Table 3.2. ORGANISATIONAL CONTINUITY AND
CHANGE IN THE CABINET

| Minister | Position existed | | No. of their junior ministers (Parl. Staatssekretäre) | |
	From/to	During chancellorship of	From/to	During chancellorship of
Chancellor's Office	1961–76 Since 1983	All chancellors	1 (1967–82) 3 (1982–7) 2 (since 1987)	Kiesinger, Brandt Schmidt Kohl Kohl
Press secretary	1989–90	Kohl		
Foreign affairs	Since 1951	All chancellors	1 (1967–72) 2 (since 1972)	Kiesinger, Brandt Brandt, Schmidt, Kohl
Interior	Since 1949	All chancellors	1 (1967–72) (1980–2) 2 (1972–80) (since 1982)	Kiesinger, Brandt Schmidt Brandt, Schmidt Kohl
Justice	Since 1949	All chancellors	1 (1969–90) 2 (1991–3) 1 (since 1993)	Brandt, Schmidt, Kohl Kohl Kohl
Finance[1]	Since 1949	All chancellors	1 (1967–72) 2 (since 1972)	Kiesinger, Brandt Brandt, Schmidt, Kohl
Economics	Since 1949	All chancellors	1 (1967–83) 2 (since 1983)	Kiesinger, Brandt Schmidt, Kohl Kohl
Federal property	1957–61	Adenauer		
Federal wealth	1961–9	Adenauer Erhard, Kiesinger		
Agriculture	Since 1949	All chancellors	1 (1969–83) 2 (1983–93) 1 (since 1993)	Brandt, Schmidt Kohl Kohl Kohl
Marshall Plan	1949–53	Adenauer		
European economic cooperation	1953–7	Adenauer		
Employment and social affairs[2]	Since 1949	All chancellors	1 (1969–80) 2 (since 1980)	Brandt, Schmidt Schmidt, Kohl

Table 3.2 *(contd)*

Minister	Position existed From/to	During chancellorship of	No. of their junior ministers (Parl. Staatssekretäre) From/to	During chancellorship of
Defence	Since 1955	All chancellors	1 (1967–82) (1983–7) 2 (1982–3) (since 1987)	Kiesinger, Brandt Schmidt, Kohl Kohl
The young, the family, women and health[3]	Since 1953	All chancellors	1 (1969–90)	Brandt, Schmidt, Kohl
Health[3]	1961–9	Adenauer, Erhard, Kiesinger		
	Since 1991	Kohl	1 (since 1991)	Kohl
Post and telecommunications[4]	1949–69	Adenauer, Erhard, Kiesinger		
	Since 1980	Schmidt, Kohl	1 (since 1980)	Schmidt, Kohl
Transport[4]	Since 1949	All chancellors	1 (1967–72) (1980–90) 2 (1972–80) (1991–3) 1 (since 1993)	Kiesinger, Brandt Schmidt, Kohl Brandt, Schmidt Kohl Kohl
Urban planning, housing[5]	Since 1949	All chancellors	1 (1969–90) 2 (1991–3) 1 (since 1993)	Brandt, Schmidt, Kohl Kohl Kohl
Expellees	1949–69	Adenauer, Erhard, Kiesinger		
Inner-German relations[6]	(1949–90)	All chancellors	1 (1969–90)	Brandt, Schmidt, Kohl
Atomic energy	1955–62	Adenauer		
Research and technology[4]	Since 1972	Brandt, Schmidt, Kohl	1 (since 1972)	Brandt, Schmidt, Kohl
Education and science[7]	Since 1962	All chancellors	1 (1969–90) 2 (1991–3) 1 (since 1993)	Brandt, Schmidt, Kohl Kohl Kohl
Third World	Since 1961	All chancellors	1 (1969–90) 2 (1991–3) 1 (since 1993)	Brandt, Schmidt, Kohl Kohl Kohl

Table 3.2 *(contd)*

		Position existed		No. of their junior ministers (Parl. Staatssekretäre)
Minister	*From/to*	*During chancellorship of*	*From/to*	*During chancellorship of*
Bundesrat	1949–69	Adenauer, Erhard, Kiesinger		
Environmental protection	1986–90	Kohl	2 (1987–93) 1 (since 1993)	Kohl Kohl
Family and pensioners	Since 1991	Kohl	1 (since 1991)	Kohl
Women and the young	Since 1991	Kohl	1 (since 1991)	Kohl

[1] Between May 1971 and December 1972 merged with the Economics Ministry into one Ministry of Economics and Finance.
[2] From 1949 till 1957 was called 'Employment Ministry'.
[3] The ministry's name in 1953–7 was 'the Family', then in 1957–69 it was 'the Family and the Young'. After 1969 the word 'Health' was added when the ministry merged with the Health Ministry. In 1986 the ministry's brief was extended to include women's interests.
[4] Post and Telecommunications was merged with Transport from 1969 till 1972 and from 1974 till 1980. From 1972 till 1974 that portfolio was administered by the Technology Ministry.
[5] In 1949–50 this was called the Ministry for Reconstruction, and then till 1961 the Ministry of Housing. The planning responsibility was added in 1976.
[6] From 1949 till 1969 this ministry was responsible for problems relating to Germany as a whole.
[7] From 1962 till 1969 this was called the Ministry for Scientific Research.
Sources: Datenhandbuch zur Geschichte des Deutschen Bundestages 1949 bis 1982, Bonn 1983, pp. 324ff.; *Datenhandbuch zur Geschichte des Deutschen Bundestages 1980 bis 1987*, pp. 314ff.; Antje Vorbeck, 'Regierungsbildung 1990–91: Koalitions- und Personalentscheidungen im Spiegel der Presse', *Zeitschrift für Parlaments- fragen*, no. 22, 1991, p. 388.

during Brandt's first chancellorship to secure partisan control over Economics and Finance after Alex Möller (SPD) had resigned in 1971 as Finance minister, rather than hand the ministry over to the FDP as coalition partner. Some mergers were the result of the planning euphoria in the early 1970s, when the Social Democrats hoped to be able to find a more effective and programme-oriented form of government organisation. The impact of these reforms, however, was limited by institutional inertia. As part of this reorganisation, the Health Ministry took over responsibility for the young and the family, a successful merger, which was extended to women's affairs under Kohl from 1986 to 1990. In 1991 the ministry was again divided into three new ministries each headed by a woman: Family and Pensioners; Women and the Young; and Health. A hotly debated and much hated merger in 1969 resulted in the fusion of the Ministry of Post and Telecommunications with that of Transport. Between 1972 and 1974, during Willy Brandt's second term, an even less promising combination of Technology and Post and Telecommunications was tried. The 1969 reform initiative had brought no observable gains, and was finally reversed by Schmidt in 1980.

Most new ministries have been created in response to urgent new social, economic and political problems. After the Second World War, for example, ministries were created to administer Marshall aid and to implement special measures to help the expellees and other Germans who had fled from areas under Soviet dominance. In 1955, when nuclear energy was adopted as the modern solution for future energy needs, Franz Josef Strauss (CSU) became the minister responsible for this programme. The creation of the Ministry of Education and Science was delayed until 1962 because of *Länder* prerogatives in these fields. This ministry, and that of Research and Technology established in 1972, provided a political infrastructure for the knowledge-based society that was envisaged by all chancellors. The latest addition to the federal ministries was Environmental Protection and Reactor Safety, set up in 1986. The creation of this ministry was both the immediate response to the Chernobyl catastrophe in the same year and a symbolic concession to the greening of German politics, which had led to a widespread opposition to nuclear power and had paved the way for the rise of the Green Party.

After unification, many expected that the chancellor would create a new ministry to oversee and promote economic reconstruction in the new German *Länder*. The Ministry for Inner-German Relations, now redundant, might have been used as the nucleus for such a ministry. Taking the view, however, that the existing government apparatus could be adapted, the chancellor rejected this option.[12] Instead, East Germans were given ministerial appointments within the existing structure. Only three such appointments were made, and these to relatively minor posts. The two East German CDU politicians regarded as possessing ministerial calibre were Günther Krause, GDR negotiator in discussions on the Unity Treaty, and Angela Merkel, cast in the role of 'woman from the east'. Krause was given the Transport Ministry, the most important of the posts allocated to easterners, while Merkel was appointed Minister for

12. See Roland Sturm, 'Government at the Centre', in G. Smith, W.E. Paterson, P. Merkl and S. Padgett (eds), *Developments in German Politics*, Basingstoke: Macmillan, 1992, pp. 103–18.

Women and the Young. Rainer Ortlep, former chairman of the Liberals in the east, was given the relatively uninfluential Ministry of Education and Science.

The two foremost representatives of the former GDR, both members of the chancellor's party, were assigned only minor roles in the political life of the new Germany. Efforts to elect the last prime minister of the GDR, Lothar de Maizière, as Speaker of the Bundestag were abandoned in the face of strong allegations concerning his involvement with the *Stasi* (GDR security police). Another prominent East German with a claim to government office was Sabine Bergmann-Pohl, Speaker of the GDR parliament and head of state before unification. She was judged by the chancellor to be lacking in ministerial calibre, but in view of her status in the former GDR her claims could not be entirely overlooked. As a compromise she was appointed to a junior ministerial post in the Health Ministry.

Constraints on Executive Leadership

The structure of the cabinet and the distribution of political territory across the ministries are just two of the variables in relations between the chancellor and the executive. Chancellors also have to take into account five other factors which impose constraints upon their freedom of manoeuvre. First, the Finance Minister is endowed by statute with a certain autonomy within the cabinet. Secondly, a chancellor's political choices can be considerably restricted by the constraints of coalition government. Thirdly, inner-executive relations can be conditioned by the influence of the chancellor's own party. Fourthly, senior civil servants can have an important bearing upon government. Finally, the dynamics of the new German polity and demands emanating from the east can be expected to exert an increasing influence on inner-executive relations.

The chancellor and his Finance Minister. Paragraph 28 (2) of the *Bundeshaushaltsordnung*[13] (the legal framework of the budgeting procedure) gives the Finance Minister a veto on all questions of finance. This can have a delaying effect, because it can force the cabinet to repeat its vote on a particular decision. As long as the chancellor sides with the Finance Minister, he cannot be outvoted.

13. See Martin Oldiges, *Die Bundesregierung als Kollegium. Eine Studie zur Regierungsorganisation nach dem Grundgesetz*, Hamburg: Heitmann, 1983, pp. 291ff.; and for a comparative perspective Roland Sturm, *Haushaltspolitik in westlichen Demokratien*, Baden-Baden: Nomos, 1989, pp. 145ff.

In reality this provision has turned out to be little more than a technicality.

Nevertheless Finance Ministers have always been strong forces in West German cabinets. Although they have never used their special privilege in the cabinet,[14] the very fact that they control the budget, which is a central interest of all other ministries, has earned them respect. Moreover, this is reinforced by the fact that chancellors have normally appointed political heavyweights to the post. The spectacular successes of Ludwig Erhard as Economics Minister in the Adenauer era overshadowed the contribution of Adenauer's first Finance Minister, Fritz Schäffer (CSU, 1949–57), who stubbornly insisted on a balanced budget. This often led to controversies with Adenauer, who wanted to spend more than Schäffer was ready to concede. When he formed his third cabinet in 1961 Adenauer decided to give Franz Etzel this portfolio.[15] During the grand coalition (1966–9) the Ministry of Finance was occupied by Franz Josef Strauss, chairman of the CSU. Strauss and Economics Minister Karl Schiller (SPD) formed a successful partnership which for the first time introduced Keynesian economic thinking into German economic policies. During the first years of the SPD/FDP coalition under Willy Brandt, the Ministry of Finance was first held by Alex Möller, then by Karl Schiller and finally in 1972 by Helmut Schmidt. The resignations of both Möller and Schiller sent shock waves through the government. With Brandt helplessly searching for consensus in economic matters, Helmut Schmidt seized the initiative. In his view, economic policy needed decisive action based on an appreciation of economic realities rather than compromises.

As chancellor, Schmidt was especially cautious over appointments to the Finance Ministry. He had seen how Karl Schiller had tried to use his reputation to outmanoeuvre the cabinet by going public when he defended his principles for the 1972 budget.[16] During his chancellorship Schmidt took care to appoint loyal supporters to this crucial post: Hans Apel (1974), Hans Matthöfer (1978) and for the final few months Manfred Lahnstein (1982), a civil servant outside parliamentary politics. Schmidt's successor, Helmut Kohl, seemed for a time to have made a tactical mistake by appointing Gerhard Stoltenberg (CDU) as Finance Minister. How-

---

14. The importance of it is, as Zunker has rightly remarked, that it exists and not that it is used in cabinet. Albrecht Zunker, *Finanzplanung und Bundeshaushalt. Zur Koordinierung und Kontrolle durch den Bundesfinanzminister*, Frankfurt am Main: Metzner, 1972, p. 47.
15. See Niclauss (1988), *op. cit.*, p. 31.
16. See Arnulf Baring, *Machtwechsel. Die Ära Brandt-Scheel*, Munich: DTV, 1982, p. 668.

ever, Stoltenberg quickly acquired a reputation for expertise and won credit for restoring stability to public finance. In opinion polls, Stoltenberg was regularly rated highest among leading politicians, easily leaving Kohl behind him.[17] Indeed, influential forces in the CDU deliberated over whether to replace Kohl with Stoltenberg, whose dependability contrasted sharply with the vulnerability of a chancellor who at the time was embroiled in a series of scandals.[18] Fortunately for Kohl, Stoltenberg himself became caught up in scandal, being implicated in the Barschel affair[19] and accused of having permitted illegal exports of blueprints for the construction of submarines to South Africa. Stoltenberg's successor in the Finance Ministry, CSU chairman Theo Waigel, is no less a heavyweight than Stoltenberg. However, he is less of a rival to Kohl since he is not in the chancellor's party and lacks his predecessor's outstanding public image. Indeed Waigel is a major asset to Kohl, since his presence helps in shifting the search for compromises between the coalition partners into the arena of the cabinet.

Coalition government. The prevalence of coalition government in the German context has forced every chancellor to seek compromises with his coalition partners. This institutionalised compromise is a Janus-faced phenomenon. On the one hand it may force a chancellor to abandon some political aims. On the other hand – as both Adenauer and Schmidt demonstrated – it may serve as a pretext for not fulfilling some of the expectations of the chancellor's own party, enabling him to blame the stubbornness of the coalition partner for the failure to achieve certain aims. Coalition compromises constitute the general framework in which political decisions are made.[20]

17. The last *Spiegel* poll before the 1987 general election gave Helmut Kohl 56 per cent (ranked seventh), compared to Stoltenberg's 66 per cent (ranked first) when respondents were asked which politician they would prefer to play a prominent part in future German politics ('*Würden Sie es gern sehen, wenn dieser Politiker im Laufe der kommenden Jahre eine wichtige Rolle im politischen Leben der Bundesrepublik spielen würde, oder würden Sie das nicht so gern sehen?*'); see *Der Spiegel*, 22 December 1986 p. 36.
18. For an overview of the debate see 'Genscher war unser rettender Nagel', *Der Spiegel*, 26 January 1987, pp. 6–22; Niclauss (1988), *op. cit.*, pp. 230ff.
19. Uwe Barschel was head of the Schleswig-Holstein *Land* government from October 1982 till September 1987. It was proved that Barschel used the resources of his office to organise a smear campaign against the candidate of the rival SPD at the 1987 *Landtag* election. Barschel committed suicide in a Geneva hotel room on 11 October. For further details see, for example, Jochen Bölsche (ed.), *Waterkantgate. Die Kieler Affäre. Eine Spiegel-Dokumentation*, Göttingen: Steidl, 1987.
20. For a detailed overview, see Peter Schindler, *Datenhandbuch zur Geschichte des Deutschen Bundestages 1980 bis 1987*, Baden-Baden: Nomos, 1988, pp. 339ff.

In the early Adenauer years this framework was a fairly informal one, partly based on an exchange of letters, which could be interpreted very much according to the chancellor's inclinations. In 1961, with FDP participation in Adenauer's government conditional upon the chancellor's early resignation, a new form of coalition agreement was introduced. The coalition 'treaty' bound the partners on policies and on organisational aspects of coalition cooperation. Moreover, it institutionalised the informal meetings on coalition affairs which had already been held under former governments and introduced a steering committee on coalition affairs (*Koalitionsausschuss*). The membership of this committee included the chairs and vice-chairs of the parliamentary parties, together with their chief whips. In addition, party chairmen were given the right to attend cabinet meetings. These formal arrangements were discontinued after 1965.

The Grand Coalition, consisting as it did of ideologically opposed parties, might have been thought to require a secure institutional base. Chancellor Kiesinger, however, initially tried to manage without any formal arrangements, attempting instead to resolve conflict in the cabinet, where leading politicians of both parties were represented. The absence of a formal coalition apparatus was partly compensated by the inclusion of the SPD's coalition terms in Kiesinger's government declaration (*Regierungserklärung*). However, the cabinet proved to be too clumsy an instrument for coalition management, and in summer 1967 the chancellor invited leading coalition politicians to his holiday resort at Kressbronn on Lake Constance, to lay down a set of guidelines for government cooperation. Out of this meeting a full-scale coalition committee emerged, meeting regularly as the so-called *Kressbronner Kreis*. Depending on the agenda, this included *inter alia* Kiesinger, Vice-Chancellor Brandt and the leaders of the parliamentary parties.[21]

With the end of the Grand Coalition, cabinet management returned to more informal structures. However, the length and detail of pre-coalition treaties were extended, narrowing the scope for interpretation, which in turn reduced the volume of controversial decisions with which chancellors had to contend. Remaining coalition differences were resolved by *ad hoc* crisis management. The major reason for the post-1969 tendency to base coalitions on detailed written accords is the eagerness of the junior coalition parties to preserve their separate identities and to present clear-cut policy profiles to their voters. This applied not only to the Liberals but also, with Franz Josef Strauss as its chairman, to the Bavarian

21. Hans Schäfer, 'Der "Kressbronner Kreis" ', *Liberal*, no. 10, 1968, pp. 862–4.

CSU. Although the Bavarian CSU and the CDU constituted a single parliamentary party, the former increasingly played the role of an internal opposition, with Strauss often (successfully) demanding coalition talks to resolve policy conflicts.

Party constraints. One important variable in the government decision-making process is whether or not the chairmen of the coalition parties are included in the cabinet. Practice has varied from one incumbent to another. During the Adenauer era it was accepted without question that the parties forming the government should participate in cabinet meetings. Adenauer, of course, was also chairman of the CDU. When he stepped down as chancellor in favour of Erhard, he retained the party chairmanship, using the position (which he held till 1966) to criticise and undermine his successor and to explore alternative government coalitions.[22]

During the period of the Grand Coalition and the years of the first Brandt government (1966–74) the original Adenauer model of including the party chairmen in the cabinet was restored. When Helmut Schmidt took over the chancellorship from Brandt in 1974, the party chairmanship of the SPD remained with Brandt. With hindsight, it has been argued that this was a major tactical mistake on Schmidt's part. Initially the Social Democratic 'troika' of Schmidt as chancellor, Brandt as party leader and Herbert Wehner as chairman of the SPD parliamentary party worked efficiently. In the later years of the Schmidt incumbency, however, Brandt and large sections of the SPD gradually distanced themselves from Schmidt's policies and increasingly identified themselves with the so-called new social movements for environmentalism, peace and disarmament. This conflict culminated in SPD opposition to the NATO decision to strengthen its defensive powers by deploying middle-range missiles in Western Europe. The conflict was all the more damaging to the chancellor since the decision had been taken at his initiative.

Helmut Kohl was keen to avoid Schmidt's problem of the party exploring the limits of its own independent political role. He favoured Adenauer's model of the Christian Democrats as a channel to transmit government decisions to the general public and to parliament. However, it was not until the death of Franz Josef Strauss in 1988 and the dismissal of the independent-minded CDU general secretary Heiner Geissler[23] that he was successful in streamlining government decision-making in this way. Until then, Geissler had

22. Konrad Adenauer, 'Möglichkeiten einer Koalition', *Politische Meinung*, vol. 10, no. 108, 1965, pp. 13–17.
23. For further details see *Der Spiegel*, 28 August 1989, pp. 14–24.

used the party headquarters in the Konrad-Adenauer-Haus as a think-tank to come up with new ideas to influence political decisions, and Franz Josef Strauss had conducted monthly meetings of CSU cabinet ministers in Munich at which they received their instructions on what to do in Bonn.[24]

The civil service. To a certain degree chancellors heading new coalitions have also faced a possible rival power centre in the senior levels of the civil service. Only twice (1969 and 1982) in the Federal Republic has there been a fundamental change in the party composition of government. These events were accompanied by an accelerated turnover of personnel in the senior civil service. Among the upper echelons of the federal bureaucracy (around 800 jobs), 9.6 per cent changed hands in 1969, increasing to 12.5 per cent in 1982. This can be compared to a turnover of 4.9 per cent in 1974.[25] The policy effects of a hostile bureaucracy should not be underestimated, especially in view of recent research findings that West German bureaucrats had more political and less technocratic attitudes than the traditionally politicised US executives.[26] Although the Federal Republic does not have an American-style 'spoils system', there is still a temptation to set aside the official 'Weberian' concept of civil service neutrality and to streamline the bureaucracy by installing government supporters in senior positions.

The dynamics of the new German polity. Discontent in the East in the aftermath of unification makes it highly unlikely that future cabinets will be appointed with as little consideration for East German interests as was shown in Kohl's 1991 cabinet. The representation of easterners can be expected to increase, if only for symbolic reasons.

Instruments of Executive Management

German chancellors are not, of course, without power resources to overcome structural obstacles in the executive arena and to organise

24. 'Fürs neue Kabinett gibt's keine Zusagen. Was CSU-Chef Strauss von seinen Ministern in der Bundesregierung hält', *Der Spiegel*, 11 August 1986, pp. 27–31.
25. See Hans-Ulrich Derlien, 'Die Regierungswechsel von 1969 und 1982 in ihren Auswirkungen auf die Beamtenelite', in Heinrich Siedentopf (ed.), *Führungskräfte in der öffentlichen Verwaltung*, Baden-Baden: Nomos, 1989, pp. 171–89, p. 173.
26. See Joel D. Aberbach, Hans-Ulrich Derlien, Renate Mayntz and Bert A. Rockman, 'American and German Federal Executives – Technocratic and Political Attitudes', *International Social Science Journal*, no. 123, 1990, pp. 3–18.

cabinet work according to their own preferences.[27] In addition to the chancellor's constitutional right to establish the guidelines of government policy (the *Richtlinienkompetenz* outlined above), he has a number of resources on which to draw: control over cabinet committees; the power to appoint and dismiss ministers; and the capacity to bring together informal circles of policy advisors. The latter are supplementary to the key power resource provided by the Chancellor's Office, which is the subject of a separate chapter in this volume.

Cabinet committees. In contrast to Britain, German cabinet committees play only a minor role in decision-making. Where they exist at all, they serve more to provide technical assistance to the chancellor than as tactical instruments at his disposal.[28] With the exception of the *Bundessicherheitsrat* (the cabinet committee on defence), all cabinet committees are open to all ministers and a written report on their activities is sent to every minister after each meeting. The chancellor is the *ex-officio* chairman of all cabinet committees and controls the agenda. He may restrict the number of ministers allowed to attend these meetings to the regular committee members, and he appoints a minister in charge of the committee.[29]

A cabinet committee on middle-range financial planning (*Kabinettsausschuss für die mittelfristige Finanzplanung*) was set up in 1969. This acquired a certain strategic importance during the late 1960s and early 1970s, when the government was trying to build up an efficient planning machinery. However, with regard to the final decision on the budget which it helped to prepare it never substituted for the cabinet as a whole.[30] Kohl reorganised the committee structure in March 1985 according to his political priorities (see Table 3.3). In 1990 the cabinet committee on the German question achieved a higher profile, because it was used to prepare the treaty between East and West Germany that launched German unification.

27. For a brief debate on the powers of the chancellor from the point of view of constitutional law, see Klaus Kröger, 'Aufgabe und Verantwortung des Bundeskanzlers nach dem Grundgesetz', *Aus Politik und Zeitgeschichte*, no. 34, 1969, pp. 28–48.
28. Ferdinand Müller-Rommel, 'Federal Republic of Germany: A System of Chancellor Government', in Jean Blondel and Ferdinand Müller-Rommel (eds), *Cabinets in Western Europe*, Basingstoke: Macmillan, 1988, pp. 151–66, p. 159.
29. *Geschäftsordnung der Bundesregierung (GOBReg), Rahmenregelungen für den Geschäftsablauf der Kabinettsausschüsse der Bundesregierung nach den Kabinettsbeschlüssen vom 31. Januar 1973 und vom 2. September 1984.*
30. See Sturm, *op. cit.*, p. 142.

Table 3.3.   MINISTERIAL MEMBERSHIP OF CABINET
COMMITTEES

BUNDESSICHERHEITSRAT (Defence)
Minister in charge: Defence
Regular members: Foreign Affairs, Interior, Justice, Finance, Economics

EUROPAPOLITIK (European Affairs)
Minister in charge: Foreign Affairs
Regular members: Finance, Economics, Agriculture

DEUTSCHLAND-UND BERLIN-FRAGEN (The German Question and Berlin)
Minister in charge: Inner-German Relations
Regular members: Foreign Affairs, Interior, Justice, Finance, Economics

WIRTSCHAFT (Economics)
Minister in charge: Economics
Regular members: Finance, Agriculture, Employment and Social Affairs, Transport,
Post Office, Urban Planning and Housing, Research and Technology, Third World

ZUKUNFTSTECHNOLOGIEN (Technologies for the Future)
Minister in charge: Research and Technology
Regular members: Foreign Affairs, Finance, Economics, Employment and Social
Affairs, Defence, Transport, Post Office, Education and Science

UMWELT UND GESUNDHEIT (Environmental Protection and Health)*
Minister in charge: Interior
Regular members: Finance, Economics, Agriculture, Employment and Social
Affairs, The Young, the Family and Health, Transport, Urban Planning and Hous-
ing, Research and Technology

---

* Organisational changes because of the reorganisation of ministeries in 1986; see
Table 3.2.
Source: Presse-und Informationsamt der Bundesregierung, *Bulletin* 61, Bonn 1985,
p. 519.

The power of ministerial appointment.   Article 64 of the Basic Law
gives chancellors the right to select their ministers. The latter do not
need individual parliamentary majorities to secure their appointment, and they do not necessarily have to be members of the
Bundestag. Hans Leussink, who was given the portfolio for education and science by Willy Brandt in 1969, was not even a party
member. Although factional interests within the chancellor's own
party, and external coalition pressures, may restrict a chancellor's
room for manoeuvre, he has a strong incentive to select his personal
following for cabinet posts. One extreme example was the last
Schmidt cabinet of 1982, which was formed after the FDP had left
the coalition and which the chancellor presented to the public as a
cabinet of fellow 'workaholics'.

As mentioned above, the dependence of individual ministers
upon the chancellor is counterbalanced by Article 65 of the Basic

Law which gives the individual minister undisputed responsibility for his or her department (*Ressortprinzip*). Ministers rarely resign over policy differences with the chancellor in the manner of Gustav Heinemann, Adenauer's first Interior Minister, who left the government in 1950 because he disagreed with the chancellor's rearmament policy. Heinemann's resignation was treated disdainfully by Adenauer, who regarded it as odd and unpolitical to give up a ministerial office over differences in political opinions.[31] Even scandals, such as the 1984 Wörner–Kiessling affair,[32] did not automatically cost ministers their jobs. Franz-Josef Strauss recalled in the context of this example that he had had to go as Defence Minister in 1962 during the *Spiegel* affair,[33] because he was accused of having lied to parliament. The circumstances then, he writes, were much less embarrassing than the damage Wörner had done. Nevertheless, the chancellor did not ask Wörner to face the consequences.[34] Under Kohl, cabinet stability has taken priority over personal and political disagreement. Cabinet posts are regarded as the precious result of coalition arrangements, even to the extent that the chancellor's prerogative of selecting his ministers is undermined. The coalition partners now claim their right to distribute their share of cabinet seats. It is feared that ministerial resignations may disturb this careful balance, and furthermore may create the impression of a lack of competence at the centre of government.

Informal advisors and 'kitchen cabinets'. The Chancellor's Office is an institutionalised support mechanism for German chancellors which facilitates control over government policy and allows the chancellor to intervene in departmental responsibilities.[35] Outside

31. This is reported by Rudolf Augstein, 'Vertrauen Sie dieser Sache Ihre beste Feder an. Rudolf Augstein über Adenauers "Teegespräche" ', *Der Spiegel*, 24 December, 1984, pp. 36–44.
32. General Kiessling, who was one of the top *Bundeswehr* representatives at NATO headquarters in Brussels, was falsely accused of homosexual practices and forced into early retirement in 1983. Manfred Wörner, the then defence minister (later NATO secretary-general), tried with dubious methods but ultimately unsuccessfully to defend this decision. See also Niclauss (1988), *op. cit.*, p. 238.
33. The journal *Der Spiegel* was falsely accused of having committed high treason by publishing an article on the NATO manoeuvre 'Fallex 62', in which it argued that the full defence of West Germany in case of an Eastern attack was not guaranteed. Without sufficient legal justification *Spiegel* journalists were arrested and the publication of the journal was blocked. Defence minister Strauss was accused of trying to get rid of critical journalists. For further details see Joachim Schöps (ed.), *Die Spiegel-Affäre des Franz Josef Strauss*, Reinbek: Rowohlt, 1983.
34. See Franz Josef Strauss, *Die Erinnerungen*, Berlin: Siedler, 1989, p. 512.
35. See Müller-Rommel in this volume (Chapter 4).

the Chancellor's Office, every chancellor has had an 'inner circle' of close friends and advisors. In economic affairs Adenauer relied heavily on the advice of bankers, especially Robert Pferdmenges and Hermann Joseph Abs.[36] On more general policy matters he called upon his 'kitchen cabinet' of close advisors, including, among others, Heinrich Krone, Walter Hallstein, Hans Globke, Herbert Blankenhorn, Josef Rust and Felix von Eckardt.[37] In contrast to Adenauer, Erhard placed more trust in the common sense of his cabinet and made a point of not confronting its members with decisions that had already been taken.[38] Heidenheimer even reports that 'there were occasions when it was publicly announced that he had allowed his cabinet colleagues to outvote him.'[39] Brandt's changing circle of close advisers showed the typical traits of *ad hoc* policy-making in kitchen cabinets.[40] A more coherent apparatus was organised by Brandt's first head of the Chancellor's Office (until 1972), Horst Ehmke. An intricate planning machinery was assembled, with the aim of making policy decisions on the basis of scientific insights.[41]

Helmut Schmidt abhorred the political structures Ehmke had built up in the Chancellor's Office, relying instead on an inner circle of three advisors, who together with Schmidt formed the so-called *Kleeblatt* (clover-leaf) team.[42] Every Tuesday afternoon they met in the Chancellor's Office to prepare policy decisions in an atmosphere which combined brain-storming and policy management. Schmidt decided in 1979/80 to discontinue the *Kleeblatt* meetings, a decision which he seems to have regretted. In the spring of 1982 he tried to revive the old decision-making structures.[43]

Kohl has restored the classic 'kitchen cabinet' to German politics. His inner circle consists of old friends, who have been close to him since childhood or at least during earlier periods of his political career, and who are available to be consulted whenever he wishes.

36. Volker Berghahn, *Unternehmer und Politik in der Bundesrepublik*, Frankfurt: Suhrkamp, 1985, p. 186.
37. See Küpper, *op. cit.*, p. 114.
38. Niclauss (1988), *op. cit.*, p. 86.
39. Arnold J. Heidenheimer, 'Adenauer's Legacies: Party Finance and the Decline of Chancellor Democracy', in Peter H. Merkl (ed.), *The Federal Republic of Germany at Forty*, New York University Press, 1983 (pp. 213–27), p. 215.
40. Wolfgang Jäger and Werner Link, *Republik im Wandel 1974–1982. Die Ära Schmidt*, Stuttgart: DVA/Mannheim: F.A. Brockhaus 1987, p. 11.
41. See Baring, *op. cit.*, pp. 520ff.
42. Helmut Herles, 'Das Kleeblatt. Des Bundeskanzlers engster Beraterkreis', *Frankfurter Allgemeine Zeitung*, 2 Dec. 1978.
43. Niclauss (1988), *op. cit.*, p. 216.

They control access to the chancellor, take on responsibilities which have nothing to do with their formal job descriptions, issue orders which they are formally not empowered to give, and have powers of patronage which extend to civil service promotions. Central to this network is Juliane Weber, *de facto* head of the chancellor's personal office.[44] Kohl dislikes working with civil servants and self-confident specialists. He much prefers to tap the potential of young and efficient collaborators. Their lack of experience may mean there are occasional mistakes, but these young advisers are and will remain loyal to him. At the centre of this network, Kohl tries to ensure that personal loyalty to him as chancellor outweighs any kind of inter-personal loyalty on the level of other political offices.[45]

'Chancellor Democracy' or 'Coordination Democracy'?

The debate over chancellor democracy goes beyond the constitutional powers of the chancellorship[46] and includes other variables – in Adenauer's case his strong personality – which contribute to the chancellor's dominance over the cabinet.[47] Those who warn against an over-zealous interpretation of Article 65 point out that leadership in politics has always been and will always remain a task of coordinating conflicting interests by making authoritative decisions. They argue that with the increase in the volume of political problems arising simultaneously, the development of competing power centres in society (formal ones such as the Federal Court, the Bundesbank and federal institutions,[48] and informal ones such as private banks and industrial concerns) and media demands for instant responses, chancellors are increasingly forced into the role of policy managers.[49] Instead of stressing the relative strength of the chancellor in the executive arena, new arguments are

44. ' "Der Kanzler wünscht das so". Wie Helmut Kohls Küchenkabinett die Bundesrepublik regiert', *Der Spiegel*, 9 June 1986, pp. 24–7.
45. Nina Grunenberg, 'Das starke Stück der Union. Der späte Start des Helmut Kohl. Vom Taktiker zum Politiker', *Die Zeit*, 5 Oct. 1990, p. 4.
46. For the earliest and 'classic' statement of the chancellor democracy hypothesis, see Wilhelm Hennis, *Richtlinienkompetenz und Regierungstechnik*, Tübingen: J.C.B. Mohr, 1964.
47. For a broader definition of *Kanzlerdemokratie* see Niclauss (1988), *op. cit.*, pp. 66ff.
48. See Peter Haungs, 'Kanzlerdemokratie in der Bundesrepublik Deutschland: Von Adenauer bis Kohl', *Zeitschrift für Politik*, no. 33, 1986 (pp. 44–66), pp. 61ff.
49. Rolf Zundel, ' "Ein Kanzler wie ein Eichenschrank". Konrad Adenauer schuf das Modell der Kanzlerdemokratie – Was ist in vierzig Jahren daraus geworden?', *Die Zeit*, 6 January 1989, p. 3.

found to support the characterisation of the political system as a
Koordinationsdemokratie.[50]

Closely interwoven with the so-called *Kanzlerprinzip* of Article 65
is the question of how different chancellors have used this prerogative. Much has been written about the different personalities of the
office-holders. Konrad Adenauer and Helmut Schmidt are usually
viewed as 'strong' chancellors who had clear ideas about their aims
and the will to get things done. At every cabinet meeting Adenauer
is reported to have stressed the general ideas that he expected his
ministers to support. He used historical arguments in his warnings
against the Soviet threat and in his praise for the new-found harmony with Israel, the friendship with France and the partnership
with the United States.[51] By the time Schmidt became chancellor
the political situation had become more complex. The hallmark of
the Schmidt chancellorship was the rational pragmatism with which
political problems were addressed.[52] In contrast to his predecessor
Brandt, Schmidt placed an emphasis on government stability and
the need to accept the limits imposed on public policy by economic
realities.[53] Thus Schmidt eschewed visionary leadership in favour
of managerial competence and tight control over the apparatus of
government.

Erhard and Brandt are regarded as 'weak' chancellors with a
limited capacity for organising the governmental process. It has

50. For the debate on these characterisations see, among others, Peter Haungs,
'Kanzlerprinzip und Regierungstechnik im Vergleich: Adenauers Nachfolger',
Aus Politik und Zeitgeschichte, nos 1–2, 1989, pp. 28–39; Wolfgang Jäger, 'Von
der Kanzlerdemokratie zur Koordinationsdemokratie', *Zeitschrift für Politik*,
no. 35, 1988, pp. 15–32; Axel Murswieck, 'Die Bundesrepublik Deutschland-
Kanzlerdemokratie, Koordinationsdemokratie oder was sonst?', in Hans-
Hermann Hartwich and Göttrik Wewer (eds), *Regieren in der Bundesrepublik*,
I. *Konzeptionelle Grundlagen und Perspektiven der Forschung*, Opladen: Leske,
1990, pp. 151–69. To some extent this disagreement about terminology reflects
the different attitudes towards the chancellorship adopted by those who take
positive or more cynical views of the political structure. *Kanzlerdemokratie*
stresses those advantages of Adenauer's chancellorship which critics have called
authoritarian or worse. *Koordinationsdemokratie* stresses those advantages of
Kohl's chancellorship which critics have called bumbling or worse.
51. Strauss, *op. cit.*, p. 517; See also Hans-Peter Schwarz, 'Adenauers Kanzlerdemokratie und Regierungstechnik', *Aus Politik und Zeitgeschichte*, nos 1–2,
1989 (pp. 15–27), pp. 16ff.
52. Theo Sommer, 'Der richtige Mann zur richtigen Zeit. Der fünfte Bonner
Regierungschef: Bilanz nach achteinhalb Jahren', *Die Zeit*, 29 October 1982,
p. 3; Golo Mann, 'Nicht Geschichte machen wollte er', *Der Spiegel*, 1 November
1982, pp. 21–3.
53. Thomas Ellwein, *Krisen und Reform. Die Bundesrepublik seit den sechziger
Jahren*, Munich: DTV, 1989, p. 126.

been said that both were hampered by their visions of new social and political structures for West German society. Kiesinger's weakness as chancellor was due less to his political style than to the fact that, as chancellor of the Grand Coalition, he was forced to come to terms with a coalition partner of equal strength.

Erhard saw himself as the mediator between the post-war period and a new Germany oriented towards the promotion of the common good. His conviction that the Third Reich should no longer be the reference point for German politics brought him into conflict with the majority of West German intellectuals and the younger generation who argued that the crimes of the Nazis could never be forgotten. Erhard also regarded pressure groups representing special interests as a potentially divisive social force. In his opinion the aim of political leadership should be to overcome these types of selfish interest and to give society a common direction (*formierte Gesellschaft*).[54] Political reality quickly prevailed, however; social pluralism was firmly entrenched and could not be ignored.

The Grand Coalition, which succeeded Erhard's conservative-liberal government, endeavoured to make strategic use of the plurality of social interests in order to realise its concept of Keynesian economic management. Brandt erroneously predicted the dawning of a qualitatively new and better kind of democracy in West Germany. However, his policies of domestic reform were soon overcome by financial difficulties and party-political cross-pressures.[35] In the face of these pressures, Brandt failed to provide effective leadership, lacking both a coherent strategic concept[56] and the political will to use his electoral triumph of 1972 as a resource for mobilising public opinion in favour of reform.[57]

Chancellors have distributed their political interests unevenly. Adenauer and Brandt developed a strong preference for foreign policy; the first with regard to the West, the latter with regard to the East. Erhard and Schmidt saw the resolution of economic problems as central to a successful chancellorship. More than any other chancellor, Kohl addresses problems in an *ad hoc* manner,

54. For details see Klaus Hildebrand, *Von Erhard zur Grossen Koalition, 1963–1969*, Stuttgart: DVA/Wiesbaden: F.A. Brockhaus, 1984, pp. 160ff.
55. For details Roland Sturm, *Gesellschaft im Aufbruch*, Tübingen: DIFF, 1990.
56. See Martin and Sylvia Greiffenhagen, *Ein schwieriges Vaterland. Zur politischen Kultur Deutschlands*, Frankfurt am Main: S. Fischer, 1981, p. 169.
57. Klaus von Beyme, 'Der Konflikt zwischen Reform und Verwaltung der Wirtschafts-und Sozialordnung', in IG Metall (ed.), *Krise und Reform in der Industriegesellschaft*, Frankfurt/Cologne: EVA, 1976 (pp. 116–33), pp. 119ff.

incurring criticism for his lack of political guidance.[58] To a greater extent than his predecessors, Kohl sees policies as instruments in a continuing party-political power struggle, whose result will shape the 'historical' dimension of his chancellorship. He therefore hesitates to get involved in decisions when the consequences are unclear. When he sees a wider perspective, however, as in German unification, he will take over and manage the whole process almost single-handed, leaving it to the cabinet to fall in line. Kohl interprets his right to determine the general guidelines of policy-making as a broad responsibility for ensuring that his ministers do their work well, but this does not necessarily mean that he intervenes personally in the details of policy formulation. On the other hand he has sometimes used this right as a convenient argument for *ad hoc* intervention, leading to a centralisation of the decision-making process under his personal control.[59]

This latter tendency means that ministers sometimes learn of the chancellor's intentions from the media. The partial exclusion of ministers from executive decision-making is not a novel feature of the political process. Indeed it was a characteristic of the Adenauer era. However, the role of the modern media has led to a fundamental change in the style of government. Adenauer used to build up a following through personal contacts and the access he allowed interest groups.[60] The latter was of particular importance in economic affairs, where the Confederation of German Industry (*Bundesverband der Deutschen Industrie*, BDI) often negotiated with Adenauer, frequently without informing Economics Minister Erhard.[61]

A Redefinition of Executive Leadership?

For each chancellor it has been important to tailor the formal powers of the office, especially those comprising the *Kanzlerprinzip* (chancellor principle), according to his own particular political needs. The *Ressortprinzip* (ministerial autonomy) and the *Kabinettsprinzip* (cabinet principle) define political territory which has

58. See, for example, Strauss, *op. cit.*, pp. 518ff.
59. Gunter Hofmann, ' "Helmut Kohl ist und bleibt Kanzler". Bonns Sommer des Missvergnügens: Seine Gefolgschaft seufzt über den Regierungschef', *Die Zeit*, 17 Aug. 1984, p. 3.
60. Niclauss (1988), *op. cit.*, p. 44. Küpper, *op. cit.*, warns, however, against putting too much stress on direct pressure group influence on Adenauer's decisions.
61. Berghahn, *op. cit.*, p. 186.

not automatically been safeguarded against the chancellor's intervention. Once in office the chancellors of all parties have been expected to fulfil their role as political leaders[62] and to create the necessary political consensus on cabinet level.[63] Important preconditions for such a consensus, for instance support for the government by the parliamentary parties of the governing coalition, mutual understanding between the coalition partners, or the public image of a chancellor, lie to some extent outside the control of the political executive. In the cabinet itself political consensus often remains a vague notion. Votes are rarely taken and a great deal of the decision-making process takes the form of written proposals, which are circulated and approved in writing. Controversial issues have usually been dealt with outside cabinet so that 'most Cabinet decisions should be described as decisions *approved* rather than *made* by government collectively'.[64] Thus the outbreak of open conflict in cabinet is all the more dramatic because it indicates not only deficiencies in crisis management procedures in the executive, but also the loss of common ground which is essential to consensus-building.

The modern German chancellorship is heavily conditioned by two features of the extra-constitutional context in which it is located. First, coalition politics casts a heavy shadow over the chancellorship. A parliamentary majority does not necessarily mean that a government is stable and secure. A failure of coalition management, or tactical or political manoeuvring on the part of the coalition partner, can result in the weakening or even the end of a chancellorship. Secondly, exaggerated media focus upon the chancellor serves to elevate his role far beyond that assigned to him in the Basic Law.

It has been observed that a tendency towards the personalisation of politics is common to all democracies with a free press.[65] In the case of the Federal Republic, Niclauss has shown that the chancellorship has always combined characteristics of direct and representative democracy.[66] What is new today is the extent to which the executive tends to be identified purely as the person of the

62. Hennis, *op. cit.*, p. 11.
63. Renate Mayntz, 'Executive Leadership in Germany: Dispersion of Power or "Kanzlerdemokratie" ' in Richard Rose and Ezra N. Suleiman (eds), *Presidents and Prime Ministers*, Washington, DC: AEI, 1980 (pp. 139–70), p. 147.
64. *Ibid.*, p. 157.
65. Fred F. Ridley, 'Chancellor Government as a Political System and the German Constitution', *Parliamentary Affairs*, no. 19, 1966, pp. 446–61. Similar arguments can be found in Hennis, *op. cit*, p. 8.
66. Karlheinz Niclauss, 'Repräsentative und plebiszitäre Elemente der Kanzlerdemokratie', *Vierteljahreshefte für Zeitgeschichte*, no. 35, 1987, pp. 217–45.

chancellor, leading some to claim there is a trend towards the presidentialisation (American style) of the chancellorship.[67] A personalised chancellorship, however, is incongruous with the increasing fragmentation of policy-making between government departments. This contradiction, between the appearance of personalised authority and the reality of fragmentation (or segmentation) in the executive apparatus, presents a demanding challenge for the chancellor. He must be simultaneously the symbol of executive unity and master of the conflicting interests and demands of resource-hungry departments in a minefield of coalition in-fighting.

Under Kohl in the last years of the old Federal Republic, a partial redefinition of the chancellorship appeared to be taking place. Against the background of diminishing expectations of executive leadership, it appeared that the role of chancellor had contracted to a point where he was responsible for establishing only the more general policy guidelines. The difficult economic and political problems accompanying unification, however, are making much greater demands upon executive leadership, requiring the chancellor to perform more than just a supervisory or coordinating role. Thus, in the new Germany the debate over executive leadership has been revived. Executive overload has also been experienced by other advanced industrial countries, especially in the face of international economic recession. In the German context, however, the pressures are intensified by unification. Moreover, positive German attitudes towards the post-war state have been founded in large part upon the success of its economic performance.

The perceived gap between the political élite and the public has widened considerably. This is underlined by the common usage of the term 'political class', which emphasises the remoteness of the relationship. Political leaders in the new Germany are widely perceived as having failed to provide the perspectives necessary to build a consensus in the new polity. For his part the chancellor has maintained that constructing visions is not the job of politicians.[68] In an age of individualism it may be true that politics cannot be expected to give meaning to the life of individuals. However, this is an unconvincing argument with which to justify an essentially passive 'wait and see' style of executive management. In periods of economic and

---

67. Uwe Thaysen, Roger H. Davidson and Robert G. Livingstone, 'US-Kongress und Deutscher Bundestag im Vergleich', in Uwe Thaysen *et al.* (eds), *US-Kongress und Deutscher Bundestag*, Opladen: Westdeutscher Verlag, 1988, pp. 517–68.
68. *Frankfurter Rundschau*, 1 Oct. 1992, p. 3.

social stability, a chancellor may choose to adopt a *laissez-faire* model of government. Experience shows that the electorate will respond negatively if the model becomes entrenched after its usefulness is exhausted. In the context of the new Germany, chancellors will have to adopt a rather more assertive and pro-active style of leadership.

4

THE CHANCELLOR AND HIS STAFF

Ferdinand Müller-Rommel

From a constitutional perspective, the federal chancellor occupies an extraordinarily strong position in the German system of government. In reality, however, his powers are limited by a number of constraints. These stem from the dynamics of coalition government and the pull of competing party interests, compounded by the sectorisation of the executive and the diffusion of power across the federal system. It is thus inconceivable that a chief executive would be able to fulfil the multiplicity of complex tasks associated with government leadership without the administrative (and often political) support of the Chancellor's Office. Although lacking a constitutional foundation in the Basic Law, the office is therefore essential to the smooth functioning of the executive authority.

The Historical Evolution of the Chancellor's Office

The *Bundeskanzleramt* (Federal Chancellor's Office) is as old as the chancellorship itself, and the two institutions have developed broadly in parallel. The first federal chancellor, Otto von Bismarck, was appointed by Kaiser Wilhelm I on the formation of the North German Confederation in 1866. Formerly minister-president of Prussia, Bismarck was given responsibility for the administrative acts assigned to the newly formed Confederation. In accordance with its constitution, the *Bundeskanzleramt* was established to support the chancellor. With unification and the creation of the German Reich in 1871, the *Reichskanzler* (imperial chancellor) assumed a much more wide-ranging role. He alone was responsible to the Kaiser; with the exception of military matters, all the affairs of state fell within his purview. Retitled the *Reichskanzleramt*, the Chancellor's Office continued to function as the personal administrative office of the chancellor.

The evolution of the early Chancellor's Office mirrored that of the state and government apparatus. Initially the office embraced the whole of the functions and responsibilities of government. As state activity expanded to include economic and social affairs, it assumed the proportions of a 'monstrous super-ministry',[1] losing its character as the administrative arm of the chancellor. Bismarck was thus compelled to re-create the office in the form of a smaller personal bureau under the title of *Reichskanzlei* (Imperial Chancellery). Subsequently, in recognition of its expanded function, the *Reichskanzleramt* was renamed the *Reichsamt des Inneren* (Office for Internal Affairs) and placed under a state secretary. With the evolution of cabinet government and the strengthening of the principle of parliamentary responsibility, the *Reichskanzlei* underwent a further transformation. During the First World War, under Chancellor Prince Max von Baden, it was restyled the *Parlamentarische Regierungszentrale* (Parliamentary Office of Central Government).

Under the liberal democratic constitution of the Weimar Republic, the character of the Chancellor's Office changed. While it continued to fulfil the role of the chancellor's personal bureau, it now took on the parallel functions of a cabinet office. Its activities expanded to include providing information resources for the chancellor and coordination between government ministries, servicing the cabinet and supervising the implementation of its decisions.

During the Third Reich, the Chancellor's Office progressively ceased to function. With the Enabling Act of March 1933 and the fusion of the offices of chancellor and president in August 1934, the way was clear for the centralisation and personalisation of government power in the hands of *Führer* and *Reichskanzler* Adolf Hitler. Administrative functions passed to Nazi party offices, and to Reich and regional commissioners acting on Hitler's personal authority. Despite the efforts of its chief to preserve his role, the Chancellor's Office was effectively marginalised, losing almost all contact with the *Führer*.

Following the military defeat of the Third Reich, and with Germany under occupation, administration passed to the victorious Allied powers. As part of the progressive restoration of self-government in their occupation zones, the British and American authorities created an embryonic Chancellor's Office (imitating the Weimar model) in the form of the Frankfurt-based *Direktorialkanzlei* (Directorial Chancellery). Established the year before the creation of the Federal Republic and the election of the first chancellor, this office was too closely associated with the occupation authorities to be accepted by Konrad Adenauer. Although the office was moved to Bonn, the new federal capital, it was sidelined by Adenauer. Appreciating the immense value of a personal office,

---

1. S. Schöne, *Von der Reichskanzlei zum Bundeskanzleramt*, Berlin: Duncker and Humblot, 1968, p. 59.

the creation of the Federal Chancellor's Office was his first act as chancellor, performed on the day of his election.

Functions and Organisation

The activity of the Federal Chancellor's Office is not specified in the Basic Law. Its functions can be defined broadly as the provision of information, the provision of inter-ministerial coordination, and the formulation and supervision of selective areas of government policy. In large part, the performance of these functions depends upon the style of different chancellors and the composition of the governing coalition. Between 1955 and 1966, for example, and especially at the time of the grand coalition, the coordination function was prominent, whereas from 1969 to 1972 the policy function of the office was uppermost.

The organisational head of the Chancellor's Office is not the chancellor but the chief of office, appointed by civil service procedure upon the proposal of the chancellor. Since 1949 there have been fourteen chiefs of the office, ten of whom have held civil service rank, whilst the remaining four have served as federal ministers with special responsibilities (see Table 4.1). The basic function of the head of the Chancellor's Office is to act as a sort of cabinet secretary. He convenes and prepares the agenda for cabinet meetings on the instructions of the chancellor. However, the role of the head of office extends far beyond the procedural domain; it includes regularly attending cabinet sessions, supervising the implementation of decisions and generally acting as the ultimate filter between the chancellor and the wider government process. As such the head of the office must distinguish between important and less important matters, keeping the latter from the chancellor, perhaps dealing with them personally. He decides what business will be dealt with by circulating written materials among ministers and what should be put before the cabinet. Finally, the chief of office is responsible for the organisation and planning of the Chancellor's Office and its day-to-day running.

The organisation of the Office rests upon a hierarchical-bureaucratic structure. The basic organisational unit is the *Referat* (policy unit), of which there are forty-one. With one exception, these are organised in fifteen *Gruppen* (sub-divisions), clustered in six *Abteilungen* (divisions). (Before unification there was an additional sub-division dealing with *Deutschlandpolitik*, under the direct control of the head of the Chancellor's Office.) The six *Abteilungen* are as follows:

(1) central division, responsible for Chancellor's Office personnel,

Table 4.1. HEADS OF THE CHANCELLOR'S OFFICE

Chancellor	Head of Chancellor's office	Duration	Months in office
ADENAUER	Dr Franz-Josef Würmeling	14.10.49–14.1.51	15
	Dr Otto Lenz	15.1.59–19.9.53	32
	Dr Hans Globke	1.11.53–16.10.63	120
ERHARD	Dr Ludger Westrick (from 16.6.64)	17.10.63–1.12.66	34
		State Secretary Minister (from 16.6.64)	
KIESINGER	Dr Werner Knieper	7.12.66–31.12.67	12
	Prof Dr Karl Carstens	1.1.68–22.10.69	22
BRANDT	Prof Dr Horst Ehmke	22.10.69–18.12.72	34
	Horst Grabert	18.12.72–15.5.74	18
SCHMIDT	Dr Manfred Schüler	15.5.72–1.12.80	103
	Manfred Laustein	1.12.80–28.4.82	17
	Dr Gerhard Konow	28.4.82–4.10.82	6
KOHL	Prof Dr Waldemar Schreckenberger	4.10.82–15.11.84	25
	Dr Wolfgang Schäuble	15.11.84–21.4.89	53
	Rudolf Seiters	21.4.89–25.11.91	31
	Friedrich Böhl	25.11.91–	

budget and organisation, and the planning of government work;
(2) foreign policy, external security, development aid;
(3) internal, social and environmental affairs;
(4) economic and financial affairs;
(5) social and political analysis, communication and publicity;
(6) federal intelligence and the coordination of the intelligence services.

The management of government work is carried out mainly within the policy units which form the organisational foundation of the Chancellor's Office. It is possible to identify two types of unit, distinguished by their relationship to the ministerial departments of government. 'Mirror units' are responsible for the policy field of a single ministry; Unit 311, for example, deals with the business of the Ministry of Labour and Social Affairs. 'Cross-sectional units', by contrast, are based on policy areas which do not correspond to individual ministerial responsibilities but cut across several ministries. The function of the cross-sectional unit is to facilitate inter-ministerial communication; a classic example is the unit responsible for coordinating government activity in the field of environmental policy.[2] The chancellor's personal bureau is an independent unit within the Chancellor's Office. Its staff work directly for the chancellor, with responsibility for his travel arrangements and personal mail. Coordinating relations between the executive and the legislature is also part of the responsibility of the Chancellor's Office. For this purpose, two parliamentary secretaries of state are attached to the Chancellery, both of whom are members of the Bundestag.

Since the end of the 1940s the Chancellor's Office has been subject to a number of organisational overhauls, creating new structures and adding to the complexity of the system. In 1949 there were just two divisions. These subdivided in 1953, but this did not prove successful and the arrangement was abolished in 1960. A new divisional structure was created in 1969 with five divisions, expanded to six in 1977. The subdivisional level of organisation was created in 1967, since which time the number of sub-divisions has risen from ten to sixteen. The number of units has increased from nine in 1949, to forty-one in 1991. At the same time, the personnel and the budget of the Chancellor's Office have increased. As can be seen from Figure 4.1, its expenditure rose more than 170-fold in the years from 1949 to 1989; between 1969 and 1989 it almost trebled.

Since its inception, there has been a steady increase in both the

2. K. König, 'Vom Umgang mit komplixität in Organisationen: Das Bundes-kanzleramt', *Der Staat*, vol. 28, 1989, p. 57.

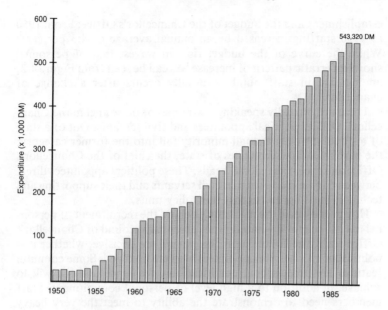

Figure 4.1.   CHANCELLOR'S OFFICE BUDGET, 1950-1989 (DM)
(non-salary costs)
Source: Bundesgesetzblatt: Haushaltspläne, 1949-1989.

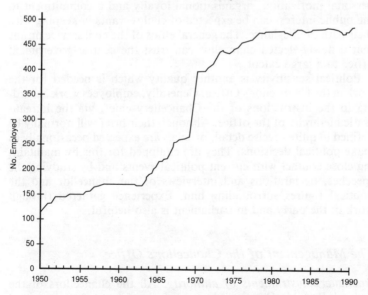

Figure 4.2.   CHANCELLOR'S OFFICE STAFF, 1950-1990
Source: unpublished Chancellor's Office document, 'Personalentwicklung
im Bundeskanzleramt, 1950-1990'.

establishment and the budget of the Chancellor's Office. From 1950 to 1990 staffing increased by an annual average of 4.3 per cent. While the curve of the budget rises in waves, that of personnel shows an erratic pattern of increase. As can be seen from Figure 4.2, an increase in staff numbers usually occurs after a change of chancellor.

There are, broadly speaking, two types of personnel in the Chancellor's Office: political appointees and civil servants. Out of a staff of around 450 only a small minority fall into the former category: the parliamentary secretaries of state, the chief of the Chancellor's Office and the six divisional heads. These political appointees direct between fifty and sixty higher civil servants and their supporting and technical staff spread across the policy units.

However diverse the mechanics behind the recruitment of personnel may appear and whatever the career background of Chancellor's Office staff, the following requirements are decisive, whether it is political or civil service appointees who are involved. Some common features are professional qualifications, resilience and the will to achieve, in addition to a high level of personal commitment. Staff members need to demonstrate the ability to meet the very heavy demands of the job; thus, with the exception of speech-writers, publicity experts and personal assistants, the majority of employees in the Chancellor's Office are experienced civil servants. In addition to personal motivation, organisational loyalty and a commitment to the public interest can be expected of civil servants in keeping with their oath of allegiance. The general ethos of the civil service means that a newly-elected chancellor can trust the central government office to a large extent.

Political sensitivity is another quality which is needed for the work in the Chancellor's Office. Generally, employees work according to the instructions of the Chancellery chief, via the bureaucratic hierarchy of the office. Although their brief will normally be defined in quite precise detail, officials are expected occasionally to make political decisions. They are equipped for this by maintaining close contact with current political events and by studying the speeches, declarations and interviews of the chancellor and the political figures surrounding him. Experience gathered through work in the party and in parliament is also helpful.

The Management of the Chancellor's Office

Adenauer's instruments of authority. All the chancellors of the Federal Republic have made use of the formal functions and organisational resources of the Chancellor's Office according to their own style of executive management. Consequently, each chancellor's style is reflected in the functioning of the office. This is particularly striking in the case of Konrad Adenauer, the first incumbent of the federal chancellorship. In his hands the Chancellor's Office was the chief instrument of a dominant leadership style which at times bordered on the authoritarian. Adenauer established the Federal Chancellor's Office on the day of his election as chancellor, prior to the appointment of his cabinet. In Adenauer's view cabinet consultation was unnecessary as the office represented an agency of the head of government, not of the cabinet. Under Adenauer, the chief task of the Chancellor's Office was to prepare the political work of the chancellor himself. For this purpose, lines of communication to government ministries, parliament, the party and interest groups were of vital importance.

The composition of the office was decisively shaped by Dr Hans Globke, Adenauer's close adviser. Initially he headed Division Two (coordination and cabinet matters) and the unit in Division One responsible for 'house and cabinet personnel'. In this capacity, Globke built up a new organisational system in the Chancellor's Office, with the power to make appointments to key posts. In the early years of the Federal Republic, appointments to the Chancellor's Office were circumscribed by four principles. First, Article 36 of the Basic Law stipulated that officials should be drawn proportionately from the *Länder*. Secondly, a fair balance was to be maintained between Protestants and Catholics. Thirdly, individuals tainted with National Socialist associations were to be excluded from government service. Fourthly, candidates had to possess appropriate professional qualifications. In appointing staff to the Chancellor's Office, not all of these principles were adhered to. One allegation made against Globke was that Catholics and those whose political affiliations were on the right were given preferential treatment.[3]

It proved particularly difficult to find the right person to head the Chancellor's Office during Adenauer's incumbency. Several office-holders failed in the early years, among them Dr Franz-Josef Würmeling, the CDU politician, and Dr Otto Lenz, who had been arrested during the Third Reich for his links with the resistance. Lenz had a background in public relations, and it was on his initiative that public relations institutions such as the Bundeszentrale für politische Bildung (Central Office for Political Education) and the

3. Karlheinz Niclauss, *Kanzlerdemokratie. Bonner Regierungspraxis von Konrad Adenauer bis Helmut Kohl*, Stuttgart: Kohlhammer, 1988, p. 38.

Institut zur Förderung der freien Wirtschaft (Institute for the Promotion of a Free Economy) were established. These institutions were later to be of some assistance to the chancellors. However, Lenz's conduct as head of the Chancellor's Office, and in particular his independence, were viewed with mixed feelings by Adenauer. It was Lenz's ambition to create a Ministry of Information which would efficiently carry out publicity work, based on systematic processing of opinion poll data and information from other sources. Erich Peter Neumann, founder of the Allensbacher Institut für Demoskopie, worked as an adviser to Lenz and the two convinced the chancellor of the political potential of public opinion research. As early as January 1950, the Chancellor's Office concluded the first contracts with the Allensbacher Institute for it permanently to report on political opinion.[4] The favourable election result of 1953 can be attributed in large part to Lenz's consistent use of opinion research.

By 1952, however, Lenz had assumed the role of political manager and his relationship with Adenauer became increasingly strained. It is widely believed that Adenauer induced Lenz to resign, with the promise of a safe seat in parliament and eventually a ministerial post.[5] Subsequently Globke was appointed as head of the Chancellor's Office, retaining the post until Adenauer's resignation in 1963.

The new chief took very great care that the chancellor was surrounded by a staff of unshakeable loyalty. The Chancellor's Office now became a finely honed instrument of executive leadership, especially in the key areas of foreign affairs and defence. At the beginning of the 1950s, both these fields were brought under the organisational umbrella of the Chancellor's Office. All important strategic decisions were concentrated here. Thus the initial confidential talks between the German and American governments concerning the setting up of a special German intelligence service took place exclusively in the Chancellor's Office.

One of the chancellor's major instruments of power was the information-gathering department, later to be named Bundespresse- und Informationsamt (Federal Press and Information Office). Adenauer was a man addicted to news information, receiving a daily *Nachrichtenspiegel* (news digest) of the press, systematically compiled in the Chancellor's Office. In the afternoon the most important excerpts from the foreign press were put before him. He also

---

4. Arnulf Baring, *Im Anfang war Adenauer*, Munich: Deutscher Taschenbuch-verlag, 1971, pp. 28ff.
5. *Ibid.*, p. 30.

regularly received a *Rundfunkspiegel* (radio digest). Staff in the Federal Press Office were instructed by the chancellor to let him have important news items constantly and promptly, whether he was at home or abroad. Through this system, the chancellor was always well informed. Moreover, he maintained good relations with journalists, without ever holding formal press conferences. From the early 1950s onwards, Adenauer used to invite around a dozen selected representatives of leading German newspapers to his so-called *Kanzlertee* (chancellor's tea circle) on Friday afternoons (journalists from opposition papers were not invited). Political problems were discussed here, and journalists would often provide the chancellor with interesting items of information which later turned up in the drafts of government policy documents.

The most important political decision-making group in the Adenauer era was the so-called 'Monday circle' which brought together the chancellor, Hans Globke as head of the Chancellor's Office, and the leader of the CDU in the Bundestag, Heinrich Krone. On Monday mornings, before eight o'clock, a variety of political issues were discussed in a frank and comprehensive session. Adenauer has often been described as a 'man of lonely resolutions',[6] but in fact most of his policies were formulated and approved in this small circle.[7]

In contrast, the CDU party bureaucracy played a subordinate role. The CDU was established as a federal party only after Adenauer had held office for a year. Collective cabinet decision-making was also downgraded during the Adenauer era. Throughout the 1950s Adenauer used the cabinet merely as a panel of experts whose opinions he could seek when he wished. The real preparatory work for his political decisions was carried out almost exclusively by the staff of the Chancellor's Office. The impact of this work reached into the ministries, and the office proved to be a smoothly functioning instrument of leadership in the hands of the chancellor.

Institutional degeneration under Erhard. Adenauer's successor, the former Economics Minister Ludwig Erhard (1963–6), saw himself as a *Volkskanzler* (people's chancellor), and the public accepted him as such. The strong polarisation between the governing coalition and the opposition which had developed during the Adenauer chancellorship now began to recede. On most issues Erhard was in broad

6. Jost Küpper, *Die Kanzlerdemokratie*, Frankfurt am Main: Peter Lang, 1985, p. 162.
7. Daniel Koerfer, *Kampf ums Kanzleramt: Erhard und Adenauer*, Stuttgart: DVA, 1987, p. 162.

agreement with his coalition partner. However, his search for an all-encompassing accord and cooperation between *all* the parties weakened his relations with his own party – of which Adenauer remained chairman until 1966 – and often brought him into conflict with coalition agreements. Erhard tried to maintain a distance from the day-to-day business of government, and in particular from organised interests. In contrast to Adenauer, the supreme power politician, Erhard was a convinced 'anti-Machiavellian'.

Upon taking office, Erhard inherited a Chancellor's Office which served as a well-running coordination centre whose employees were accustomed to taking clear instructions from the head of government. Thus Erhard had little need to make any personnel changes, but merely established new posts for some of his personal collaborators. Among these were his closest advisors, Dr Ludger Westrick and Karl Hohmann, and his press officer, as well as two younger civil servants from the Economics Ministry. Westrick was appointed head of the Chancellor's Office and Hohmann put in charge of the personal bureau. Subsequently, however, Erhard created twenty-three new posts, the first increase in staff numbers in the Chancellor's Office.

The Erhard chancellorship saw the breakdown of the intimate and confidential contact which Adenauer had established with the staff of the Chancellor's Office. Erhard had no talent for organisation, mastering detailed briefs only rarely and with some reluctance. Nor was he a natural cabinet chairman.[8] His inclination to discuss issues with scientific thoroughness and rigour frequently led to decisions being postponed. Although his relations with cabinet ministers were friendly and cooperative, Erhard allowed his ministers to carry more responsibility than they had done under Adenauer, thereby weakening the position of the Chancellor's Office. Gradually it degenerated into little more than a research and information-gathering bureau, with no significant influence over ministerial departments. This style of leadership made Erhard vulnerable to criticism. Secondary power centres emerged and conflicts of loyalty arose within the party. Some of these were provoked by Adenauer, resentful to the end of his life at his loss of office.

Reorganisation and professionalisation: Kiesinger and Knieper. Erhard's successor, Hans-Georg Kiesinger (1966–9), led a Grand Coalition under political and institutional conditions which made it almost impossible for him to develop strong leadership. First, the

8. *Ibid.*, p. 756.

governing coalition now consisted of two almost equally strong parties, with sharply different programmes and objectives. Kiesinger
was thus restricted to attempts to find compromises between the
coalition parties. In the words of Conrad Ahlers, Erhard was little
more than a 'walking mediation committee'. Secondly, two key
ministries, Foreign and Economic Affairs, were in the hands of
highly competent Social Democrats, Willy Brandt and Karl Schiller,
in comparison with whom Kiesinger's stature was diminished.
Thirdly, the chancellor was marginalised within his own party. Formerly minister-president of Baden-Württemberg, Erhard had close
ties with the regional CDU rather than the national party. Initially
he was able to use his favourable public image and some good *Land*
election results to neutralise the party's reservations. By 1968–9,
however, his lack of support in the party began to tell against him.
Fourthly, there was a shift in the political decision-making process
from the cabinet to informal power centres, a classic example of
which was the *Kressbonner Kreis*. Established in 1967, this group
consisted of the chancellor and vice-chancellor, the parliamentary
chairmen of both coalition parties, senior ministers, and two parliamentary secretaries of state.

Upon taking office, Kiesinger made an immediate attempt to
reorganise the Chancellor's Office. Following a suggestion by the
head of the Federal Accounts Bureau (*Bundesrechnungshof*), the
chancellor tried to introduce a planning bureau, responsible both
for formulating long-term strategy and for addressing more immediate issues. Kiesinger was sceptical of the capacity of the Chancellor's Office to provide the broad overview which he believed was
a pre-requisite of effective policy-making. The planning bureau was
charged with this task, under the organisational oversight of Chancellery chief Dr Werner Knieper, an exponent of modern management methods who had previously worked in the Defence Ministry.
Knieper was responsible for a far-reaching restructuring of the
Defence Ministry at the behest of Kiesinger and Willy Brandt.
Altogether twenty-six posts in this ministry were taken over by the
Chancellor's Office, which thereby received its second substantial
increase in personnel. At the same time the recruitment policy of
the office changed: regional and confessional balance now assumed
less importance than previously. Kiesinger and Knieper set out to
assemble a more professionally oriented staff. They thus placed a
premium on administrative experience, drawing personnel from
Länder ministries and local government. In 1967, as a further innovation, Kiesinger and Brandt introduced the so-called 'political' civil
servant, enabling the chancellor and ministers to appoint close political confidants (such as personal aides and secretaries of state) to

leading administrative positions. (In this way these appointees acquired the status of lifetime civil servants, although they could be temporarily retired when there was a change of chancellor or government.) Political appointments of this kind enabled the chancellor to place loyal and sympathetic personnel at key points in the upper echelons of the Chancellor's Office, and the practice was subsequently regularised in federal law.

Although Kiesinger and Knieper acted in unison in executing these reform initiatives, relations between the two quickly became strained. Conflict arose because of differences in their personalities and styles of leadership. The 'modern manager' had difficulty in adapting to Kiesinger's neo-feudalist manner. Moreover, the professional standards of the Chancellery staff failed to meet Knieper's high expectations. In his view, the shortcomings of his staff undermined the coordination function of the Chancellor's Office, and the planning bureau failed to operate in the way that had been envisaged. Thus, under Knieper the office served as little more than a sort of 'letter box' through which cabinet proposals passed without adequate scrutiny. On account of these technical and organisational shortcomings, the cabinet became hopelessly overburdened, and both Kiesinger and the Chancellor's Office acquired a reputation for political incompetence.[9] Finally, in December 1967, Knieper was relieved of his duties as head of the Chancellor's Office.

The position was filled by Professor Dr Karl Carstens, who enjoyed an excellent relationship with the chancellor and who was more successful than his predecessor in orchestrating the Chancellery staff in the coordination of government business. Carstens held weekly discussions with the heads of policy units and took part in the monthly meetings of the personnel council.[10] However, the idea of setting up a formally organised planning bureau, as initially envisaged by Kiesinger, was quietly dropped. Towards the end of his incumbency, the chancellor made more intensive use of his staff than he had previously done. But organisational and technical limitations prevented the Chancellor's Office from becoming an effective centre for political management under Kiesinger.

The emergence of the modern Chancellor's Office: Brandt and Ehmke. The leadership style of the Brandt chancellorship (1969–74) underwent a distinct change midway through his incumbency. It

---

9. Kenneth Dyson, 'The German Federal Chancellor's Office', *Political Quarterly*, vol. 45, 1974, pp. 367.
10. K. Seemann, *Enzaubertes Bundeskanzleramt*, Munich: Verlag Politisches Archiv, 1975, p. 31.

is therefore necessary to distinguish between the first and second terms of his chancellorship. During his first term (1969–72) Brandt exercised a leadership role similar to that of Adenauer in terms of strength, although he achieved this without acting in an authoritarian fashion. Once again the cabinet became the centre of decision-making, and decisions were generally arrived at collectively. Brandt was predominantly concerned with foreign policy and especially with *Ostpolitik*, leaving domestic politics largely to his ministers. Brandt's engagement in foreign affairs helped to distinguish the government coalition from the opposition, but it also led to tensions between the chancellor and the FDP Foreign Minister, Walter Scheel. Moreover, Brandt was increasingly hampered by tensions within the SPD. In his capacity as party chairman, Brandt tried to mediate between the various intra-party groupings, but personal and policy differences increased towards the end of the life of his first cabinet. His positive public image reached its climax in 1971, when he received the Nobel Peace Prize. This accolade marked the turning point in his chancellorship. Previously he had been seen as a man of charismatic character in the mould of John F. Kennedy; soon afterwards he was accused of indecision and weakness.

The success of Brandt's *Ostpolitik* relied to a large extent on the support of the Chancellor's Office. On assuming office he announced plans to modernise the apparatus and operational practices of the office. In this he was much influenced by the ideas of the new Chancellery chief, Horst Ehmke. Ehmke undertook a far-reaching overhaul of the organisation, laying the foundations of the modern Chancellor's Office. The apparatus he inherited was organised in three divisions: foreign affairs, defence and *Deutschlandpolitik* (relations with the GDR); economics and finance; and domestic politics and Chancellery administration. There was also a planning bureau somewhat on the lines of that created by Kiesinger. Ehmke reorganised the three divisions, added a new one for administration and law, and reorganised the planning bureau as a new 'planning division' (*Planungsabteilung*). In the course of these changes, the number of staff in the Chancellor's Office grew from around 250 to nearly 400.

Brandt insisted that the leadership of the office should be based on a clearly defined division of labour between three key figures who were also his closest advisors. Egon Bahr, with the rank of secretary of state, was responsible for foreign affairs, defence and relations with the GDR. Katharina Focke became parliamentary secretary of state with responsibility for contacts with parliamentary parties on issues related to Europe, research and education. Ehmke, who had ministerial status, was to play the coordination role between the

Chancellor's Office and the ministries.

Ehmke's new planning division had two main functions: policy coordination from the initiation stage, and the long-term planning of individual policy projects. The rationale behind this system was that ministries should coordinate the handling of front-line government projects from the outset. In this way, it was hoped that a realistic schedule for policy implementation could be established, taking account of the financial and personnel resources available. For the purposes of longer term planning, it was important to have an overview of government activity so that new priorities could be fitted into the general frame. Initially this planning apparatus operated quite successfully, due to the professionalism and involvement of Ehmke and the head of the planning division, Professor Reimut Jochimsen. However, the orchestration of government activity by the Chancellor's Office quickly aroused resentment among ministers and departmental civil servants.

During Brandt's first term, the essentials of *Ostpolitik* were accomplished, but the objective of making the Chancellor's Office the chief centre of government planning was not fully realised. After the 1972 elections, the early planning euphoria was never rekindled. For his second term, Brandt selected a new leadership team for the Chancellor's Office. Ehmke was succeeded as head by Horst Grabert, previously the Berlin representative in the federal government. Egon Bahr remained as minister with special responsibilities for *Ostpolitik* and relations with East Germany. Jochimsen left the planning division to assume responsibility for economic policy. The planning division degenerated into little more than a small staff of advisers, headed by Albrecht Müller, manager of the successful 1972 election campaign. New arrivals in the Chancellor's Office included two influential journalists, Günter Gaus, who became second secretary of state, and Klaus Harpprecht, the chancellor's speech-writer.

Grabert, as Chancellery chief, was the only leading figure in the office with real administrative experience. However, he lacked the strength of personality to convince the chancellor of the political potential of the office. Moreover, Brandt's new journalistic advisers were temperamentally much closer to him than Grabert was.[11] Rivalries emerged within the Chancellery team and Brandt appeared to lack the will to reassert discipline. During his second term his authority progressively diminished, and he displayed a marked clumsiness in handling advisors and ministers. Policy issues were not addressed with the necessary decisiveness and the cabinet was

11. Niclauss, *op. cit.*, p. 149.

uncoordinated, characterised by lengthy and inconclusive discussion. In May 1974, a bitter Brandt left office after his personal secretary Günther Guillaume was revealed as a GDR spy.[12] The underlying reason for his resignation, however, was his loss of control over government, of which the degeneration of the Chancellor's Office was symptomatic.

The hub of executive management under Schmidt. Helmut Schmidt (1974–82) was an activist chancellor who was particularly concerned with foreign policy and with monetary and economic policy. He was a pragmatist; he was also in the habit of speaking frankly and demanded clear answers, expecting ministers to arrive in cabinet well briefed.[13] Deputy chairman of the SPD, he had a close working relationship with Brandt, who was party chairman (see Chapter 2). However, many Social Democrats mistrusted Schmidt on account of his pragmatism and his scepticism of party ideology.

Although Schmidt's style of government had authoritarian characteristics, resembling Adenauer's in some respects, he placed a high premium upon cabinet cohesion and discipline. He demanded to be informed about ministerial initiatives from the moment of inception. In maintaining tight cabinet coordination, he relied heavily on his Chancellery team. Head of the Chancellor's Office was Dr Manfred Schüler, whom Schmidt had brought with him from the Economics Ministry. Schüler's was an inspired appointment. His highly developed administrative capacity was combined with human qualities and impressive expertise in economic and financial policy. Highly regarded among his Chancellery colleagues, and by the chancellor himself, Schüler held his post for over eight years. Without his assistance it is inconceivable that Schmidt would have been able to exercise the sort of efficient crisis management which become the hallmark of his chancellorship.

At least as important was the role played by Klaus Bölling, government spokesman and close personal adviser to Schmidt. He had previously been a TV foreign correspondent in Washington and Moscow and was one of the most loyal and dedicated of the chancellor's aides. It has been said of Bölling that he had more of the *homo politicus* in him than most professional politicians in the

12. Seemann, *op. cit.*, p. 53.
13. Renate Mayntz, 'Executive Leadership in Germany: Dispersion of Power or "Kanzlerdemokratie" ' in R. Rose and E.N. Suleiman (eds), *Presidents and Prime Ministers*, Washington, DC: AEI, 1980, p. 158; see also P. Berry, 'The Organisation and Influence of the Chancellery during the Schmidt and Kohl Chancellorships', *Governance*, vol. 2, 1989, p. 341.

cabinet.[14] Schmidt's Chancellery team was completed by the appointment in 1976 of Hans-Jürgen Wischnewski as secretary of state. Alongside Schmidt, Schüler, Bölling and Wischnewski were nicknamed the *Kleeblatt* (clover-leaf) team at the heart of the Chancellor's Office. Their supremely efficient collaboration was based upon the pragmatic understanding of politics which was the common ground between them.

Under Schmidt, the Chancellor's Office became a finely honed instrument of executive coordination and leadership. The chancellor maintained close personal contact with the heads of divisions, sub-divisions and policy units (*Abteilungen, Gruppen, Referate*) in the Chancellor's Office, often inviting them to accompany him to public and private meetings – though not to party meetings. Together with the recruitment policy of Schmidt and Schüler this involvement promoted team spirit and a sense of responsibility amongst the Chancellery staff, encouraging them to develop initiatives. Channels of communication and operation ran along the lines of a hierarchical-bureaucratic organisation, from policy units via subdivisions and divisions to the head of the Chancellor's Office. However, formal processes were not slavishly adhered to when benefits could be derived from informal variations. For instance, although communication between one specialised unit and another was formally expected to take place at subdivision level, policy units were encouraged to communicate directly with each other. Moreover, subdivisions were assigned according to areas of policy, which meant that their role went beyond that of merely directing and coordinating. Assigned policy responsibilities, their role became similar to that of a policy unit, enhancing collegial cooperation at subdivisional level.[15] Another non-hierarchical element in the organisational pattern was the so-called 'working group' (*Arbeitsstab*). From 1978, for example, there was a working group for *Deutschlandpolitik* (inner-German policy) working directly under the leadership of the head of the Chancellor's Office and available for consultation at short notice. The working-group model was particularly well adapted for work in policy areas affecting different ministerial departments and where prompt reaction was important.

Another example of organisational flexibility in the Chancellor's Office under Schmidt was the so-called *Lage* (situation) meeting, a review of the general political situation, which took place every morning between top-level administrative and political officers in

14. C. Rang, *Ertl kam stadig zu spät . . . und andere Kabinettsstücke*, Bonn: Lamuv Verlag, 1986, p. 53.
15. König, *op. cit.*, p. 58.

the Chancellery. Bringing together the head of the Chancellor's Office, ministers of state and secretaries of state, the heads of the divisions, and the head of the chancellor's personal secretariat, this forum functioned as a link between politics and administration. Issues of a general nature affecting more than one division were discussed, insecurities were dispelled and new instructions were issued.

Other organisational innovations came about in response to the domestic crises provoked by the wave of political violence in the middle to late 1970s. An 'extended circle of political consultation' (*grosser politischer Beratungskreis*) was introduced, made up of party chairmen, the leaders of the parliamentary party groups, and the minister-presidents and interior ministers of the *Länder* directly affected by terrorist activities. Another innovation was the *kleine Lage*, an operational group which met in the Chancellor's Office under the chairmanship either of the chancellor himself or of the Minister of the Interior. Regular members were Foreign Minister Genscher and Justice Minister Vogel. Other cabinet members were invited if required. In October 1977, when the domestic crisis seemed to be at an end, the two crisis committees were discontinued.

During these years, the Chancellor's Office saw a considerable increase in the numbers of its personnel. Some services were transferred there from the federal intelligence office, and the unit dealing with intelligence services was elevated to the rank of a sixth division. These moves came as a response to the Guillaume affair and the need for greater intelligence coordination which had been identified by the subsequent commission of inquiry. The terrorist crisis also saw an expansion in the Chancellery establishment. A centre for crisis management, the *Lagezentrum*, was set up. Permanently manned, operating weekends and night shifts, the centre entailed further recruitment and the Chancellery staff increased by around twenty between 1976 and 1978.

After the 1980 Bundestag elections, Schmidt changed his leadership team in the Chancellor's Office. Klaus Bölling became permanent representative of the Federal Republic in East Berlin, Manfred Schüler went to the Kreditanstalt für Wiederaufbau in Frankfurt and Hans-Jürgen Wischnewski took over the deputy chairmanship of the SPD. The new head of the Chancellor's Office was Manfred Lahnstein, formerly head of the economics division. Lahnstein was a young, experienced civil servant who had served his political apprenticeship in Brussels as *chef de cabinet* to an EC commissioner. Second in command was Günter Huonker from the SPD left, chosen by Schmidt in order to keep peace with those in the party who were already somewhat critical of government policies.

As a new government spokesman the chancellor appointed a journalist from *Die Zeit*, Kurt Becker, who was inexperienced in administration.

The new team proved unsuccessful, and Bölling and Wischnewski were quickly recalled to their former posts. They, together with the chancellor and Lahnstein, made up the new foursome which fashioned government policy until the end of the Schmidt chancellorship. Schmidt made skilful use of the Chancellery for the purposes of information-gathering and advice, the promotion of his own policy preferences and the protection of his position within the government. Departmental ministries were obliged to accept the authority of the Chancellor's Office. One indication of its efficiency is that the office was able to deny the FDP any pretext for the termination of the coalition, which finally occurred in autumn 1982.

The personalisation of the Chancellor's Office under Kohl. When he became chancellor in 1982, Helmut Kohl lacked experience in any ministerial department. As a 'generalist', he is uninterested in the details of cabinet proposals in their developmental stages. He allows the departments more independence in decision-making and the consequent decentralisation of responsibility often results in conflicts reaching the cabinet and the public before they have been resolved. Kohl sees himself less as a policy manager than as a political and moral leader of the nation. CDU party chairman since 1976, he remains first and foremost a party politician. His ties with the party are as close as were those of Adenauer. There were few open disagreements between Kohl and the CDU till 1989, when a group of ministers and minister-presidents of some *Länder* tried to launch a revolt against the chancellor. The rebels included Rita Süssmuth, Lother Späth, Ernst Albrecht and Heiner Geissler. The failure of this attempted 'coup' only served to confirm Kohl's authority. He is very much a power politician. Potential competitors are kept at a distance, and he frequently delays passing on items of information for tactical reasons. These characteristics have been reflected in Kohl's handling of the Chancellor's Office.

The first chief of Kohl's Chancellery was Professor Waldemar Schreckenberger, a close confidant of the chancellor since student days. Schreckenberger had been head of the *Land* chancellery of Rhineland-Palatinate in Mainz when Kohl was minister-president there. Beneath him, the most important person in the Chancellor's Office was the chief of Division Five, Eduard Ackermann. He had earlier been press spokesman of the CDU *Bundestagsfraktion*, popular with the Bonn journalists and already close to Kohl, then chairman of the parliamentary party. His responsibilities in the

Chancellor's Office included social and political analysis, communication and publicity. A third important figure was the Berlin political scientist Dr Horst Teltschik, from the CDU central office. He took over Division Two, which had responsibility for foreign and GDR relations, development politics and external security.

Under Schreckenberger, the Chancellor's Office effectively ceased to function as a coordination centre. Virtually nothing remained of earlier attempts to harmonise activity between ministerial departments and Chancellery policy units. Instead, the chancellor now used the Chancellery almost exclusively as a source of information. Moreover, the hierarchical-bureaucratic structures of the Chancellery were progressively weakened in the face of Kohl's tendency to consult the few people in whom he placed trust, mainly Teltschik and Ackermann, irrespective of their rank and hierarchical position. At times the chancellor communicated with heads of divisions or sub-divisions without the knowledge of the Chancellery chief. In the first years of Kohl's chancellorship this bred rivalries and dissatisfaction in the office, demotivating staff. The failure of coordination led at times to chaos, and this was partly responsible for some of the political breakdowns in 1984.

Schreckenberger was downgraded to the rank of secretary of state (without special assignment) and Dr Wolfgang Schäuble, formerly chairman of the CDU *Bundestagsfraktion*, became the new head of the office. This experienced administrator soon improved links between the office and the ministries, thereby raising the motivation of staff. He also displayed considerable competence and sensitivity in his dealings with politicians of all parties in the Bundestag, and with those in East Germany. In April 1989, Kohl promoted his 'friend' Schäuble to the post of federal minister of the interior. His successor in the Chancellor's Office was Dr Rudolf Seiters, previously secretary of the parliamentary party. On the instruction of Chancellor Kohl, the preparatory work for the unification treaty between the Federal Republic and the former GDR was carried out in the Chancellor's Office. The failure to consult ministerial departments over the draft treaty was a source of resentment and criticism in those quarters. There is a parallel for this, however, in the preparation of the draft for the European monetary system which took place under Helmut Schmidt in the Chancellor's Office – the Bundesbank and interested ministries were then informed of the process, but not of all the details of the discussion. Similarly the handling of preparatory work on the *Ostverträge* (eastern treaties) under Brandt was carried out in the Chancellor's Office under the responsibility of Minister of State Egon Bahr.

Chancellor Kohl has never made full use of the potential of the Chancellor's Office, relying instead on the expertise of his closest collaborators. It has been left to Schäuble and Seiters to engage the specialised competence of the Chancellery in the interests of political planning and policy guidance. Thus during the Kohl chancellorship there has been no increase in the size of the Chancellery staff. (Indeed there was even a slight decrease in the years 1988 and 1989.) The intensification of political problems on the post-unification agenda, however, may lead to a further increase.

Under Kohl, new personnel have normally been appointed from the ranks of *Bundestagsfraktion* or the party organisation, rather than by promotion from within the Chancellor's Office or ministerial departments.

Conclusion

The functioning of the Federal Chancellor's Office has been subject to considerable variation from one incumbency to another, depending on the leadership style of individual chancellors. In particular, the emphasis on coordination and planning has varied widely, reflecting similarly wide variations in executive leadership. The influence of the office within the executive arena has depended wholly upon the authority of the chancellor himself. At no time has the Chancellery been able (or indeed attempted) to exert an independent political influence. Over time the Chancellery has maintained its character as an instrument of executive leadership, without itself appropriating power. Generally, it can be concluded that an efficiently run office has served to strengthen chancellor authority. Efficiency offers protection against external criticism and prevents the emergence of competing power centres. A well-ordered and efficiently run Chancellor's Office may thus be regarded as a precondition for the maintenance of the chancellor's authority.

5

THE CHANCELLOR AND FOREIGN POLICY*

William E. Paterson

The conduct of foreign policy is always centred on the executive. The feature that distinguishes the Federal Republic from other states has been the absolute centrality of foreign policy, reflecting the Federal Republic's genesis as more a foreign policy in search of a state than a state in search of a foreign policy. The division of Germany meant that the Federal Republic was centrally preoccupied with the external environment in its efforts to bring about reunification. Moreover, the absence of a comprehensive peace settlement at the end of the Second World War also involved successive federal governments in protracted negotiations about the status of their own eastern and western boundaries and, in relation to Poland and Russia, the borders of a Germany that corresponded to the map of Europe in 1937. West Berlin's singular position continually pulled the Federal Republic into the international arena. Beyond the pre-occupation with borders, the new German state had to forge its policy response to the existential needs of security and the economy in the international environment through participation in NATO and the EEC.

The first years of the Adenauer government were the crucial defining moment in the evolution of the institutional structure of the Federal Republic. A continued occupation status which precluded the establishment of a Foreign Ministry until 1951 and postponed the appointment of the first Foreign Minister until 1955 clearly robbed the ministry of the unchallenged pre-eminence in foreign policy matters customary in long-established West European states. The chancellor was thus assigned a role in the foreign policy field that has only recently come to be identified with heads of government elsewhere in Europe.

* The author would like to thank His Excellency Dr Peter Hartmann; Dr W. Bitterlich, now in charge of Division Two of the Chancellor's Office; Dr Uwe Kaestner and Dr R. Löhr of *Referat* 211 in the Chancellor's Office; and Dr Wilhelm Grewe and Dr B. Seebacher-Brandt for granting him interviews on the role of the Chancellor in external policy. He would also like to thank Dr Bernd von Staden for his comments on an earlier draft of this chapter.

Perhaps even more striking than the inter-ministerial rivalry that will be examined in detail below has been the degree to which foreign policy has preoccupied successive chancellors in a way suggestive of post-war American presidents rather than their West European counterparts. Part of the reason for this lies in the nature of the Federal Republic. Much can also be explained by the definition that Konrad Adenauer gave to the role by his success and concentration on external policy. Adenauer created the public image of the chancellor and confronted his successors with the problem of responding to high public expectations about the manner in which the chancellor can determine 'the guidelines of policy' under Article 65 of the Basic Law (see Chapter 3). Since then, external policy has often been the preferred route to meeting these expectations. It is of course true that the two major constraints on the chancellor's position – coalition government (and the dominance of the FDP in the Foreign Ministry) and the departmental principle – continue to operate, but the departmental principle is a little weaker given the Foreign Ministry's lack of monopoly status in this area. Two other important constraints are, however, largely absent. Foreign policy rarely requires the passing of laws and thus largely escapes the constraints imposed by the dual majority of Bundestag and Bundesrat, except in the case of treaties and EC directives. Interest groups are normally relatively inactive and ineffective in this area in comparison to their role in domestic politics. There are two major exceptions to this. Agricultural interest groups have boxed in successive chancellors on reform of the Common Agricultural Policy (CAP), while policy on the German question was influenced by refugee organisations in 1949–69 and again in the early years of the Kohl government.

The Role of the Chancellor in Foreign Policy-Making

The primacy of the chancellor in the Adenauer era

'In the beginning was Adenauer.' (Arnulf Baring)[1]

The dominant characteristic of foreign policy-making in the early years of the Federal Republic was its extreme, not to say excessive, centralisation in the person of the first chancellor, Konrad Adenauer, and the Chancellor's Office. While this centralisation was not different in kind, it was different in degree from that prevailing in domestic politics. This centralisation was foreshadowed

---

1. Arnulf Baring, *Aussenpolitik in Adenauers Kanzlerdemokratie. Bonns Beitrag zur Europäishen Verteidigungsgemeinschaft*, Munich: Oldenbourg, 1969, p. 1.

in various provisions of the Basic Law, notably Article 65, under which the chancellor was made responsible for 'determining the guidelines of policy', and Article 64, under which he proposed to the president the appointment and dismissal of ministers.

This 'chancellor principle' was modified in Article 65 by two further principles, the *Kollegialprinzip* or cabinet principle, and the *Ressort* or departmental principle. The *Kollegialprinzip*, according to which the federal government resolves disputes between ministers, was rendered largely inoperative by Adenauer's mode of government. He himself took over the function of settling disputes and in general showed a preference for 'lonely decisions' (that is, those taken by himself with no advisers). He was also very reluctant to use cabinet committees, which have subsequently played only an occasional role in German policy-making. The departmental principle, according to which, subject to the chancellor's policy guidelines, ministers shall manage their departments on their own responsibility, was irrelevant in the field of foreign policy in the early years of the Federal Republic, since Adenauer was his own Foreign Minister until 1955.

The special position of the chancellor *vis-à-vis* his ministers was only latent in the Basic Law; its realisation depended on the personality of the first chancellor and the electoral dependence of the CDU/CSU on him (see Chapter 2). This dependence was much more apparent in the field of foreign policy than in that of domestic policy. In domestic policy support was attracted to the CDU/CSU by a whole range of personalities and conceptions. In foreign policy, on the other hand, there was only one conception, one personality that mattered. This position was reinforced by the decision of the SPD leadership to oppose Adenauer primarily in the field of foreign policy, since it meant that it was much easier for him to integrate the CDU/CSU around his personal foreign policy programme than would otherwise have been the case.

Adenauer's position was further strengthened by the peculiar situation of West Germany at that time. West Germany only possessed contingent-dependent sovereignty until its entry into NATO in 1955. This meant that foreign policy had to be carried on, if at all, with very close reference to the wishes of the Allies and their representatives in West Germany, the High Commissioners, a situation which Adenauer exploited to the full.

The fact that Adenauer was able to monopolize access to the High Commission for his own Federal Chancellor's Office represented a great and well exploited power advantage, since the High Commission was the real government in Germany until 1955. He could easily counter any objections

from his opponents with the contention, whether true or false, that the
situation was in reality quite different, but that as Chancellor he was
required to treat certain information as confidential.[2]

Until the formal creation of the Foreign Ministry in March 1951,
external affairs had been handled by various agencies operating
inside the Chancellor's Office. The largest of the agencies, the
Dienststelle für Auswärtige Angelegenheiten, headed by Herbert
Blankenhorn, formed the central core of the new Foreign Ministry
and handled relations with the High Commissioners. There were
other very important agencies, however, such as the Verhandlungs-
ausschuss für die Ablösung des Besatzungsstatuts under Professor
Wilhelm Grewe. The fact that there were a number of these agencies
reflected both the constitutional position, in which West Germany
was officially precluded from carrying on external relations, and
Adenauer's desire to split responsibility among his subordinates. In
the reconstituted Foreign Ministry, Blankenhorn and Grewe were
each made head of one of the main political departments while
Walter Hallstein, who had already played a major role in the conduct of foreign policy from within the Chancellor's Office, became
state secretary. In the period up until 1955, then, the main lines of
foreign policy were exclusively formulated by Adenauer, to whom
Hallstein reported. Coordination was still very largely in the hands
of the Chancellor's Office and Hallstein operated as a quasi-Foreign
Minister. (At the Messina conference, the launching conference for
the EEC in 1955, five states were represented by their Foreign Ministers, and the Federal Republic was represented by State Secretary
Hallstein.)

When Heinrich von Brentano was appointed as the Federal
Republic's first Foreign Minister in 1955 he was expected to have a
considerable say in foreign affairs; in fact neither he nor the ministry
were able significantly to expand their role in the period 1955–61.
The weakness of his position was underlined in the Geneva Conference of 1955, when Wilhelm Grewe presented the position of the
FRG despite von Brentano's presence, and is apparent from the
following:

'If and when the Minister of Economics considers it necessary to become
politically active, he must first consult with the Ministry of Foreign Affairs;
possibly my decision has to be sought, since I determine the guidelines of
policy.'[3]

2. Arnulf Baring, 'The Institutions of German Foreign Policy', in K. Kaiser and R.
   Morgan (eds), *Britain and West Germany: Changing Societies and the Future of
   Foreign Policy*, Oxford University Press, 1971, pp. 151–70 at p. 163.
3. Letter from Adenauer to Erhard, 20 June 1959.

There were three main reasons for this weakness. First, Adenauer continued to dominate the making of foreign policy because his political position continued to be exceptionally strong, though after reaching a high point in 1957 it tailed off sharply in the period after the erection of the Berlin Wall in 1961. This political dominance more than made up for the loss of the advantages he had enjoyed over his rivals by virtue of his privileged access to the Allied high commissioners. Adenauer was also exceedingly well served by his Foreign Policy Bureau (*Aussenpolitisches Referat*). Although not part of the normal departmental structure (it is not a chancellery division), it enjoyed privileged access to Adenauer. Secondly, the Foreign Ministry was challenged by the rise of other powerful ministries, notably the Ministries of Economics and Defence. The relative position of ministries was a function of the standing of their ministerial heads and their centrality in the policy-making process. The first challenge to the Foreign Ministry came therefore from the Economics Ministry, which wanted to play an equal part in the negotiations for the EEC. The Foreign Ministry was able to beat off this challenge and it was primarily responsible for coordinating the West German negotiating team. However, after the EEC was set up the ministry had to share the coordination of EEC policy with, in the first instance, the Economics Ministry and, to a much lesser extent, the Ministries of Agriculture and Finance. The situation of the Economics Ministry was especially powerful, as the Ministry for the Marshall Plan and the responsibility for the EEC were transferred to it in the government reshuffle of 1957.

In the second half of this period the monopoly position of the Foreign Ministry came under more sustained attack from the Ministry of Defence. At that time West Germany had only two real fields of foreign policy, Western Europe and NATO. After the signing of the EEC and Euratom treaties and the rejection of the Free Trade Area, alliance policy was probably more central to West German foreign policy than European policy was. Under these circumstances any minister of defence was likely to have played an important role; but it is clear that the fact that the minister was Franz Josef Strauss led to a much deeper involvement. The influence of the Foreign Ministry was further reduced by divided loyalties among its officials. Strains were imposed upon the Foreign Ministry by virtue of the fact that a large number of officials gave their loyalty directly to Adenauer rather than to the Foreign Minister. This group included Walter Hallstein until his departure for Brussels in 1958 as first president of the EC Commission. This was true both of those who had worked with Adenauer in the Chancellor's Office and those whom Adenauer had selected for the Foreign Ministry because of their Rhenish background, the so-called *'Kölner Klüngel'*. Brentano's attempt to take advantage of Hallstein's departure to carry out a reorganisation of the Foreign Ministry in order to cut down the power of the state secretary and to increase the proportion of those at the top who owed their position to him was a failure. Perhaps even more important were the quasi-political feuds in the Foreign Ministry arising not out of party political differences (since appointments were almost exclusively reserved for CDU/CSU and, to a very limited extent, FDP adherents), but out of differing experiences in the Third Reich. This was particularly important in the Foreign Ministry since, while there was a great deal of continuity with the old Wilhelmstrasse, more 'outsiders' were brought in here than they were to the other Bonn ministries, because of the exigencies of overseas representation.

Over the Adenauer era as a whole there was an increase in the influence both of the Foreign Minister and of the ministry itself. This increase in influence was less marked, however, in the last two years of Adenauer's incumbency. Heinrich von Brentano, a man by this time with much reduced influence, had been dropped as one condition for FDP entry into the government. Although his successor, Gerhard Schröder, was a much stronger figure, with a powerful *'Hausmacht'* (power base) in the Protestant Working Circle of the CDU, and had begun to distance himself from Adenauer during his time as Interior Minister, he was not entirely successful in asserting himself against Adenauer and Defence Minister Franz Josef Strauss.

The assertion of the departmental principle under Erhard. Strauss's resignation as defence minister in the aftermath of the *Spiegel* Affair (see p. 97 above) and Adenauer's withdrawal in October 1963 created a much more favourable environment for Schröder. Both the new chancellor, Erhard, and the Defence Minister, von Hassel, held opinions on foreign policy that were very close to his own and they were prepared to accord him primacy in the foreign policy field. Similarly Mende, the Minister for Inner-German Affairs, accepted Schröder's leadership except in the period immediately before the 1965 election. Mende was able only to play a subordinate role because of his own position as leader of a small party and because the Foreign Ministry and Chancellor's Office had sufficient expertise and were not dependent on his ministry. Moreover any actual external contacts were of such overwhelming national importance that they required coordination both with the Western allies and the other ministries.

At the same time, the influence of the Economics Ministry declined as Erhard's successor inevitably failed to carry the same weight. The Schröder era was an unusual one in that Erhard alone of post-war chancellors was relatively uninterested in foreign policy matters and, despite the urgings of his policy planning division (which sought to apply its expertise to both domestic and foreign policy decisions), was content to leave the running to Schröder. There were challenges to this arrangement but they came largely from the 'outs', that is, Adenauer, Brentano and Strauss, rather than from other office-holders, and it was clear that they were really objecting to the policy rather than to the increased influence of the foreign minister. Schröder also benefited from the obvious support of the United States administration, which more than compensated for his poor relations with de Gaulle.

Kiesinger and the Grand Coalition.

'The trouble with this government' is that we have a Foreign Minister who would also like to be Chancellor, and a Chancellor who would also like to be Foreign Minister.'[4]

The period of the Grand Coalition is an exceptionally interesting one in the formulation of West German foreign policy. The situation was a novel one in which the CDU/CSU were confronted by a partner nearly equal in weight. This was reflected in the disposition of offices: the CDU provided the chancellor and the Minister of Defence, while SPD candidates held the Foreign Ministry and the Ministry for Inner-German Affairs. Under these circumstances foreign policy could be dominated neither by the chancellor principle, as under Adenauer, nor by the departmental principle, as under Schröder, but of necessity had to stress the collegial principle. In internal affairs the necessary collegiality was often achieved by the so-called *Kressbronner Kreis*, a group of top party leaders drawn from both camps (see Chapter 2). In foreign policy collegiality was created partly by informal contacts (particularly between Herbert Wehner and Baron von und zu Guttenberg) but also for the first time by cabinet committees. Two of the most contentious issues were handled within this framework. The Non-Proliferation Treaty was considered by the *Bundesverteidigunsrat* (set up in 1955 as an imitation of the US National Security Council, but normally relatively inactive) and its decisions were usually accepted as government policy. In the equally contentious area of 'inner-German relations the influence of the Committee for Inner-German Relations was very important.

4. *Der Spiegel*, no. 26, 1967, p. 54.

Willy Brandt's long experience of foreign affairs, the calibre of the staff he brought with him, Bahr and Rehs, and the strong position of the SPD in the coalition, made him a much more influential Foreign Minister than Brentano had been. He was, however, constrained by the needs of the coalition as a whole and the importance of maintaining a credible degree of overt unity on policy. He was also constrained by the involvement of Kiesinger and the Chancellor's Office.

As the bastion of the CDU/CSU, the Chancellor's Office was the main check on the Foreign Ministry, particularly as both its state secretaries were foreign policy experts. It could, and did, for instance, ask for confidential studies to be undertaken on foreign policy questions by the Stiftung Wissenschaft und Politik, a government-sponsored research organisation similar to the Rand Corporation.

Within the Chancellor's Office, the key foreign policy adviser to Kiesinger was Baron von und zu Guttenberg, the CSU Gaullist and a leading opponent of Schröder's foreign policy under the Erhard administration. Although Guttenberg was only the parliamentary state secretary he played a greater role as policy adviser than did Karl Carstens, the state secretary in the Chancellor's Office. In particular Guttenberg had a close personal relationship with Kiesinger, while Carstens had been Schröder's state secretary in the Foreign Ministry and had at first gone with Schröder to the Defence Ministry at the beginning of the Grand Coalition. Guttenberg also acted as a watchdog for the CSU.

The restoration of chancellor primacy under Brandt and Schmidt. In the first Brandt–Scheel government of 1969–72, the chancellor and the Chancellor's Office again gained in influence *vis-à-vis* the Foreign Ministry. Brandt himself had been Foreign Minister and his principal adviser, Egor Bahr, who became state secretary in the Chancellor's Office, had been head of the planning staff in the Foreign Ministry. Scheel, by contrast, had been out of power since 1966 and was leading a party which had only just managed to secure representation in the Bundestag.

Arrangements for foreign policy-making, particularly in the early period of the Brandt–Scheel government, reflected a new dominance of the Chancellor's Office. The state secretary of the Foreign Ministry had to report to the daily situation conference in the Chancellor's Office, while Egon Bahr took part in the so-called *Direktorenbesprechungen* (directors' conference) in the Foreign Ministry. This pattern of relationships, reminiscent of the Adenauer era, was modified after the incident in April 1970 when it became known that the state secretary of the Foreign Ministry had conducted a secret correspondence with Wladyslaw Gomulka, the Polish Prime Minister, at Brandt's behest, without the foreign minister being informed. Thereafter Scheel's influence increased, since it became a matter of first priority that the FDP should be seen to be achieving some measure of success in the field of foreign policy, although Egon Bahr continued to undertake much of the detailed negotiation of *Ostpolitik*.

In the second Brandt–Scheel government (1972–4) the position of the Foreign Office was strengthened, reflecting the greatly increased strength of the FDP. At the same time Bahr was accorded a much less prominent role in foreign policy-making. The responsibility for the coordination of European policy, which had resided *de facto* in Frau Focke while she was parliamentary state secretary in the Chancellor's Office, was formally transferred to the newly created parliamentary state secretary in the Foreign Ministry, Hans Apel.

Brandt's successor, Helmut Schmidt (1974–82), was an unusually forceful, competent and popular chancellor. Moreover, he had ministerial experience at the highest level in both economics and defence. Schmidt came closer than any chancellor since Adenauer to making a reality of Article 65 by determining 'the guidelines of policy'. He was constrained by the coalition nature of the government and by a growing distance, especially on defence, between himself and his own party, the SPD (see Chapter 2), which often made him dependent upon the support of the FDP. His intervention in foreign policy was thus necessarily selective. Schmidt was greatly aided by a succession of very able advisors. Bernd von Staden came back from the United States, where he had been ambassador, to head the foreign policy division in 1979; when he left to be state secretary in the Foreign Office in 1981 he was replaced by his deputy, Otto von der Gablentz. Schmidt had a major impact on West German policy towards the EC, where he cultivated a Paris–Bonn axis and stressed intergovernmentalism at the expense of supranationalism. The introduction of the European Monetary System was the most notable outcome of the close cooperation between Schmidt and the French president, Giscard d'Estaing. His other major area of intervention was in European–American relations. Here he intervened constantly to attempt to correct what he saw as a failure of American leadership, especially in the monetary field, but he was also very active in alliance issues and launched the debate on the modernisation of theatre-nuclear weapons which led to the NATO dual-track resolution of 1979. Policy towards the East was largely dominated by Hans-Dietrich Genscher, who was foreign minister for the entire period of the Schmidt chancellorship.

Kohl: from shared authority to chancellor dominance. The advent of the CDU/CSU/FDP government initially saw a revival in the influence of the Foreign Ministry. Helmut Kohl displayed relatively little interest in policy details and lacked the interventionist bent and broad policy grasp of his immediate predecessor as chancellor. His was initially a government run on the departmental principle. Moreover, having been Foreign Minister since 1974 and with his unrivalled experience in the area, Genscher was in a very strong position.

The FDP was also central to Kohl's governmental strategy. Without the FDP there would have been no majority; almost as important, the FDP was able to act as an ally of the chancellor against the pressures imposed by the CSU. Genscher and the Foreign Ministry thus dominated the making of foreign policy in the first period of the Kohl government.

The chancellor sporadically attempted to intervene, bringing in Horst Teltschik, with whom he had collaborated over a long period, to head the foreign policy division. Differences between the chancellor and the Foreign Minister surfaced most frequently on questions of alliance policy. Kohl was much more favourably disposed towards the Strategic Defence Initiative (SDI), more popularly known as 'Star Wars', and to West German participation in the project than was the Foreign Ministry, a very determined backer of Eureka and Esprit, the European-based schemes for scientific and technological collaboration. Sharply divergent views were also apparent in the reaction to the arms negotiations between the United States and the Soviet Union in 1987, when the chancellor for a time insisted that the Federal Republic hold on to its seventy-two Pershing IA missiles, while the Foreign Ministry was much more prepared to give them up in the interests of a negotiated settlement.

Over time, Kohl's influence gradually increased and his interventions became less selective. This partly reflected a changing agenda; he had always been decisive on alliance and European integration issues. Alliance issues remained important but the key issues from 1989 onwards were German unity, for which the chancellor was constitutionally responsible, and the European Community. This agenda shift was much more favourable to the chancellor than it was to the foreign minister.

Kohl's position was also strengthened by two other factors. The rapid growth in international summit meetings from the mid-1970s onwards focused attention on the role of the chancellor, most obviously in the meetings of the European Council and Group of Seven (G7) economic summits. This was a transnational development, increasing the role of heads of government. A further factor in the domestic arena was the growth of Division Two of the Chancellor's

Office under ministerial director Teltschik. Officially titled Division Two: External and Inner-German Relations, Development Policy and External Security,[5] it was the direct descendant of the arrangements set up under Adenauer. Teltschik had worked with Kohl in Mainz but the division was largely staffed by diplomats on secondment. It expanded under Kohl and was subdivided into five groups and an *Arbeitsstab* (working group), with responsibilities as follows:

- Group 21: coordination with the Foreign Ministry and the Ministry for Economic Cooperation.
- *Referat* 211: European unity; bilateral relations with West European states; servicing the cabinet committee on European policy.
- *Referat* 212: East–West relations and arms control.
- *Referat* 213: the UN and bilateral relations with Asia, Africa, Latin America.
- *Referat* 214: development policy and North–South issues.
- Group 23: coordination with the Defence Ministry and servicing the Federal Security Council.
- *Arbeitsstab* 20: German policy (although in Division Two it was directly responsible not to ministerial director Teltschik but to Rudolf Seiters, the minister in the Chancellor's Office).

Division Two is primarily concerned with fleshing out suggestions from the chancellor in order to enable him to play his role in external affairs. It takes an important part in preparing the daily-situation meeting in the Chancellor's Office, where foreign policy issues have played an increasing role. Officials in Division Two have suggested that the increased centrality of the chancellor in external issues is due to two factors. The first is the changing issue agenda and the increasing intractability of issues. When issues are very difficult, ministers are keen to shift the responsibility to the chancellor, otherwise they are keen to claim the credit themselves. One example cited by officials was missile deployment. Other examples include development aid, where the specialist ministries are caught between a Church lobby in favour of increasing aid, and an unenthusiastic public. Another issue where the relevant ministries have allowed the chancellor to take responsibility is the 'out of area' deployment of German armed forces. Secondly, officials in Division Two point to public expectations (the 'Adenauer legacy') and to the institutionalisation of international summits as reasons for the increased centrality of the chancellor in foreign affairs.

Occasionally the chancellor will over-rule other ministers. Recent

5. The reference in the title to 'Inner-German Relations' was dropped after unification in 1990.

examples include Kohl over-ruling the Defence Ministry on the length of national service, and on South Africa – where left-liberals had persuaded Foreign Minister Genscher to back the maintenance of sanctions, but where the chancellor felt sanctions should be lifted.

The key external area in which the chancellor exercised dominance was that of German unity, an issue very well adapted to chancellorial influence. The chancellor had always enjoyed a privileged position in the German policy arena, which was further strengthened during the Brandt chancellorship. The GDR government rejected any contact with the Ministry for Inner-German Relations, instead dealing directly with the Chancellor's Office. For its part the Chancellor's Office communicated with the GDR government through the two *Vertretungen* (representations) in Bonn and East Berlin. This meant that the Inner-German Ministry had little in the way of operational responsibilities; the most important exception was 'humanitarian cases', involving purchasing the freedom of dissidents in the GDR. The chancellor thus had an unassailable internal position which combined with his strong position in external affairs to place him absolutely at the centre of German policy on unity. He alone had the requisite authority to launch the Ten-Point Plan of November 1989, envisaging eventual German unity, and thereby to take the initiative on the issue. In launching this plan, Kohl was motivated by the desire to exert leverage on events in the GDR. There was great concern in the Chancellor's Office after the breaching of the Berlin Wall in that month that events could run completely out of control, with the attendant dangers of a violent backlash on the part of the GDR authorities. German policy-makers still had vivid memories of 17 June 1953, when Soviet troops had crushed an uprising in East Berlin three months after the death of Stalin had seemed to presage a more relaxed Soviet régime. From this perspective, Kohl's plan was an attempt both to accelerate unification and to moderate opinion in the GDR. The plan established Kohl's unchallenged ascendancy on the issue and greatly encouraged hopes of unity in the East.

Although the chancellor enjoyed a clear ascendancy on the unity issue, Genscher chaired the foreign and security sub-committee of the cabinet committee on German unity. The imperatives of coordination gave that committee a crucial role. For example, it was the subcommittee which took the decision on 19 February 1990 that the EC treaties should apply automatically to the entire German territory after unity, and that Germany would not press either for extra commissioners or for increased votes in the EC

Council of Ministers.[6]

While the Foreign Ministry was, of course, responsible for negotiating the various treaties necessary to effect German unity, the influence of the chancellor was pervasive. In relation to the European Community, Kohl twice met with the whole Commission and also had a number of separate meetings with Jacques Delors. It was Kohl who negotiated the Stavropol agreement with Gorbachev in July 1990 (see below). Much of the informal ground work leading to the overall agreement on German unity was worked out between Kohl, Bush, Gorbachev and their staffs. The Foreign Ministry was involved, especially Genscher and State Secretary Kastrup, but comparatively little use was made of the embassy network; more reliance was placed on direct contacts with the Chancellor's Office. Dr Hartmann of the Chancellor's Office always attended any negotiations being conducted by the Foreign Ministry.

The Chancellor and the Länder in Foreign Policy-Making

The role of the chancellor in external policy has been challenged but not seriously threatened by the desire of the *Länder*, especially Bavaria, to participate in foreign policy decisions. Most of the *Länder* minister-presidents have in recent years undertaken foreign tours and some German commentators have spoken of *Nebenaussenpolitik* (parallel foreign policy). This is to accord the *Länder*'s policy an importance that it does not warrant, since the *Länder* are constitutionally barred from concluding agreements. In two areas, however, they can play a role. The association of the individual *Länder* with *Land* central banks gave them access to West German–East German relations by virtue of their ability to extend credit to the GDR. The Bavarian minister-president, Franz Josef Strauss, was notably active in this area. Much more worrying for the chancellor, the foreign minister and the federal government as a whole has been the desire of the *Länder* to increase their involvement in the formulation of German policy towards the European Community.

The Federal Republic is the only member state of the EC which has a federal constitution, and intrinsic to the Bonn government's way of integrating EC business with its own has been its familiarity with federalism and its different layers of authority. The *Länder* have been consistent supporters of European integration. Adenauer's domination of European policy meant that there were no major *Länder* objections to the effects of integration, although

6. H. Teltschik, *329 Tage*, Berlin: Siedler Verlag, 1991, p. 152.

there had always been concern about the channels through which their views would be articulated. From the late 1960s onwards the EC's impact upon the *Länder* has increased, creating difficulties in certain policy areas, such as regional and environmental policy. Prior to the debate about the Single European Act (SEA), the constitutional-legal basis of *Bund–Länder* cooperation on EC affairs had been disputed but, in practice, it had followed the spirit of cooperative federalism. On occasions the federal government had to defer a policy pronouncement or withhold agreement in the EC Council due to the position of the *Länder*.

The SEA was perceived by the *Länder* as a threat to their constitutional status. It allocated some of their policy responsibilities, as set out in the Basic Law, to the EC without the federal government having any guarantees for increased *Länder* involvement in policy-making. There was a feeling among the *Land* governments (especially Bavaria) that their powers, on environmental policy for example, had been negotiated away by the federal government. This also reflected, of course, Strauss's aspiration to reduce Helmut Kohl's authority as chancellor. Ratification of the SEA thus gave the *Länder* a lever to prise some concessions from Bonn on a long-standing grievance. The significance of this is that relations between federal government and the *Länder* over European policy are becoming harder to manage. This could constitute a further serious impediment to the realisation of Germany's potential leadership role in the EC.

The *Länder* signalled their objections in a Bundesrat resolution of 21 February 1986 on the ratification of the SEA. In this resolution they suggested that their agreement to the ratification would be dependent on improvements to the policy-making machinery in the Federal Republic, and to *Länder* representation in international institutions such as the EC. In the Bundesrat's first debate on ratification on 16 May 1986 the *Länder* sought to introduce an article providing for their constitutionally guaranteed *Mitwirkung* (involvement), including the introduction of *Länder* representatives in West German negotiating teams at the Council of Ministers. Although this campaign was led by Bavaria and the SPD-governed states, the resolution was passed unanimously. In the event, the federal government agreed to legal provision for restricted *Länder* participation in policy-making and the Bundesrat ratified the SEA in December 1986.

The consequences of this arrangement for European policy have been put well by Renate Hellwig, who argues that this formal consultation procedure will inevitably slow down the process of European policy-making within the Federal Republic. Agreeing a position between the *Bund* and the *Länder* would make a prompt and coherent German response to EC initiatives even more difficult than before, especially if there was a disagreement between the majority view in the Bundesrat and the view of the federal government. Hellwig also points to the possibility that individual states would employ their new rights of co-decision to defend specific *Land* interests.[7] The *Länder* have also set up individual state representations in Brussels alongside the German permanent representation, further institutionalising the plurality of German representation in the European Community.

The federal government responded to these challenges by appointing a minister of state in the Chancellor's Office to liaise between federal and *Länder* governments. However, with a junior minister in the Foreign Office having responsibility for coordinating overall European policy, and the Economics Ministry coordinating most of the routine business, the allocation of a new coordinating role to the Chancellor's Office could only have been intended to indicate the seriousness with which the federal government viewed *Länder* concerns.

The issues raised at the time of the ratification of the Single European Act resurfaced even more strongly during the debates on the ratification of the Maastricht Treaty. The position of the chancellor was significantly weaker than it had been in the earlier debates, with Kohl's popularity at a low ebb. Moreover, while public opinion remained broadly in favour of integration, there was a great deal of unease about the European union treaties, especially the envisaged replacement of the Deutschmark by the ECU in the final stage of European monetary union. Furthermore, Kohl was seen to be even more closely identified with the European union treaties than he had been with the SEA. The government was in a minority in the Bundesrat and the treaty ratification process offered a good opportunity for the SPD to inflict damage on the government. The *Länder* accordingly pressed for a much stronger *Mitwirkung*. They had been represented in treaty negotiations, but now wished to take part on a regular basis in Council of Minister meetings and not just when subjects of obvious *Länder* concern were at issue. They also pushed for a more explicitly political function for the Brussels representations. Disagreements between the *Länder* and the chancellor on their role in EC decision-making continued throughout 1992 and were a central preoccupation of the regular meetings between the chancellor and the minister-presidents. Ultimately, the government conceded the stronger *Mitwirkung* which was being asked for.

7. Renate Hellwig, 'Die Rolle der Bundesländer in der Europapolitik. Das Beispiel der Ratifizierung der Einheitlichen Europäischen Akte', *Europa-Archiv*, 1987, no. 10, pp. 303-12.

The Chancellors and their Foreign Policy

Adenauer's Westpolitik. Before assuming the chancellorship, Adenauer's experience was almost exclusively in domestic and municipal politics, although in the 1920s he had been involved in quasi-international negotiations on the question of the future status of the Rhineland. Despite this restricted background, he established the basic lines of the foreign policy of the Federal Republic, founded on a vision of Europe and Germany's place within it. Adenauer's Europeanism revolved around a deep but narrow complex of sympathies and antipathies. His Europe was a Western Catholic one radiating out from his beloved Cologne; symbolically, from Adenauer's house in Rhöndorf it was possible to look only westwards over the Rhine. This Western Europe was seen to rest on the basis of a Franco–German entente.[8] His enduring anti-communism also meant a very close identification with the policy of the United States and an unwavering hostility towards the Soviet Union. In the field of external relations it was possible for Adenauer to shape a coherent policy out of this bundle of conflicting prejudices. There was at that time no tension between his reliance on the French in the field of European integration, and on the Americans for security. The French were content to follow the American lead in security matters in the face of the Soviet threat, and the Americans were the most committed supporters of Western European integration.

Thus, Adenauer's foreign policy stressed a clear-cut option for the West. He believed that Germany's interests were essentially identical with those of the Western powers and that they would be willing to grant Germany a genuine partnership by gradually dismantling the discriminatory status of the occupation regime. This had to be preceded by an unmistakable German commitment to the West, for only then would the Western powers trust Germany enough to repeal the discriminatory legislation. Adenauer's genius was to see that the emergence of Germany as a political force had to be identified with the pattern of cooperation that was being established in the Western world. This meant above all a willingness by Germany to make concrete concessions to the French, the main opponents of Germany's rapid return to playing a major role on the world stage, in return for France's intangible trust and goodwill; without these no progress could be made.

Adenauer was to be the main architect of European integration.

8. W. Weidenfeld, 'Die Europapolitik Konrad Adenauer's', *Politische Studien*, vol. 1, 1979, pp. 303–12.

He responded favourably to an invitation from the Council of Europe for Germany to become an associate member in 1950, although many counselled that the simultaneous entry of the Saar would mean that Germany was legitimising the permanent detachment of the Saar from Germany. Adenauer's handling of the issue of the Saar, which had in effect been annexed by France after 1945, is a good example of his general policy on European integration. In his view, the tension between legitimate French demands for security against the possibility of a too-powerful Germany and the traditional 'Germanness' of the Saar could be resolved only by its Europeanisation. He was to hold this view even after it had become apparent to most people that the Saarlanders wished to join the Federal Republic.

Moreover, Adenauer's enthusiastic embracing of the ideas of Robert Schuman, put forward in May 1950, was crucial in making the European Coal and Steel Community possible. This plan for the pooling of French and German heavy industry under a common European authority combined all the elements close to Adenauer's heart; indeed it was very similar to his own proposals. It was a way of giving more freedom of manoeuvre to the German coal and steel industry; it allayed French anxieties over their security; and it had the full and enthusiastic support of the American government and of its representative in Germany, John McCloy. Adenauer's greatest disappointment was the failure of the plans for a European Defence Community. These plans would have taken Western Europe far along the road towards a federal state, but were rejected by the French National Assembly in August 1954.

In taking Germany into the European Economic Community and Euratom, Adenauer was faced with opposition, not from the Social Democrats but from his erstwhile coalition partners, the Free Democrats, and with distinct reservations from his Economics Minister, Ludwig Erhard. More important perhaps than his victory over domestic opposition was his insistence on major concessions to the French in the negotiations. He saw that without these concessions the weak French government could not lead France into the EEC. Walter Hallstein, who became president of the Commission of the EEC, was the chief German negotiator and Adenauer's closest foreign policy confidant. This period represents the high point of the chancellor's success.

The weakening of the Adenauer chancellorship was synonymous with the erosion of foreign policy certainties in the early 1960s. The newly-elected US president, John F. Kennedy, had made it clear that he intended to press for détente with the Soviet Union, despite the continued division of Germany. Adenauer attempted to hold the

United States to the priority of overcoming German division but with little success, and Wilhelm Grewe, his ambassador to Washington, had to be recalled. Unity with the West was no longer necessarily seen as identical with a concern for German reunification.

In this new situation de Gaulle acted as a catalyst of the forces of change. If he had limited himself to asserting French interests within the existing framework, he would not have threatened the cohesion of Germany's foreign policy. However, he went further, presenting a rival programme which contained a competing vision of a *Europe des états* (Europe of the states), rather than a supranational Europe. The other part of his programme offered an eventual solution to the German question within the framework of East–West détente, which appealed to different groupings in the Federal Republic, although there was no consensus in support of the total package.

The conflict between Gaullism and Atlanticism. De Gaulle's challenge to the United States, his attack on NATO and his animus against the supra-national elements of the European Community embarrassed the German government. De Gaulle's stance threatened to disrupt the links between the bases of Adenauer's foreign policy: between security alignment with the United States and entente with France, and between the French–German rapprochement and the commitment to European integration. Faced with these conflicts, Adenauer was in a much less happy situation than he had been among the certainties of the 1950s.

After an attempt to deny the tension between these competing views, the chancellor indicated that while West Germany must continue to depend on the United States for security, Germany's interests in West European integration lay with France and thus with de Gaulle. This implied a lesser commitment to supra-nationalism and an endorsement, however unwilling, of the French exclusion of Britain – a major blow to the Community idea. This endorsement was symbolised by Adenauer's insistence on signing the Franco-German Treaty, against considerable internal opposition, including that of his foreign minister, Schröder, just after the French veto on British entry in January 1963.

Adenauer's successor, Ludwig Erhard, had very little interest in external policy and was content to leave the running to Foreign Minister Gerhard Schröder. Erhard, Schröder and Defence Minister von Hassel were, unusually, all Protestants and lacked the easy identification with the Europe of Adenauer and Kohl. Erhard's period of office was characterised by a contest between the Atlanticists (who included Erhard and Schröder) and the Gaullists, who argued for a more European-oriented policy. The chancellor's policies were motivated less by any lack of enthusiasm for France than by the need to prevent foreign policy from drifting towards conflict with the United States. (This imperative has weighed heavily with all governments of the Federal Republic.) In any case the force of 'the Gaullist attack' was blunted by its own incoherence. This rested in the contradiction between support for very close links with France and support for supra-nationalism, given Gaullist antipathy towards the latter. It was also the case that no West German politician at that time would have risked serious conflict with the United States, given the Federal Republic's dependence on the American security guarantee.

Despite his great interest in and knowledge of foreign policy issues, Kurt-Georg Kiesinger (1966–9) was not able to make a decisive impact on German foreign policy. European integration had entered a period of stagnation after de Gaulle's rejection of supranationalism, underlined by French withdrawal from Community meetings in 1965. The resolution of the conflict in the Luxembourg Compromise of 1966 in practice excluded majority decision, thereby retarding the process of integration. On the German question, the running was made by Brandt as Foreign Minister in Kiesinger's Grand Coalition. It was Brandt who was responsible for the loosening of the Hallstein Doctrine, by which the federal government had regarded recognition of the GDR by a third state as an unfriendly act. Although Kiesinger talked of a new *Ostpolitik* and emphasised the Federal Republic's friendly intentions towards Eastern Europe, he remained committed to the Hallstein Doctrine, the openness of the borders issue and a general policy of non-recognition of the reality of the GDR, all of which undermined his attempts to put relations with Eastern Europe on a new footing.

Brandt's Ostpolitik. With the exception of Erhard, all West German chancellors have had a selective interest in external policy, but Brandt came closest to Adenauer in his almost exclusive focus on external affairs and his pronounced lack of interest in domestic policy. While this was surprising in Adenauer's case, given the provincialism of his previous background, almost all of Willy Brandt's political experience in exile, in Berlin and as Foreign Minister had been in foreign affairs. Brandt's exclusive focus on foreign policy provided the basis for his electoral triumph in November 1972 but was to prove his undoing in the wake of the oil price rise in 1973 which demanded firm action at the domestic level. Brandt also resembled Adenauer in imposing his own imprint upon a central area of German foreign policy. Whilst Germany's *Westpolitik* was defined by Adenauer, Brandt will always be identified with its *Ostpolitik*.

Before the Brandt chancellorship, *Ostpolitik* had been fatally constrained by the imperative of non-recognition of the GDR. In his governmental declaration of October 1969, Brandt referred to 'two states of one German nation', which, while stopping short of full international recognition of the GDR, also, by implication, ruled out German reunification for the foreseeable future. Indeed Brandt's government declaration of 1969 was the first not to use the term 'reunification'. The chancellor argued that the pursuit of Adenauer's policies emphasising the primacy of reunification had resulted in atrophy in contacts between East and West Germany by encouraging the government of the GDR to maintain its defensive posture. Explicit acceptance of the fact that reunification was not practical policy would, it was hoped, enable the East German government to feel free enough to liberalise contacts between the two states and thus strengthen the sense of *Zusammengehörigkeitsgefühl* (feeling of belonging together). Historically, this feeling had not, as Brandt constantly emphasised, depended on living within the same frontiers. In other words, the new government, in the hope of preserving the German nation as a *Kulturnation* (nation defined by culture), refrained from stressing the pursuit of *Staatsnation* (nation defined by citizenship). The primary goal of *Ostpolitik* was and remained throughout a new relationship with East Germany. The new relationship with the GDR, although central to Brandt's plans, was likely to be the most difficult to achieve and depended on the prior settlement of relations with the Soviet Union.

For Brandt, the normalisation of relations with Eastern Europe was an over-riding priority on three principal grounds. First, normal relations with Eastern Europe were seen as a pre-condition for progress on the central plane of German–German relations, including some easing of the Berlin problem. Secondly, it was part of a process of emancipation and would decrease the reliance of the Federal Republic on the Western allies, who hitherto had acted as its interlocutors with Eastern Europe. Finally, there was an important moral dimension, symbolised by Brandt's gesture of throwing himself on his knees at the site of the Warsaw Ghetto during his visit there in 1970. This moral dimension recognised that German action in Eastern Europe in the Second World War had not only fatally compromised German territorial rights in the area but had been of such a traumatic character that it continued to impose obligations on the Germans to make some sort of recompense.

The basic thrust of the new *Ostpolitik* was not only to offer, as the CDU/CSU/FDP government had done in 1966, a renunciation of force, but to buttress this by a recognition of realities, in effect a recognition of existing frontiers in Europe. It was this, of course, which was of key interest to the Soviet and Polish governments and which formed the central element in the Moscow Treaty, the four-power agreement on Berlin and the Warsaw Treaty.

The crucial negotiations which led to the Moscow Treaty were carried out on the German side by Egon Bahr, Willy Brandt's foreign and German policy adviser in the Chancellery, between January and May 1970. Bahr had first acted as a foreign policy advisor to Brandt in Berlin and then followed him to the Foreign Ministry in 1966. The so-called 'Bahr Paper', setting out the points of agreement, was leaked in May 1970. In this paper, which anticipated the later Moscow Treaty, the federal government committed itself to respecting the territorial integrity of all European states and the inviolability of their frontiers, including the Oder–Neisse line and the demarcation line between the Federal Republic and the GDR. In the Bahr Paper the Federal Republic also committed itself to support the admission of the two German states into the United Nations, while not accepting the Soviet demand for full international recognition of the GDR.

The Moscow Treaty itself was negotiated and signed in July/ August 1970 by Walter Scheel, the Foreign Minister. The position of the Federal Republic was strengthened in two ways by Scheel. In order to safeguard the long-term position of the federal government and to quieten domestic opposition, a 'letter on German unity' was presented to the Soviet government at the signing of the treaty, reaffirming the federal government's commitment to German unity. Equally significantly, ratification was made subject to a successful outcome of four-power negotiations on Berlin – an issue of central concern to the federal government.

The coupling of the four-power negotiations on Berlin with the Moscow Treaty gave the Soviet Union an interest in a speedy outcome for the former. Neither German state took part in the Berlin negotiations but they were, of course, intensively consulted. The Western position was very largely worked out by the Bonn group of Western ambassadors, plus the federal government and the Berlin Senate. After prolonged negotiations the agreement was signed in 1971.

The key element in the negotiations between the Federal Republic and Poland was the question of the recognition of Poland's western frontiers. The Polish government desired an explicit and unconditional recognition of the frontier line (the Oder–Neisse line) established in practice after 1945. The federal government was unable to meet this demand fully without making ratification impossible. In the event German consciousness of historic guilt weighed heavily on the negotiators and the final formula went very far towards meeting Polish aspirations. In Article I it was stated that the Oder–Neisse line 'shall constitute the western state frontier of the People's Republic of Poland'. The recognition of Poland's western frontier was flanked by provisions for economic and technological coopera-tion and measures designed to make it easier for citizens of German origin to leave Poland.

The central goal of Brandt's *Ostpolitik* was to make progress on German–German relations. Negotiations moved very quickly after the conclusion of the Berlin Agreement in September 1971 and the ratification of the Moscow and Warsaw treaties in May 1972. The Basic Treaty (*Grundlagenvertrag*) between the two German states was negotiated on Brandt's behalf by Egon Bahr and was concluded in early November 1972. In the Basic Treaty both states agreed to support each other's membership of the United Nations and to establish diplomatic relations with each other, although their repre-sentatives were to be known as high commissioners rather than ambassadors. This formula had already been anticipated in the Bahr Paper during the Moscow negotiations. *Ospolitik* and especially the Basic Treaty were central to Brandt's resounding election triumph of November 1972 and represented the historic legacy of his chancellorship.

Schmidt: a foreign policy of of interdependence. Helmut Schmidt's chancellorship followed on the oil price rise of 1973 and the failure of Brandt to address Germany's changed situation. In external policy terms its key concept was interdependence, which meant, first, ensuring that German domestic economic policy accurately reflected external imperatives. More originally, the concept meant ensuring that external economic policy reflected growing interna-tional economic interdependence. This second aim was pursued through the establishment of the European Council in 1974 and the first world economic summit at Rambouillet in 1975. Schmidt was ideally suited to pursue both forms of interdependence. His unrivalled political experience as minister of defence, of economics and of economics and finance, as minister at the *Land* level in Hamburg and as parliamentary party leader of the SPD in the Grand Coalition, had given him a very strong grasp of policy interconnections. At the regional and global levels his strong intellectual grasp of defence and economics issues made him a very powerful advocate of the logic of interdependence and the necessity of averting protectionism.

Schmidt's chancellorship coincided with a period of declining

American leadership and his combination of intellectual arrogance and combative personality emboldened him to make a significant contribution to filling the vacuum that had been created. In raising the volume of the German contribution to the international policy debate, Schmidt was also, of course, the beneficiary of *Ostpolitik*, which had steeply reduced the degree of dependence on the Federal Republic's Western allies.

However, Schmidt's contribution to the development of German policy on European integration was somewhat paradoxical. In a very important sense he played down interdependence. Since Adenauer and Hallstein, the Federal Republic had been the strongest advocate of the EC Commission, stressing the supranational potential of the European institutions. Schmidt was a stern critic of the Commission, whom he accused of financial irresponsibility and administrative incompetence. The central thrust of Schmidt's policy was therefore to increase the role of the European Council and to return to the Franco–German axis characteristic of Adenauer's last years as chancellor.

Yet in another sense Schmidt increased interdependence. A long series of struggles with successive US administrations, and a profound intellectual contempt for President Carter's grasp of economics, convinced him that the United States was no longer able to play its former role in global monetary management. Schmidt became increasingly attracted to the idea of a European Monetary System (EMS), and he and the French president Giscard d'Estaing played the key role in its creation in 1978. The EMS in Schmidt's view had two obvious advantages. First, it created a zone of monetary stability in Europe which was unattainable at a global level. Secondly, it avoided the risks of Germany being perceived as pursuing national interests too clearly. In particular he wished to avoid clearly assigning the deutschmark a role as a clearly identifiable reserve currency, because of potential negative monetary, political and psychological consequences.

Reflecting both his own prudent fiscal instincts and West German public opinion as a whole, Schmidt's European policy was geared to capping Community expenditure and tying any increases to reform. In the most important area of EC reform, however, the CAP, he failed to follow his own instincts; coalition with the FDP precluded change in this crucial policy area. The chancellor's failure to press for the reform of the CAP reflects another major constraint. Although more assertive than previous German chancellors, Schmidt was convinced that other Community members would refuse to accept explicit German leadership. His solution was further to institutionalise and deepen the Franco–German relationship.

Under Schmidt, *Ostpolitik* faltered; while Brandt's central goals had been peace and political change in Europe, Schmidt was preoccupied with maintaining economic success. This necessarily involved a downgrading in the importance of *Ostpolitik*, since Western Europe and the United States provided the context for the German economy. The treaty basis of *Ostpolitik* had already been accomplished by Brandt; the accent was now more on gradual and routine consolidation, and this was essentially the business of the Foreign and Economic Ministries. The change of American administration in 1980 and events in Afghanistan precipitated East–West confrontations which threatened to reverse the achievements of *Ostpolitik*, and Schmidt spent much of his last two years in office attempting to rescue détente in Europe from the rupture in superpower relations.

In his policy on the US alliance and deployment of nuclear missiles, Schmidt was distinctive in acting against the wishes of large sections of his own party, the SPD – a notable contrast to the support Adenauer enjoyed from the CDU/CSU on Europe and Willy Brandt received from the SPD on *Ostpolitik*. The dispute on the issue of intermediate nuclear forces began with the chancellor's speech to the International Institute for Strategic Studies meeting in London in 1977. Schmidt, like other German defence policy-makers, was worried by a growing imbalance between the capacities of the Warsaw Pact and NATO in medium-range nuclear systems. By 1977 the Soviet Union had deployed some 1,300 medium-range weapons, including the SS20 and 'Backfire' bomber, while NATO only had less than 400 ageing weapons. Schmidt drew attention to this gap and suggested that policy attention be given to dealing with it. Schmidt's initiative was taken up by NATO, which in 1979 adopted the so-called twin-track decision. This resolution envisaged negotiating with the Soviets to persuade them to remove their SS20 missiles from Eastern Europe with the threat that, should these negotiations fail, then NATO would deploy intermediate-range nuclear missiles, including a large number of Pershing 2 and Cruise missiles, in the Federal Republic.

The NATO decision provoked a great deal of opposition in the Federal Republic. It gave rise to a large peace movement which organised a hectic programme of petitions and demonstrations. More threateningly for Schmidt, there was considerable opposition from within the SPD. NATO's move attracted predictable criticism from Bahr and Brandt, who in the 1970s had become increasingly critical of US policy and had already clashed with Schmidt on the neutron bomb issue. Especially worryingly for Schmidt, it attracted very bitter criticism from Herbert Wehner, the leader of the SPD *Bundestagsfraktion*, who complained that the deployment of these weapons would turn the Federal Republic into a kind of stationary aircraft-carrier for the United States.

The SPD had opposed nuclear weapons in the late 1950s but the new opposition from significant sections of the SPD had a novel character. In the 1950s the SPD protest had been largely a moral one. The opposition now to the enhanced weapons and, even more clearly, to the stationing of Cruise and Pershing 2 missiles, was clearly linked to the desire to preserve détente. Opposition to the stationing of the weapons became increasingly bound up with accusations that the Reagan presidency had brought détente to an end and thus it continued to increase, particularly as negotiations proved fruitless and plans for deployment went ahead. A demonstration in Bonn against the imminent stationing of the missiles in October 1981 was the largest in the history of the Federal Republic and was supported, much to Schmidt's anger, by almost a quarter of the SPD *Bundestagsfraktion*.

A possible defeat for government policy at the Munich conference of the SPD in April 1982 was staved off by a compromise which left the decision to a special conference in November 1983. These conflicts with the SPD seriously weakened the Schmidt chancellorship in its later years.

Alliance conflicts under Kohl, 1982–1989. Helmut Kohl came to power in 1982 with a set of foreign policy assumptions which bore the clear imprint of Konrad Adenauer. His immediate goals were to speed up progress towards European integration, to re-establish amicable relations with the American administration and to reduce the priority given to détente. In his first years of office, Kohl was able to make only modest progress towards realising the first goal. His key role in carrying through the deployment of the Pershing missiles did help to re-establish close and amicable relations with the United States and this repositioning was accompanied by a much more sceptical view of détente than had obtained under Schmidt and which was still maintained by Foreign Minister Genscher.

If the first Kohl government represented a return to old certainties, the second saw dramatic changes. On Europe, the chancellor played an important role in the formulation of the Single European Act (1986). Relations with the United States came under increasing strain after the conclusion of the Soviet–US Agreement on the scrapping of intermediate-range nuclear missiles (the INF Treaty) in early 1988. The preference of the United States and its other principal allies was to move on from the INF Treaty to a treaty on strategic missiles. In this scenario, deterrence would be preserved by the modernisation of short-range battlefield nuclear weapons in Europe. This position was publicly and fiercely rejected by the chancellor. It was argued that an agreement on strategic nuclear weapons would significantly reduce the risks of a nuclear strike for the United States and so might encourage limited nuclear war. Shorter-range missiles were very heavily concentrated in the two Germanies; their presence was a constant reminder to the West German population of their terribly exposed position. This was expressed by the CDU general secretary, Volker Rühe, in the telling epithet: 'The shorter the range, the deader the German.' It was pointed out that the removal of long- and medium-range weaponry would not affect the short-range missiles which were based in and targeted on the Federal Republic. The chancellor feared that modernisation and a stress on short-range missiles would be unacceptable to the West German public, since the risks inside NATO would manifestly be spread unevenly and this would underline the 'singularity' of the Federal Republic – its unique susceptibility to the dangers posed by the concentration of shorter-range missiles on German soil.

Tension between the Federal Republic and its leading NATO allies on the modernisation issue deepened considerably in 1989. A succession of poor election results increased the electoral vulnerability of the chancellor and, by raising the possibility that the FDP might not attain 5 per cent of the vote in the 1990 elections, paradoxically increased its leverage in the coalition. Both developments increased the pressure on Kohl not to yield to Anglo-American demands for the modernisation of short-range missiles. In April 1989 Kohl went much further and called for negotiations with the Warsaw Pact for the removal of short-range missiles altogether. This move was supported by some smaller NATO allies but gravely alarmed the British and American governments, who took the view that there should be no negotiations on short-range missiles until the Warsaw Pact's superiority in conventional and chemical weapons was eliminated. In the period immediately after Gorbachev's accession to power in the USSR, Germany's relations with its NATO allies continued to be tense. The conclusion of the INF Treaty and the re-establishment of harmony between the superpowers removed the main impediments to good relations, however. For his part, conscious of the crippling weakness of the Soviet economy, Gorbachev increasingly relied on the Federal Republic for support.

The 'chancellor of unity'. From the publication of his Ten-Point Plan on 28 November 1989, Chancellor Kohl made the running on

German unity. There were a number of formidable external obstacles, of which the most challenging was the necessity to gain the agreement of the Allied powers, especially the two superpowers. The Soviet Union's opposition to German unity was one of the great 'givens' of post-war politics; the principal factor in its move away from that position was its own gathering internal weakness. Kohl, however, played a crucial role in helping Gorbachev to work out the logic of this weakness in a way which would not immediately precipitate a coup by hard-liners and it was Kohl who worked out with Gorbachev at their meeting in Stavropol in July 1990 an agreement on the future of German security arrangements which was the last great building block of unification. Relations with the United States were also crucial. Although Kohl had developed different views on the missiles issues, he continued to place a very high priority on close and friendly US–German relations and he continued to be seen as a close and trusted ally in Washington in a way that was emphatically not true of Genscher. Without Kohl as chancellor, it is unlikely that President Bush would have given such immediate and consistent support to German unification.

German unity was also achieved within the framework of the European Community; here again Kohl played a key role. His close and friendly relations with Jacques Delors were one factor in Delors' consistent support for unification. Kohl was also crucial to the process by which the EC, principally the Commission, formulated the arrangements for the incorporation of the GDR into the Community. The Chancellor's Office was a key player in the negotiations and Kohl visited the Commission in March 1990 to brief it.[9]

While Kohl's overall handling of the external dimension of the unity process was magnificently assured, he showed some uncertainty over the Polish borders issue, where, worried by electoral support for the Republican Party, he appeared at times in early 1990 to be unwilling to endorse the finality of the Polish–German border – a position from which he retreated under international pressure.

The ascendancy established by Chancellor Kohl in the unity process remained in post-unification Germany. Foreign Minister Genscher's core agenda of pan-European détente was decisively overtaken by the collapse of communism and the achievement of unification. In the period of just over a year and a half that Genscher remained in office after unity, he appeared a tired and increasingly less influential figure. He was replaced by the experienced but rather grey Klaus Kinkel, who lacked a political base, having only joined

9. D. Spence, *Enlargement without Accession: The EC's Response to German Unification*, London: Royal Institute of International Affairs, 1992.

the FDP in 1991. Kinkel devoted a great deal of energy to making up for this deficit, and the resignation of Jurgen Möllemann left him as unchallenged favourite to succeed to the leadership of the FDP. However, the declining influence of the CSU in a united Germany has reduced the importance of the FDP's role as counterweight. The position of the Foreign Minister was further challenged by the appointment of Volker Rühe (CDU), an ambitious ally of Chancellor Kohl with pronounced views on a wide range of foreign policy issues, as Defence Minister in early summer 1992.

After unification Kohl faced three major foreign policy challenges. His central preoccupation with the deepening of European integration stemmed from a conviction that this was the mission of his generation and one that could not safely be entrusted to a successor generation. In the German unity process he had linked the achievement of German unity with progress on European unity by pushing, together with President Mitterrand, for treaties on economic and monetary union and political union. In the negotiations for the European Union treaty, Kohl consistently stressed that progress on political union was as crucial as that on economic and monetary union (EMU). The negotiations at Maastricht in December 1991 were a major disappointment to Kohl because, while agreement on EMU was far-reaching, little was achieved on political union. Moreover, the commitment to replace the Deutschmark by the ecu in the final stage of EMU alarmed significant sections of German domestic opinion. Further damage to the chancellor's vision was inflicted by the internal and external difficulties that have attended the ratification process.

Kohl's second preoccupation was the issue of changing the constitution to enable German forces to play a role outside the NATO area. The Gulf crisis of 1990–1 placed the Federal Republic in an unenviable position, since intervention on the Allied side was both difficult under Article 87A of the Basic Law and domestically very unpopular. The failure to intervene and the difficulty in framing a subsequent response seriously damaged Germany's international standing. The chancellor invested considerable personal authority, with some degree of success, in preparing German opinion to change the constitution in readiness for out-of-area intervention:

As things are nowadays, it would be a fatal mistake to close our eyes to the way in which peace and freedom are now endangered. This is no corner of the world in which Germans could shelter from the cold blast of world affairs; neither do we want such a refuge.[10]

---

10. Helmut Kohl, *Our Future in Europe*, Edinburgh and London: Europa Institute/ Konrad Adenauer Foundation, 1991, p. 17.

The third of Kohl's foreign policy priorities was to buttress the position of President Gorbachev in an increasingly unstable Soviet Union. Kohl was very conscious of the role played by Gorbachev in bringing about unification, and this sense of indebtedness was a feature of all the chancellor's major speeches after 1989. His sense of shock during the attempted coup against Gorbachev in August 1991 was palpable. The grounds for supporting Gorbachev were of course deeper than mere gratitude. Germany had a vital interest in the smooth completion of the Soviet military withdrawal by 1994, which could have been endorsed by the restoration of hard-line rule in Moscow. The Federal Republic is also obviously deeply concerned that total breakdown in, and mass migration from, the Soviet Union should be avoided.

Taken together, these factors influenced the chancellor in providing strong support for Gorbachev. Conscious that the difficulties of the Soviet economy were too profound to be dealt with by Germany alone, Kohl lobbied incessantly for the other Western powers, especially Japan and the United States, to share the burden of the economic transformation of the Soviet Union. The condition of the US budget made a positive US response extremely unlikely and Japan still had territorial arguments with the Soviet Union. It was Kohl who insisted that Gorbachev make his ill-fated plea to the G-7 conference in July 1991. Germany itself had by 1991 provided over DM60 million in economic aid to the Soviet Union, approximately 56 per cent of all Western aid up to the time of unity.

However, in this decisive phase of developments, in this process of the opening of this huge country, we must not sit back as pure spectators saying that what is happening there is something on which we shall keep a watching brief and that later on when decisions have been made we will come in and help them. We must help them help themselves sensibly and feasibly. I am absolutely persuaded that this is vital at this point in time. This will help the Soviet Union to develop in a way that will ensure peace for us all. This is a point I have also made in Washington time and time again, because there are western voices suggesting something different. But I think any policy aimed at bringing about the dissolution of the Soviet Union as a whole is political folly.[11]

Kohl's support for Gorbachev led to a major contradiction in his policy. Whereas German policy generally stressed self-determination, the federal government was very muted in its support for the Baltic republics and little pressure was exerted on the Soviet leadership to move quickly on that issue. 'The Soviet leadership will realise that in the end the right to self-determination will prevail.'[12]

11. *Ibid.*, p. 13.
12. *Ibid.*

The eclipse of Gorbachev as Soviet leader and the break-up of the Soviet Union has left the chancellor without a coherent policy in regard to that area. Given Germany's greater exposure to risk, it is little comfort to know that this problem is shared by other states.

Conclusion

The distinctive role played by successive chancellors in the formulation of foreign policy, and their disproportionate interest in foreign policy issues, reflected the abnormal character of the Federal Republic. The successful achievement of unity transformed that status and swept away all the remaining vestiges of conditional sovereignty and provisional status. It is, however, unlikely that normalcy will reduce the role of the chancellor in external policy. Germany may no longer be divided, but foreign expectations of its role have increased correspondingly. Only the chancellor has the authority to move a rather quietist German public opinion some way towards fulfilling these expectations. This is, of course, a much more difficult task than that faced either by Adenauer in giving policy expression to the generally positive public orientation towards European unity or by Brandt in relation to recognising the realities of Eastern Europe. Faced with an increasingly intractable domestic environment, however, post-unity chancellors will continue to seek foreign policy success to bolster their position.

6

THE CHANCELLOR AND ORGANISED INTERESTS

Heidrun Abromeit

Organised Interests and the Centre of Power

In textbooks on organised interests it is often observed that pressure groups and lobbyists tend to approach virtually all the actors in the political arena, in order not to miss the slightest chance of exerting their influence. At the same time, however, being rational actors, their major efforts are channelled towards the centre of power. Thus, in most parliamentary systems organised interests direct their attentions largely to the executive.

In the Federal Republic, the chancellor is the constitutional power centre of the executive. Article 65 of the Basic Law endows him with sole responsibility for establishing the guidelines of government policy (*Richtlinienkompetenz*). Article 64 confers the power of appointment. It might be expected, therefore, that in a system of *Kanzlerdemokratie*, lobbyists would queue at the doors of the Palais Schaumburg or at least of the Chancellor's Office in pursuit of their interests. However, the Federal Government's Standing Orders (para. 10) clearly state that direct contact between the chancellor and interest group delegations is restricted to 'special cases'. The normal procedure prescribed by these Orders, as well as by the Common Standing Orders of the Federal Ministries (*Gemeinsame Geschäftsordnung der Bundesministerien*, or GGO), is that pressure groups should make their voices heard through an approach to the relevant department (para. 23 GGO II). This constitutes the foundation of the close clientelistic relationship between organised interests and government departments that is commonly found in all parliamentary systems.

The statutory provisions have not prevented lobbyists from finding their way to chancellors more frequently than the prescription 'only in special cases' would suggest. Nevertheless, the practice does bear some resemblance to the formal rules in so far as the normal way of exerting influence is through a more or less continuous contact with the relevant government department (or respective division of the department). This applies particularly to the stage of initiating and preparing legislation. It is only when these attempts to shape policies are unavailing that organised interests need to approach the chancellor directly.

The Autocrat and his Advisers: Adenauer

Contemporaries of the first federal chancellor have expressed somewhat contradictory views on his treatment of pressure groups. According to one view, Adenauer was perfectly ready to accept them as legitimate and even necessary and to listen to them, yet he was not ready to grant them 'a decisive influence on the direction his policy should take'.[1] The other more critical view is that Adenauer maintained such close contact with organised interests that he effectively 'degraded' his ministers.[2] Much of this apparent contradiction can be understood in terms of organised interests using an approach to the chancellor as a last resort. Whenever possible, Adenauer remained aloof from day-to-day politics. Equally, the lobbyists saw his role as that of a sort of 'fire brigade' in cases where all other channels of influence had been exhausted. At this point, Adenauer might come to the assistance of the interest groups concerned by using his authority in cabinet – sometimes to the point of publicly undermining his ministers.

The 'fire-brigade' style of interest group activity is graphically illustrated by the *Mitbestimmung* issue of 1950/1.[3] Initially Adenauer had trusted that he could leave the formulation of a system of worker participation in industrial management to direct negotiations between the peak associations of the unions and the employers, if necessary with assistance from the Federal Department of Labour. With unions and employers unable to agree upon a mutually acceptable formula, however, and with the unions on the point of taking industrial action in order to press their claims, Adenauer was alerted. After an exchange of letters between him and the DGB leader Hans Böckler over the question of whether or not such a strike would be illegal, the two met for lengthy discussions on 11 January 1951. During these talks Böckler managed to con-

1. Theodor Sonnemann, 'Adenauer und die Bauern', in Dieter Blumenwitz *et al.* (eds), *Konrad Adenauer und seine Zeit*, Stuttgart: DVA, 1976, p. 267.
2. Theodor Eschenburg, in *Kölner Stadtanzeiger*, 6 May 1960. This latter view is supported by Jost Küpper, *Die Kanzlerdemokratie*, Frankfurt am Main: Peter Lang, 1985, pp. 183ff.
3. For details see Horst Thum, *Mitbestimmung in der Montanindustrie*, Stuttgart: DVA, 1982; Volker Berghahn, *Unternehmer und Politik in der Bundesrepublik*, Frankfurt am Main: Suhrkamp, 1985, pp. 218ff.

vince Adenauer that the framework of workers' participation which already existed in the iron and steel industry ought to be maintained and extended to the coal-mining industry. A few days later Adenauer met leading representatives of the employers to establish their position. On discovering that they were by no means of one mind on the issue, he persuaded them to meet the unions once more. Assisted by his friend and adviser, the banker Robert Pferdmenges, Adenauer himself was in the chair when these talks were renewed. When they ended without result, Adenauer resolved to see the matter through. Negotiating separately with the two sides, he eventually brought the employers to accept the system of worker representation on company boards which subsequently became the core of 'co-determination' in the steel and coal-mining industries.

The resolution of this issue was facilitated by a fairly good personal relationship, even 'a strange sort of friendship',[4] between Adenauer and Böckler. After Böckler's death shortly afterwards, the trade unions lost practically all influence on the shaping of industrial relations law. The initial success of the trade unions had strengthened the employers' resolve to resist union demands. Moreover, Adenauer himself lost all interest. Neither Böckler's successor, Christian Fette, nor any subsequent trade union leader was able to replicate Böckler's personal relationship with the chancellor.

Personal chemistry often appeared to be an important ingredient in Adenauer's relations with pressure groups. It was not, however, always the decisive one. For instance, Andreas Hermes, first president of the German Farmers' Association, had been one of Adenauer's rivals for the post of party chairman. Subsequently, the two detested each other and avoided contact as much as possible. Hermes' successor, Edmund Rehwinkel, was not much liked either, probably because of his tendency to exaggerate the farmers' needs and demands in public.[5] Nevertheless, the farmers' association was a formidably effective pressure group.[6] Its success was due in large part to its close relationship with the federal Ministry of Agriculture. Theodor Sonnemann, first secretary of state in the ministry, had been a leading member of the association and remained its faithful ally. Most civil servants in the ministry saw their role primarily as that of trustees of the farmers' interests. Yet occasionally even the Minister of Agriculture had to accept a compromise in cabinet.

4. Ludwig Rosenberg, 'Adenauer und die Gewerkschaften', in Blumenwitz *et al.*, *op. cit.*, p. 257.
5. See Sonnemann, *op. cit.*, pp. 267ff.
6. See, for instance, Hans Peter Schwarz, *Die Ära Adenauer, 1949-57*, Stuttgart: DVA, 1981, p. 173.

Those were the occasions when agricultural lobbyists approached Adenauer directly, to achieve – in more than one instance – higher price increases for agricultural products than their own ministry had dared to ask for: 'Experience showed that the leaders of the German Farmers' Association could count on the chancellor when things got rough.'[7]

Other groups were also able to 'count on the chancellor'. In the question of *Lastenausgleich* (the equalisation of burdens between the refugees from the East and the rest of the population), Adenauer supported the Association of Refugees against both his Minister of Finance and his Foreign Minister. As in the case of the farmers' association, Adenauer's readiness to exert his authority over ministers for the benefit of interest groups had little to do with personal affinities. Nor did it derive from the valuable expertise represented by the respective organisations. Rather, the influence of these two associations rested – and continues to do so – upon their electoral importance.

It is somewhat doubtful whether Adenauer judged the doctors to be another such group. Nevertheless, the *Kassenärztliche Bundesvereinigung* (a federation of about 52,000 medical practitioners) was also able to rely on the chancellor's support. In the 1958–9 reform of the health insurance funds, the federation sought direct contact with Adenauer. Negotiating directly with the doctors' federation, the chancellor made undertakings without consulting the relevant minister. Subsequently, the planned reform was abandoned in 1961.[8] Adenauer was often ready to lend an ear to lobbyists who appeared to him, as 'practitioners', a refreshing contrast to the bloodless bureaucrats and theorists from government departments.

This was particularly true in matters of economic policy. Although in forming cabinets he could not exclude the extremely popular Ludwig Erhard, self-styled 'father of the German economic miracle', Adenauer seems never to have trusted or liked his economics minister. Given to abstract theorising, Erhard was the antithesis of Adenauer, with his pragmatic down-to-earth approach. Consequently, the chancellor found ways to counterbalance Erhard's influence. As early as 1949 he formed a cabinet committee for advice on economic matters. Alongside Erhard and the ministers of finance and of economic cooperation, Adenauer appointed two representatives of the Bank Deutscher Länder (the central bank) and two close personal friends, the bankers Robert Pferdmenges and Her-

---

7. *Ibid.*, p. 175.
8. See Theodor Eschenburg, *Das Jahrhundert der Verbände*, Berlin: Siedler, 1989, pp. 112ff.

mann Josef Abs. The two last-named were Adenauer's permanent and most-trusted economic advisers, always present when economic policy issues were discussed. Pferdmenges and Abs were also the most prominent members of the 'small circle' of economic advisers, formed in 1954 and consisting of leading members of the central bank, the Confederation of German Industry (BDI), the Hamburg and Berlin Chambers of Commerce, and the Association of German Craft Industry and Trades.

The third principal economic adviser, besides Abs and Pferdmenges, was Fritz Berg, president of the BDI. Whereas Adenauer had justified his strong reliance on Abs with the words 'I like to ask you because I know that you don't make demands on me',[9] he could hardly have given the same justification in the case of Berg. However, in a speech in October 1959 he expressed his thanks to Berg, who had always 'advised him well' and had never been 'a representative of one-sided interests'.[10]

In fact, throughout Adenauer's chancellorship Fritz Berg manifestly pursued the interests of the industrial hardliners on the conservative wing of the BDI. In a tough seven-year battle he did his best to fight the proposed Federal Competition Act (*Gesetz gegen Wettbewerbsbeschränkungen*), marching in and out of the Palais Schaumburg and abusing Erhard, to whom the Act constituted the centre-piece of the market economy.[11] In the end, Erhard got the Act through (in 1957), but with its teeth drawn. That was, however, not the end of the fight between Erhard and German industry; it continued over almost all aspects of Erhard's economic policy, culminating in the 'Gürzenich affair' of 1956 and the 1960–1 debate on the revaluation of the deutschmark.[12]

In the Gürzenich affair, the chancellor openly and publicly took the BDI's side against his ministers Erhard and Schäffer over the question of increasing the bank discount rate to curb inflation. In common with the BDI, he judged the measures superfluous. In May 1956 Adenauer was invited as a guest of honour to speak at the BDI's annual conference in the Gürzenich Hall in Cologne. After Fritz Berg had thoroughly abused Erhard (who had not been invited) in his own speech, Adenauer surpassed his invective, reproaching

9. Hermann Josef Abs, 'Konrad Adenauer und die Wirtschaftspolitik der frühen fünfziger Jahre', in Blumenwitz *et al.*, *op. cit*, p. 245.
10. Quoted in Daniel Koerfer, *Kampf ums Kanzleramt*, Stuttgart: DVA, 1987, p. 504.
11. For details see Viola Gräfin von Bethusy-Huc, *Demokratie und Interessenpolitik*, Wiesbaden: Franz Steiner, 1962, pp. 36ff.; Berghahn, *op. cit.*, pp. 152ff.
12. See Koerfer, *op. cit.*, pp. 109ff., 464ff., 503ff.

Erhard, *inter alia*, for his lack of sangfroid in dealing with the business cycle. Against public expectations, Erhard stayed on, only to be let down again over the question of the revaluation of the deutschmark in 1960-1. In the talks and consultations leading to the revaluation of 6 March 1961, Adenauer dealt with his ministers and the BDI in very different ways. Berg, Abs and Pferdmenges attended cabinet committee meetings and the *Konjunkturgespräche* (talks on the business cycle) initiated by Adenauer. Consequently, Erhard found himself in a minority even within his own circle. The BDI, on the other hand, was granted the privilege of private negotiations with Adenauer, without the knowledge of his Economics Minister. When Erhard privately criticised the way Adenauer indulged lobbyists, the latter informed Berg, who was so sure of his influence on the chancellor that he publicly taunted Erhard with it, remarking to the Bonn Press Club: 'I just have to go to the chancellor to get the whole revaluation issue off the agenda once and for all.'[13] Although this rather overestimated his influence in the matter, the following day's headlines asked the now familiar question: 'Erhard or Berg?' Speculation increased when no rebuke was issued by the Chancellor's Office.

One of the principal reasons for what Theodor Eschenburg has described as 'the chancellor's kowtowing to the business associations'[14] was his party's dependence on donations from industry. Thus, in the cabinet meeting after the Gürzenich affair of 1956, Adenauer tried to justify his strange behaviour by pointing to the overwhelming necessity not to estrange industry, the party's chief sponsor, shortly before the federal elections (of 1957). In this instance it was money that explained the influence which organised interests had on the chancellor; in other cases (as seen above) it was electoral considerations that were decisive.

Another reason for the easy access that lobbyists had to the chancellor was Adenauer's leadership style. An autocrat in cabinet, he did not hesitate to undermine his ministers publicly, or even to repudiate them. Rather than seeking advice from this quarter, he preferred to listen to 'pragmatic practitioners' and to his personal friends who happened to be bankers. Personal chemistry explains many of the peculiarities of Adenauer's style of governing. And his personal relations were frequently better with people outside rather

---

13. Quoted in F.U. Fack, 'Entwicklungstendenzen des industriellen Lobbyismus in der Bundesrepublik', in Carl Böhrel and Dieter Grosser (eds), *Interdependenzen in Politik und Wirtschaft. Festschrift für Gert von Eynern*, Berlin: Duncker and Humblot, 1967, p. 488.
14. Eschenburg (1989) *op. cit.*, p. 114.

than inside his cabinets. Thus it is not surprising that journalists and political scientists referred to the 'rule of pressure groups'[15] and saw grave dangers for the common good on the horizon.

Erhard as an 'Old-Fashioned Corporatist'

In his dealings with organised interests, Adenauer can be characterised as a conservative pluralist with a definite preference for working with bankers and business people. His successor Erhard was, in this respect at least, much more old-fashioned – an old-fashioned corporatist, one might say.

From the beginnings of his political career in the 1940s – first as a minister in Bavaria, then as director of economic affairs in the administration of the 'Bi-Zone' – up to his days as chancellor, Erhard seems always to have felt profoundly uneasy in the presence of lobbyists. Though he would sometimes force himself to cooperate with pressure groups, and even tried to use them in an attempt to introduce some kind of economic self-regulation, he never lost his strong misgivings about them.[16] In his eyes, organised interests were the incarnation of group egotisms which could never be reconciled with the 'common good', but were inevitably detrimental to it. Worse still, each group tended to make demands that conflicted with the claims of the others, and these conflicting demands put a pressure on the economy which was wholly incompatible with economic stability. At the same time, pressure groups heralded the age of collectivism which threatened to devour individuals and 'the personality'. The words 'personality' and 'moderation' recurred frequently in Erhard's vocabulary.

In contrast to Adenauer, Erhard was not prepared to accept the necessity of maintaining a tolerable working relationship with organisations representing either party sponsors or important sections of its electorate. Instead he claimed: 'I would never allow myself to be influenced if somebody approached me, saying: We have some hundreds of thousands members. . . . To me, this does not

---

15. Theodor Eschenburg, *Herrschaft der Verbände?* Stuttgart: DVA, 1955. In this book, however, Eschenburg never once mentions the BDI's and other associations' close contacts with Adenauer.
16. See Albrecht Düren, 'Ludwig Erhards Verhältnis zu organisierten wirtschaftlichen Interessen', in Rüdiger Altmann *et al.* (eds), *Ludwig Erhard. Beiträge zu seiner politischen Biographie*, Frankfurt am Main: Propyläen Verlag, 1972, pp. 42–66. See also Ludwig Erhard's numerous speeches, in Ludwig Erhard, *Deutsche Wirtschaftspolitik*, Düsseldorf: Econ Verlag, 1962.

count.'[17] To give way to pressure groups appeared to him immoral as well as irreconcilable with parliamentary democracy; the latter would become a 'farce' if policies were 'dictated' by the wishes of 'social, economic or political groups'[18] (a statement which left room for one to wonder whether, for Erhard, political parties came under the same heading).

Erhard's instinctive aversion to interest politics led him, upon becoming chancellor in 1963, to attempt not to appoint Werner Schwarz, a leading member of the farmers' association and former Minister of Agriculture, to the same ministerial post in his first cabinet. On this occasion, however, he was forced to give in to group pressure when the association threatened that the fifty of its members in the CDU parliamentary group would cast their votes against him when the Bundestag met to elect him as chancellor. The result was that Erhard was elected, and Schwarz duly remained Minister of Agriculture.[19]

Among those groups which Erhard once characterised as 'the real enemies of the German people',[20] the trade unions ranked highest. The unions, in his view, combined the evils of egotism, immoderation, lack of economic expertise, the 'faceless masses' and 'popular pressure'. However, a gulf of 'irreconcilable antagonism'[21] separated him from the BDI as well, leading to endless bickering between Erhard and BDI leaders. Instead of narrowing, the gulf had widened during the 1950s, since Erhard's total lack of sympathy for the way the BDI tried to promote industry's interests was increasingly tinged with disappointment. In his early years he had made some effort to cooperate with industry and relied on the advice 'of a circle of businessmen'.[22] Furthermore, he had always particularly favoured manufacturing industry, regarding it as 'the elder brother' among all 'his children' in the economy.[23] Obviously he felt that so much loving care deserved gratitude, which the BDI was lamentably slow to demonstrate.

During the short time of his chancellorship (1963–6) Erhard's attitude towards pressure groups did not change. Indeed, his impatience with their immoderate demands grew. Nor did he think much of advice coming from those quarters. In accordance with his own

17. In a speech before young artisans, 6 Dec. 1952; quoted by Düren, *op. cit.*, p. 48.
18. Radio speech of 11 November 1952, in Erhard, *op. cit.*, p. 99.
19. See Eschenburg (1989), *op. cit.*, p. 109.
20. In an article in the *Frankfurter Allgemeine Zeitung*, 27 Aug. 1960; quoted in Erhard, *op. cit.*, pp. 503ff.
21. Düren, *op. cit.*, p. 63.
22. Open letter to Otto A. Friedrich; quoted in Erhard, *op. cit.*, p. 119.
23. Speech on the BDI annual conference of 17 May 1954; quoted in *ibid.*, p. 237.

'professorial' appearance, he preferred listening to professors rather than to practitioners. There were no bankers or business people to play a role comparable to that of Abs, Pferdmenges or Berg under Adenauer's chancellorship. Instead, Erhard consulted the professors Götz Briefs and Eric Voegelin and, especially, the publicist Rüdiger Altmann: men who were not even economists but conservative thinkers and philosophers. Preferring grand designs and structural (if somewhat nebulous) concepts to pragmatic and *ad hoc* decisions, he found kindred souls in these three.

These advisors comprised the think-tank behind the grand design that Erhard presented in his governmental address of 10 November 1965: the vision of the *Formierte Gesellschaft* (disciplined society) and the *Deutsches Gemeinschaftswerk* (common national undertaking). It is the first which is of particular interest here, since it describes what to Erhard appeared to be the ideal condition of an advanced, democratic society. Democracy in its present, disorderly shape was to be thoroughly reformed; the chaos of pluralist groups was to be transformed into a disciplined, quasi-corporatist state where the groups cooperated under the guidance of government experts for the benefit of the common good.[24] This meant that organised interests were no longer to represent and promote group egotisms, but instead they were to be the instruments through which government would teach their members the kind of behaviour necessary for the attainment of the common good.

In part, the concept resembles what political scientists, more than ten years later, were to describe as 'neo-corporatism'. However, the latter visualises a system in which major interest groups have a decisive say in societal decision-making and are acknowledged partners of governments (hence the concept of 'tripartism' in which business associations, trade unions and the government negotiate policies). Neo-corporatist systems are, therefore, basically bargaining systems. Erhard's *Formierte Gesellschaft* did not conceive of pressure groups as the government's partners, nor did it acknowledge group interests to be legitimate. Rather it conceptualised interest organisations as mere 'shells', useful only in so far as they might be the means through which the interests of society as a whole could be transmitted to the people. It was not a bargaining system,

---

24. For details see Erhard's speeches of 31 March 1965 (on the CDU party conference in Düsseldorf) and 10 November 1965 (in the Bundestag), *Gesellschaftspolitische Kommentare*, no. 13/14, 1965; Reinhard Opitz, 'Der grosse Plan der CDU. Die "Formierte Gesellschaft" ', *Blätter für deutsche und internationale Politik*, no. 9/1965.

but basically an authoritarian conception that sought to break the
'rule of pressure groups' and to reinstate 'the state' as the principal
and decisive political actor.[25]

Though this concept was, in principle, an assault on all pressure
groups, the BDI, interestingly enough, kept a surprisingly low profile in the debate. This may be explained by the fact that the concept
visualised a leading role for industry. Moreover, the *Formierte
Gesellschaft* might have provided an instrument to chasten the
unions. In the event, however, the grand design was never put into
practice.

While Adenauer had dealt personally and pragmatically with
organised interests, Erhard dealt with them on a conceptual basis
– which is to say that as chancellor he did not deal with them
at all. Thus, the relationship between government and pressure
groups was restored to that intended by the statutes in that lobbyists approached government departments, rather than appealing
directly to the chancellor. The behaviour of lobbyists – particularly
of the business lobby – reflects their perception of who or what is
the centre of power. In the days of Adenauer, business people
shunned their sponsoring minister – Erhard – and went instead to
the chancellor. With Erhard as chancellor they found their way back
to the Economics Ministry, using their weight in the CDU as a
second line of influence. It was not altogether accidental that the
CDU's *Wirtschaftsrat*, an auxilliary party organisation representing
business interests, was founded in the early days of Erhard's
chancellorship, in December 1963. Nor did this spearhead of
industry within the party remain inactive when the party élite
prepared Erhard's downfall as a chancellor.

Confrontation and Cooperation: the Social Democratic Chancellors

During the Grand Coalition and for most of Willy Brandt's chancellorship, the business community quite naturally approached not
the chancellor but the Economics Ministry. Where their interests
were concerned, they quite rightly judged the minister, Karl Schiller,
to be the centre of power. Neither Kurt-Georg Kiesinger nor Willy
Brandt showed any interest in economic matters.[26] However, they

25. See Klaus Hildebrand, *Von Erhard zur Grossen Koalition 1963–69*, Stuttgart:
    DVA, 1984, pp. 162ff., 167ff.
26. Willy Brandt was said to evince 'an ostentatious lack of interest in all matters of
    economic and fiscal policy': Arnulf Baring, *Machtwechsel. Die Ära Brandt-
    Scheel*, 2nd edn, Stuttgart: DVA, 1982, p. 655.

gave Schiller enough support and discretion to enable him to develop a Keynesian system of *Globalsteuerung* (global guidance) which was entirely new to Germany. Its purpose was to come to grips with the business cycle generally and the 1967 recession in particular. He invented the 'contingency budget', steering (federal) public investment. Business thus had an inducement to be on good terms with him.

Schiller also introduced *Konzertierte Aktion*, vaguely reminiscent of Erhard's *Formierte Gesellschaft*. This was a tripartite arrangement between business associations, trade unions and government, designed to streamline incomes policy. The institution has since become the model for theorists of neo-corporatism, although it did not long outlast Schiller's days as economics minister.

Kiesinger's chief role as 'mediation agency' between the partners of the Grand Coalition left him little room or energy to busy himself with mediation between interest groups as well; while Brandt's major interest lay in foreign policy, above all in achieving a reconciliation between Germany and the East European nations. This over-riding task led him to distance himself from day-to-day domestic politics. Aloof from interest group politics, his charisma and the high esteem in which he was held prevented those groups which might have felt marginalised or neglected from voicing open discontent. In particular, the trade unions, historic allies of the SPD, had sufficient reason to feel ill treated. During the 1967 recession and the early years of *Konzertierte Aktion* they had been persuaded to forego wage increases in the interests of the economy as a whole. With the restoration of economic growth and business profitability, however, their claims for social symmetry went unheeded. In 1969 and 1973 workers reacted with wild-cat strikes, while union leaders still felt bound to the *Konzertierte Aktion* and remained loyal to the government.

In contrast to the early years of the Adenauer era, union leaders could not 'go to the chancellor', for he was plainly not interested. Facing the dilemma of how to deal with 'their' government, which on the one hand had to be supported, but which on the other hand failed to deliver support for their claims, the unions responded with a strategy of 'limited conflict'. In 1974, the public sector workers' union ÖTV launched a strike aimed partly against the government itself (thus adding to the problems which led to Brandt's resignation).[27] Subsequently, in 1977, the trade unions left *Konzertierte*

27. See Frank Grube and Gerhard Richter (eds), *Der SPD-Staat*, Munich: Piper, 1977, p. 87; interview with ÖTV president Heinz Kluncker, *Der Spiegel*, no. 44/75, 27 Oct. 1975, pp. 46ff.

Aktion, bitter at economic policies which appeared closer to employer interests than to their own objectives. While some policy initiatives originated from FDP Economics Minister Hans Friderichs, some of the blows which estranged the labour movement from the Social–Liberal government came from the chancellor himself. When, after the 1976 election, Minister of Labour Walter Arendt resigned, Scmidt appointed Herbert Ehrenberg, without the customary consultation with the DGB.[28]

The Ehrenberg appointment was indicative of the distant relationship between Schmidt and the trade unions. Another example was the chancellor's handling of the sensitive issue of pension adjustments. According to press reports,[29] union leaders had been at the chancellor's bungalow for discussions on the night when SPD and FDP coalition negotiators had come to terms over the postponement of a promised increase in pensions. The SPD had previously committed itself to a 10 per cent increase, and the issue was close to traditional trade union concerns. Discussions had ranged over the pensions issue, yet the chancellor had given no indication of this *volte face*. This was by no means the only instance of Schmidt sacrificing trade union concerns without prior consultation, a habit which led to a progressive souring of relations between the trade unions and the Schmidt government. Ultimately, it has been argued, the consequent loss of faith in the SPD amongst its core clientele contributed to the electoral decomposition of the party.

Whilst SPD chancellors distanced themselves from the trade unions, their relationships with business interests were often acutely strained. This was particularly true of Brandt. Preoccupied with *Ostpolitik*, Brandt's full attention was never focused on economic policy, allowing policy differences in the cabinet to go unresolved. Conflict surfaced between Economics Minister Schiller and Finance Minister Alex Möller, the latter urging fiscal discipline and resigning when Schiller refused to accept his exhortations. Subsequently, as 'super-minister' presiding over both the Economics and the Finance Ministries and by now converted to a tight fiscal course which left him in a minority in the cabinet, Schiller also tendered his resignation. These vicissitudes of economic policy, and the chancellor's apparent inability to exercise cabinet authority, exposed Brandt to the hostility of business interests. In addition, his hands-off style and identification with the Social Democratic reform agenda left ministers a free hand to introduce programmes, many of which

28. See the bitter complaint of DGB president Heinz Oskar Vetter, in *Der Spiegel*, no. 50/76, 6 Dec. 1976, pp. 85ff.
29. See *Frankfurter Rundschau*, 5 Jan. 1977.

incurred expenditure commitments. Finally, business interests were appalled at Brandt's tolerance of the SPD left and its rhetoric of 'testing the capacity of the economy to bear tax burdens'.[30]

Brandt's isolation from the business community was exacerbated by his predisposition (which he shared with Erhard) to take advice from writers and journalists rather than practitioners. Moreover, there was still a considerable social distance between industrialists and Social Democratic politicians. Business people like Philip Rosenthal, who expressed public support for Brandt, were rare exceptions. More significantly, in contrast to the CDU, the SPD was not dependent upon corporate donations. Business associations thus lacked the usual sanctions against the government, and responded to this new experience in November 1971 with a press campaign under the slogan 'We can no longer keep silent', coupled with an assault against 'the union state'.[31] It has been suggested also that business interests backed CDU efforts to win over parliamentary deputies from the government parties in order to erode the government's majority in the Bundestag. These campaigns continued until the motion of no confidence against Chancellor Willy Brandt was defeated in spring 1972.

This defeat did not end the business associations' strategy of confrontation, but led instead to a change of tactics. The government could not be brought down, but it could be undermined in the all-important field of economic policy until it 'saw reason'. Circumstances were favourable for such a strategy. After the 1973 oil crisis, the economy slid into an ever-deepening slump. Growing unemployment exacerbated the government's dependence on the goodwill of the business community. From September 1974, the government made various attempts to boost the economy, with programmes of public investment and premiums for private investment.[32] However, the instruments deployed by Schiller with such success in 1967 now failed to elicit the intended upturn. Keynesian economics was denounced by virtually all the business associations as futile, so long as the government was unwilling to create a climate favourable for private business. By this they meant tax reductions and, above all, a retreat from the Social Democrats' reform programme. The confrontation escalated to the point where an 'investment strike' was openly threatened.

---

30. See the respective demands of left-wing politicians at the SPD Conference on Taxes, November 1971.
31. See Institut der deutschen Wirtschaft (ed.), *Auf dem Weg in den Gewerkschaftsstaat?*, 2nd edn, Cologne: DVA, 1974.
32. For the following see Heidrun Abromeit, 'Interessendurchsetzung in der Krise', *Aus Politik und Zeitgeschichte*, B 11/1977, pp. 15–37.

Upon assuming the chancellorship, Schmidt's response was a combination of admonishment and conciliation. In a speech before the annual conference of the Federation of German Employers' Associations (BDA) in December 1975, Schmidt invited employers, between biting criticisms and heavy irony, to reconsider their stance towards the Social-Liberal government, to drop their posture of studied pessimism, and to mend their own public image.[33] The lecture was similar in style to that delivered a few weeks previously to the DGB, emphasising discipline and the unions' duty to support the government.[34]

Schmidt had already begun to ring the changes in the political climate demanded by business. After discreet talks between his confidants and leading members of the BDI, he invited a group of carefully selected bankers and industrialists to accompany him in October 1975 to China and the United States. In November he accepted an invitation from the BDI president Hans-Günther Sohl to talk to about 100 managers of Germany's biggest firms. These blandishments, assisted by the intermediary efforts of FDP ministers (above all Hans Friderichs), eventually broke the ice. Business leaders and bankers (Ernst-Wolfgang Mommsen of Krupp AG, Edzard Reuter of Daimler-Benz, Jürgen Ponto of the Dresdner Bank) let it be known that they belonged to the circle of the chancellor's advisers. Peter von Siemens even conceded that in some respects industry 'could not wish for a better chancellor'.[35]

It may be supposed that the chancellor's influential allies, such as Bundesbank president Karl Klasen and his ex-colleagues in the Deutsche Bank, had paved the way for this change of atmosphere. Moreover, Schmidt thought along business lines, comparing his role as chancellor to that of a company manager. As 'managing director of the Federal Republic', his task was to direct the 'firm' efficiently.[36] Unlike Brandt or Erhard, he did not follow grand designs and he was ready to agree to compromises. Like Adenauer, he was a pragmatist who avoided alienating powerful groups. More than any of his predecessors, Schmidt impressed the business community by his unassuming air of administrative competence.

The change was not merely one of style. Chancellor and Economics Minister paid the price the business associations had named for their compliance with the government's economic policy, withdrawing or reducing the scope of key reform projects. The 1974 government bill on workers' participation, the biggest bone of con-

33. See *Frankfurter Rundschau*, 12 Dec. 1975.
34. *Der Spiegel*, no. 42/75, 12 Oct. 1975, p. 32.
35. *Der Spiegel*, no. 44/75, 27 Oct. 1975, p. 44; no. 48/75, 24 November 1975, p. 38.
36. In an interview with *Die Zeit*, 22 Aug. 1980.

tention between the SPD and industry, was amended in line with the employers' wishes, which meant dropping the principle of parity representation. (Nevertheless, the employers fought the law in the Constitutional Court.) Another controversial piece of legislation, on industrial training, was modified, and a planned reform of the entire system of vocational training was abandoned. The package was rounded off with provisions for reducing corporate tax burdens. The unions, meanwhile, retreated in the face of rising unemployment and agreed to exercise discipline and restraint.

The new spirit of cooperation between the Schmidt government and business interests was consolidated with the restoration of economic growth from 1976. This was the era of *Modell Deutschland*, and some SPD ministers visualised the extension of cooperation into other policy areas, in particular industrial, structural and 'high-tech' policy. But the honeymoon did not last very long. New conflicts arose, over nuclear energy and environmental policy, for instance, on which the chancellor, as his business friends noted with some misgivings, did not see eye to eye with his party, or even with some of his cabinet. Old confrontations reappeared, as the economy faltered around 1980 and the government tried to force investment programmes upon an unwilling industry. Ultimately, Schmidt's personal accord with business leaders could not save him from the consequences of his loss of control over his party. Business associations decided that their interests would be better served by a party which caused less trouble and which had no strong links with trade unions or other movements with interests antithetical to their own. When it became apparent that Schmidt had lost his previously strong grip on the SPD, business associations, leading FDP politicians and even the Bundesbank looked towards a change of government and chancellor.

Although Schmidt restored the chancellorship to its status as the undisputed centre of power,[37] it does not appear that lobbyists naturally 'went to the chancellor' as they did in the Adenauer era. Direct contact seems, on the whole, to have been limited to two groups, but with a decisive distinction. While the trade unions were more or less summoned to the chancellor's office (or to his private residence) to receive instructions as to where their duties lay, business leaders were courted with concessions to win them over to his side. In both cases, however, it was less a case of interest groups 'going to the chancellor' than of the chancellor inviting them for his own purposes.

---

37. See Wolfgang Jäger, 'Von der Kanzlerdemokratie zur Koordinationsdemokratie', *Zeitschrift für Politik*, 35, 1/1985, pp. 25ff.

Schmidt's strategy of disciplining the unions and winning the support of business met with only short-term success. The consensus which he achieved in the middle 1970s was fragile and was not born of conviction. Ultimately the result was frustration in the trade unions, arising out of broken promises concerning reform and 'social symmetry', and a realisation among business interests that it was not worth their while to carry on with a difficult partner when a much easier one was available. Some observers have speculated upon whether the Schmidt government would not have been wiser to have adhered to its old alliance with the trade unions.[38] Alienating them after 1976 meant that there was little to counterbalance the political influence of 'big business'. It also weakened the SPD's position in the coalition. While the FDP was backed by industry, the Social Democrats lacked equivalent supportive patronage.

Kohl as 'Adenauer's Grandson'?

Of all German chancellors, Schmidt's successor Helmut Kohl probably had the most intimate connections with the world of organised interests. At the same time that he embarked on his political career as a member of the parliament of Rheinland-Pfalz in 1959, he began a ten-year term as secretary of the *Landesverband Chemische Industrie Rheinland-Pfalz* (Chemical Industry Association)[39] which he ended only when he was elected minister-president of Rheinland-Pfalz in 1969. In this capacity he was a kind of lobbyist himself, paid by a pressure group to represent its interests in parliament.

Since then, Kohl has been good friends with a number of leading members of the business world, including Hanns-Martin Schleyer (the BDA president who was murdered in 1977), the Flick manager Eberhard von Brauchitsch (who played a prominent part in the protracted affair over illegal party funding) and the chairman of the Deutsche Bank, Alfred Herrhausen (also murdered, in 1989). The latter especially seems to have played a significant role as economic advisor to Kohl. Of course, as chairman of a party heavily dependent on donations from industry, Kohl was bound to be quite close to the major donors. Not surprisingly, those donors formed a habit of going either directly to the chancellor or to his confidants[40] whenever they saw the necessity to do so.

After Kohl won the constructive vote of no confidence in October

---

38. See Carola Schulz, *Der gezähmte Konflikt*, Opladen: Westdeutscher Verlag, 1984, pp. 220ff.
39. See Werner Maser, *Helmut Kohl*, Berlin: Ullstein, 1990, pp. 75ff.
40. *Frankfurter Rundschau*, 1 Sept. 1990.

1982, industry supported the chancellor in every possible way. The business associations immediately made plain their view that the climate for investment had considerably improved. When Kohl fought his first election as chancellor in March 1983 they made it equally plain that new investment would be seriously endangered should the SPD return to power: projects would be withheld until 6 March and cancelled in case of an SPD victory. Never before, observed *Der Spiegel*, had the employers' lobby cooperated so closely in an election campaign with the CDU.[41] For its part, the government was not slow in fulfilling its pledge to reduce corporate taxation.

The extent to which the chancellor personally took steps to satisfy his business clientele is unclear. It appears, however, that he was instrumental in the government's decision in 1988–9 to exempt the Daimler-Benz merger with the armaments group Messerschmitt-Bölkow-Blohm (MBB) from control under federal competition law. He seems also to have intervened personally to shield the Howaldts-werke-Deutsche Werft against the consequences of its sanctions-breaching submarine deal with South Africa in 1984–5. It seems likely, too, that he backed the Volkswagen attempt to win a major order from the *Bundeswehr* in 1988. Moreover, attempts to reform the financing of medical care have been undermined at times by chancellor intervention, behind which the hidden hand of the pharmaceutical industry may be detected.

Despite his generally close relationship with industry and commerce, Kohl has not been immune from criticism from this quarter. Irritation at the chancellor's autocratic and sometimes inconsistent style of leadership, and its uneven results, spilled over in the late 1980s from the party to the business community. The BDA lamented the absence of a 'really solid market-oriented policy', and Edzard Reuter of Daimler-Benz censured the 'appalling lack of competence in economic policy'. Some leading members of the BDI went so far as to launch an 'offensive against ignorance and amateurism in economics'.[42] It was Kohl's good fortune that unification spared him from the consequences of industry's dissatisfaction with his performance.

On occasions, Kohl has been over-attentive to lobby groups. The refugees' associations, for instance, were behind his reluctance to give unconditional guarantees to Poland over German's eastern borders during the unification process. The chancellor's attempts to pacify the refugee associations were part of a manoeuvre designed

41. *Der Spiegel*, no. 6/83, 7 Feb. 1983, p. 19.
42. *Der Spiegel*, no. 5/88, 1 Feb. 1988, pp. 28ff.

to staunch the flow of CDU voters to the Republican Party. However, it brought him into conflict with his foreign minister and threatened to stall unification negotiations with the Allied powers.

The farmers' association was notably successful (as it has been with virtually all post-war governments) in repelling threats of subsidy-reduction. However, its president, Konstantin von Heeremann, was personally disappointed in his aspiration to be appointed agriculture minister. The bid was thwarted when Kohl was forced to bow to party considerations, appointing a figure from the Bavarian CSU instead.

The trade unions have been conspicuously distant from Kohl, regarding him as the 'chancellor of industry'. In the climate of political polarisation following the *Wende* of 1982–3, union leaders refused any meeting with the chancellor, and subsequently the relationship between Kohl and the DGB has remained arctic. Making little attempt to mend fences, Kohl publicly derided union policies, in particular the campaign for a reduced working week, as 'stupid and foolish'. It took almost a decade to overcome the total breakdown of relations. In 1991 Kohl addressed the engineering union IG Metall on the occasion of its centenary celebrations. The chancellor's speech was an exercise in studied caution, and his audience was under injunction from the union leadership to repress its protests.

The nadir of Kohl's relationship with the trade unions came in spring 1992, when the government was drawn into a bitter industrial dispute with the public sector workers' union ÖTV. In the face of inflationary pressures related to unification, the public sector pay round was brought forward with the intention of establishing a bench-mark of wage restraint for subsequent private sector negotiations.

The industrial conflict which followed was the most acute and extensive since the early 1970s, paralysing public services and creating an atmosphere of crisis which Kohl hoped would have a salutory effect upon subsequent pay bargaining. The calculation misfired, however, when after eleven days of strikes the government was forced to back down in a settlement in excess of one that it had previously rejected.[43] Since then Kohl has been more circumspect, eschewing confrontation in favour of a more conciliatory approach and calling for 'concerted action' by both sides of industry to meet the economic challenges of the post-unification period.

43. Stephen Padgett, 'The New German Economy' in G. Smith, W.E. Paterson, P. Merkl and S. Padgett (eds), *Developments in German Politics*, Basingstoke: Macmillan, 1992.

are ready with seemingly impartial expert advice. Nearly all chancellors have had such outside advisors, amongst whom bankers have figured particularly prominently. Most studies on organised interest in Western democracies demonstrate a structural asymmetry between business and the trade unions in their capacity to influence government policy. The German chancellor's relationship with organised interests merely accentuates this general asymmetry.

7

THE CHANGING PARAMETERS OF THE CHANCELLORSHIP

Gordon Smith

A Choice of Approaches

How can the performance of a chancellor best be evaluated? There is no easy answer to this question, since the number of variables is considerable, as are the criteria on which judgements can be based. Variables such as the public standing of a chancellor and his rapport with the electorate are obviously relevant, as are his relationships with his own party and his ability to manage it. Beyond that there is the structure of the party system: is it conducive to the formation of stable government? If it is not, then – whatever the personal qualities of the chancellor – his government may be short-lived and 'success' will consist chiefly in being able to keep a fragile coalition intact. In German circumstances the 'coalition variable' has almost always been a key consideration for chancellors, and the ability to manage the coalition successfully has proved to be almost as important as being able to manage the chancellor's own party.

Electoral and party relationships are central to making assessments about chancellor performance. However, the support they give to a chancellor depends on the perceived success of the government in implementing its policies and in dealing with problems as they arise. A chancellor's freedom of action is, moreover, limited by constitutional constraints – for instance, by the restrictions of the federal system and by the jurisdiction of the Federal Constitutional Court. Nevertheless, success in managing government is related to factors over which the chancellor does have a large measure of control. For example, the quality of advice supplied to the chancellor by the *Kanzleramt* (Chancellor's Office) depends critically on the chancellor's selection of its personnel, and the *Kanzleramt* has become a vital instrument for the chancellor to direct policy and to secure the coordination of government.

This listing of variables could be extended without too much difficulty, but it may be sufficient at this point to refer to five major dimensions: those relating to the constitutional position of the chancellor; the electorate; his party; coalition and government management; and to chancellor prerogatives in particular spheres of policy. These can be described as the chancellor's principal 'areas of resource'.[1] How well they are exploited depends in part on the abilities of the individual chancellor, but their availability will vary from one period to another, and a 'resource' may in certain conditions turn out to have a negative rather than a positive value. The advantage of using an approach such as this is that it provides a systematic way of evaluating a chancellor's performance, and it also enables direct comparisons to be made between chancellors.

A quite different approach, but one which is also in a way 'systematic', is the use of the 'chancellor democracy' model. This model has been applied to make explicit comparisons between Konrad Adenauer on the one hand, and one or more of his successors on the other. There can be few parliamentary systems where the influence of one head of government has been so pervasive over a long period as that of Adenauer in Germany. Over the years he has provided a stable point of reference for analysing the powers and role of the chancellor and he is the one against whom the performance of all others has been judged.

'Chancellor democracy' refers in various ways to Adenauer's style of governing: the rapport he had with the electorate, his patriarchical and authoritarian image, his disposition to take 'lonely decisions', the independence he maintained from his own party, the domination he exercised over his ministers, his stubbornness (and usually success) in pursuing favoured lines of policy, and the key part he took in dealing with the demands made by interest groups: 'Adenauer personally acted as the master integrator who satisfied group demands as he saw fit.'[2] All these attributes, and probably others, can be conflated to give a picture of 'chancellor democracy' that is far removed from the normal working of parliamentary democracy.

Ironically, the Basic Law itself does not endow a chancellor with such sweeping powers as would result in or justify a chancellor democracy. The chancellor's constitutional powers are not significantly different from those of other heads of government in parliamentary systems. Indeed, the constitutional constraints facing German chancellors appear to limit their freedom of action to a far greater extent than any restrictions placed on, say, British prime ministers. The latter do not have to work within the rules of a federal

---

1. G. Smith, 'The Resources of a German Chancellor', in G. Jones (ed.), *West European Prime Ministers*, London: Frank Cass, 1991, pp. 48–61.
2. P. Merkl, 'Interests and Adenauer's Survival as Chancellor', in M. Dogan and R. Rose (eds), *European Politics: A Reader*, London: Macmillan, 1971, p. 372.

system or deal with a powerful upper house, such as the Bundesrat representing the interests of the *Länder* governments; nor do they have to face a constitutional court armed with sweeping powers or a central bank charged with implementing an independent monetary policy.

It is reasonable to query what kinds of comparison are implied in using chancellor democracy as a method. Does it imply a positive or a pejorative judgement on chancellor authority? Or is it to be used as a basis for a neutral evaluation? If the latter, the model has to be taken apart so as to isolate the individual factors. But in that case the outcome is bound to be defective, since it neglects the central characteristic of chancellor democracy: that all the ingredients (electoral, party, governmental, policy) were for Adenauer strongly inter-linked. He was a virtuoso performer, using his strengths in one field to consolidate his position in others. There is no objection to applying the label 'chancellor democracy' to a large part of the Adenauer era, but it is not very helpful to allow the concept to travel much further.

There is, too, a danger that comparisons of this kind can be misleadingly static because they take little account of different circumstances prevailing during different incumbencies. The importance of changing circumstances becomes apparent in looking at the contrasting records of chancellors in the Weimar Republic in comparison with those in the Federal Republic. If chancellors had been expended at the same rate as during the Weimar Republic, there would have been no fewer than forty-two chancellors since 1949, instead of six. The high turnover during Weimar reflected the acute polarisation and fragmentation of the party system, which in turn reflected the social and economic circumstances of Weimar Germany. Society was heavily divided, the economy was always fragile, Germany's international position was never properly secured, and the constitutional provisions gave little support to the chancellor. These features persisted throughout the life of the Weimar Republic, and no individual chancellor could expect to rise much above a short-lived mediocrity. The contrasts with the experience of chancellors in the Federal Republic are striking on all counts. The two large, moderate parties have been dominant from the beginning, thus allowing long periods of stable government. The parties have drawn their strength from the high level of social cohesion and the strong performance of the economy. From the outset, the Federal Republic was firmly secured within an international alliance system, and the Basic Law was designed to give chancellors maximum support, compatible with the federal and parliamentary system of government. These favourable influences have all persisted, and –

given relative continuity in the basic circumstances of the Federal Republic – the performances of individual chancellors are more easily compared. The major exception is Adenauer, and it is important to appreciate how his impact marked out the path taken by his successors.

Adenauer and the Concept of Strategic Change

There is no doubt that a gulf separates Adenauer from other chancellors. In the context of the early post-war years and with the problems of making the transition to democracy, the demands on the political system differed substantially from those made when the democratic system was fully established, since they required quite fundamental choices to be made.

As a way of emphasising the long-term significance of decisions made during the early and critical post-war years, Dahrendorf introduced the concept of a 'strategic change'.[3] In the West German case these decisions proved to be strategic in two senses. First, the changes they introduced had permanent effects on the functioning of the whole system. Secondly, once they had become fully institionalised, any subsequent departure or reversal became increasingly difficult to make. None of the strategic changes (or choices) made in the late 1940s was a necessary corollary of the democratic order, although in fact they were to become strongly supportive of it. In the field of international relations, Adenauer took the initiative of binding the Federal Republic firmly into the Western alliance system – politically as well as economically and strategically. Adenauer aimed not only at winning security for the Federal Republic, but also at gaining strength and sovereignty. The policies – and the motivation behind them – were for some years disputed by the SPD in opposition, but they were not challenged later by SPD chancellors, and Brandt's *Ostpolitik* did not result in a weakening of the Federal Republic's Western commitments.

The second strategic decision was the adoption of the doctrine of the social-market economy on the part of the Christian Democrats and its incorporation as the central plank of the socio-economic institutional order. The ramifications of this decision were far-reaching, since it laid the basis for the integration of a pronounced social dimension into the market system, and it proved to be an important factor in promoting industrial harmony. At first, the

3. R. Dahrendorf, *The Modern Social Conflict*, London: Weidenfeld and Nicolson, 1988. However, Dahrendorf is more concerned with strategic change as a function of positive social and economic policy rather than with all kinds of fundamental change.

ideology of the social market was the preserve of the CDU and was rejected by the SPD, but gradually, as the political implications of its success became apparent, the SPD accepted its tenets. The social-market philosophy secured a prominent place in orthodox thinking.

A third strategic choice for the Federal Republic, but not attributable to Adenauer, consisted in the provisions of the Basic Law which, taken together, make up the closely articulated system of checks and balances. These three elements – the Western commitments, the social-market economy and the Basic Law – formed the basis of the 'institutionalised consensus' that underpins the German political system. It was in the early phases of the republic, and largely due to the part played by Adenauer, that the essential parameters for later chancellors were put in place; not to observe them would be to threaten the established consensus.

Chancellors of Consolidation?

From several points of view, the whole period from the early 1960s until some point in the 1980s can be labelled a time of consolidation, following and building upon the strategic decisions of the Adenauer era. Adenauer's legacy was not an entirely comfortable one, and both Bracher and Pulzer draw attention to its uneven achievements. Thus, Bracher found that: 'The Adenauer era was a vital transitionary period. It succeeded in identifying the people with the system . . . however, primarily by excluding from discussion the basic policy questions – reunification and the eastern frontier.'[4] It was indeed the shelving of these two fundamental issues that affected the policy-making of chancellors for decades afterwards. Peter Pulzer, in commenting on Adenauer's political style and its consequences, concluded: 'In the short term the semi-competitive chancellor plebiscites may have inhibited the German citizen's growth of democratic self-confidence; in the long run the conventions of present-day German politics would be unthinkable without the first decade of "chancellor democracy".'[5] On this reckoning the unfinished business left over for the period of consolidation was to rectify the retarded development of a democratic political culture.

The consolidation took place after the strategic choices had been made, the institutional structures were becoming rooted and popu-

---

4. K. Bracher, *The German Dilemma*, London: Weidenfeld and Nicolson, 1973, p. 153.
5. P. Pulzer, 'Responsible Party Government in the German System', in H. Doring and G. Smith (eds), *Party Government and Political Culture in Western Germany*, London: Macmillan, 1982, p. 25.

lar attachment to the democratic system was growing. Evidence of consolidation provided by the development of the party system was also fairly conclusive: the concentration of the popular vote on the three parties of government, the high levels of electoral turnout, and the stability of governing coalitions throughout the 1970s and 1980s.

Admittedly, to describe a whole line of chancellors from Ludwig Erhard through to Helmut Schmidt as 'consolidators' does less than justice to the extent of their individual contributions; nor does it square too well with the fact that their incumbencies were punctuated by periodic crisis and uncertainty, which could convey a different impression of how the Federal Republic was developing. These reservations point to the need for caution in applying a broad-brush treatment: if the idea of consolidation is to be retained, it is necessary to give a differentiated account of the performance of individual chancellors. None the less, in retrospect and with an awareness of the dramatic changes brought about by German unification, a good case can be made for treating the years after Adenauer and before Kohl as a composite whole.

Erhard and Kiesinger, Adenauer's immediate successors, were essentially interim figures, although they paved the way for the SPD to come to office, and the SPD's entry to government signified an important phase of consolidation. The core of the post-Adenauer era is, in fact, represented by the two SPD chancellors, Willy Brandt and Helmut Schmidt, who between them led the governing coalitions from 1969 till 1982. Consolidation thus refers largely to the performance of the SPD in office during these years. In addition, account must be taken of three *prior* determinants of the party's outlook and behaviour: the acceptance of the doctrine of the social-market economy; the commitment to the policy of Western integration; and the readiness of the party to enter into coalition with the CDU or the FDP – well aware of the constraints involved – in order to show itself to be *regierungsfähig*, a responsible party of government. Taken together, these three determinants almost entirely robbed an SPD chancellor of the ability to promote radical initiatives for his government.

A major exception in Brandt's case was the launching of his *Ostpolitik*, and it was precisely this initiative that led to the sharp political polarisation in the 1970s, for on one level it rejected the part of Adenauer's foreign policy stance which implied a negative relationship with the Soviet bloc countries and the GDR. On another and more fundamental level, however, Brandt's initiative did not contradict Adenauer's basic premise: the unswerving alliance with the Western powers. The fact that the CDU subsequently came to accept the outcome of the *Ostpolitik* led to a greater stabilisation of the Federal Republic in the international system once the immediate crisis had passed.

In domestic politics the SPD had set out to make far-reaching social reforms, but in addition to the coalition constraints imposed by the Free Democrats the SPD continually found itself hemmed in by economic factors. For the party to maintain its hard-won image of being a responsible party of government, it was imperative to give precedence to economic and financial prudence, especially since the decade of the 1970s was dogged by international economic crisis. Thus, the SPD began to lose its reputation as a party of reform. For Schmidt, unlike Brandt, the constraints on the party's reform agenda seemed no great sacrifice; for Schmidt, 'the maintenance of economic security was given almost absolute priority over social and economic reform'.[6]

Chancellor Schmidt has frequently been characterised in terms of his 'managerial efficiency', for being a 'crisis manager' and for showing a reactive leadership style rather than an innovative one, particularly in relation to domestic politics. Effectively, the SPD and its chancellors were managing a political system and a socio-economic structure created and nurtured by the CDU since the foundation of the republic. The contribution of the SPD chancellors was to firm it up.

However, an over-emphasis on consolidation masks changes and tensions in German society which had a decisive influence upon the chancellor's position. The causes of tension were located on three levels. First, there was the increasing assertiveness of economic and social interests. Although their conflicts of interest are common in mature democracies, in German perceptions this 'new pluralism' appeared as an unwelcome threat to the consensual traditions of 'institutionalised pluralism', one of the hallmarks of the West German style. The second level of tension was located within the SPD itself and was already apparent towards the end of Brandt's chancellorship: the failure of the SPD to generate social reform caused unease and dissension among party activists. With Schmidt, these intra-party tensions became acute. Divisive issues, such as those concerning nuclear energy and support for NATO policy on nuclear weapons, increasingly alienated the rank-and-file of the party from Schmidt. The divisions within the SPD were a reflection of the changes taking place in German society as expressions of the 'new pluralism' – the rise of a variety of new social movements, especially the ecological and peace movements. The third level concerns the

6. S. Padgett and T. Burkett, *Political Parties and Elections in West Germany*, London: Hurst, 1986, p. 61.

changes in electoral behaviour and the effects on the party system. It was in the latter part of Schmidt's tenure that signs of electoral disaggregation became marked: a decline in electoral participation and in the aggregate vote for the major parties. Symptomatic of the changing aspirations and priorities affecting wide sections of German society was the rise of the Greens, based in the ecological movement but representative of the new social movements and their values as well.

As chancellor, Schmidt was generally popular and respected for his forceful style. Unlike Brandt, he was also skilled in coordinating the work of government, but also unlike Brandt, he lacked the ability (or inclination) to carry the SPD with him – the leadership of the party he left in Brandt's hands. The immediate cause of his fall from office in 1982 was the defection of the FDP to the CDU, but the downfall of Schmidt should also be related to his estrangement from the SPD. This in turn can be related to changes in German society, especially those sections whose sympathies lay with the political left. As a consolidator, Schmidt was still well suited to the needs of the Federal Republic up to the 1970s; by the 1980s, however, large sections of society were looking for something else. Schmidt's decline and fall can thus be explained in terms of the ending of the era of consolidation.

The Three 'Lives' of Chancellor Kohl

In analysing the long period of CDU government under Helmut Kohl, a totally different perspective is required. The Kohl chancellorship presents a number of problems of evaluation. Is Kohl merely a fortunate 'survivor', largely reliant upon the electoral weakness of the opposition? Or does he display some qualities which, if not in the mould of 'chancellor democracy', none the less point to strengths that other chancellors have lacked? Two final questions relate to the circumstances of the new Federal Republic: to what extent has unification redefined the role of the chancellor, and, if it has done so, what kinds of parallel are to be found with the early years of the republic?

When he first became chancellor in 1982, Kohl was intent on making a decisive break with the kinds of policy associated with SPD-led governments since 1969. Kohl argued that there should be a complete change in the direction of policies. The *Wendepolitik* was aimed, among other things, at reducing the levels of state intervention in economy and society. The problem was to cut state subsidies and government expenditure so as to redress the balance in favour of the market in a social-market economy that had seemingly

become tilted in favour of the 'social' element. Yet the impetus of
this policy quickly faltered, not primarily because of lack of purpose, but through the inherent tendency to immobilism in the German political and governmental system when radical changes in
policy are attempted. This feature in part results from the diffusion
of authority across the institutional structures of the Federal Republic, and the powerful consensus-inducing mechanisms that serve to
frustrate radical change. In part, too, it stems from the character of
the party system in Germany, which severely limits the available
choice of coalition partners. Douglas Webber, in examining the
limited achievements of Kohl's *Wendepolitik*, highlights the problems of coordination in the context of the German political system;
he concludes that they are due to

coalition government, containing parties and factions of parties seeking to
represent interests of clients with conflicting socio-economic interests; to
the existence of an idiosyncratic form of federalism which gives the state
governments a high capacity to veto policy initiatives which offend regional
interests as they define them; and to the presence of 'sectoral corporatism'
or collective 'self-administration', that is to say the negotiation of policy
between the government and a limited number of highly organised interests
which typically also play a central role in policy implementation and which
are normally privileged by the status quo.[7]

A consequence of these arrangements is that an active executive-
led consensus has to be mobilised if the natural inertia of the system
is to be overcome. Seen in this light, the problems encountered by
Kohl in trying to change the basic direction of government are more
readily understood. A charge of weak leadership would be appropriate if from the outset Kohl had been content to be a *laissez-
faire* chancellor, but, in view of the ambitions he had for the
Wendepolitik, this was hardly the case. Faced by the resistance of
entrenched interests, public and private, Kohl's government for-
feited its radical purpose. There are parallels here with the experience of the SPD in office and its failure – the obverse of the
CDU's – to promote radical social reform.

The decline in the public esteem with which Kohl was regarded
stemmed from a perceived deficiency of leadership qualities. Whilst
Schmidt was consistently more popular than his own party, for Kohl
the reverse was true. The need to accommodate the interests of the
two fractious coalition parties (the FDP and the CSU), and Kohl's
at times embarrassing performance at international level, eroded his

---

7. D. Webber, 'Kohl's *Wendepolitik* after a Decade', *German Politics*, vol. 1, no. 2,
   August 1992, pp. 149–80.

public standing. Kohl's survival was due largely to the buoyancy of the economy and to the poor showing of the SPD in both the 1983 and 1987 elections. The weak electoral performance of the CDU in 1987, with a drift to the FDP and an increase in the number of people who did not vote, contributes to a picture of the chancellor's party winning despite its lacklustre performance in office. Kohl's fortunes reached a nadir in the first part of 1989, with reverses in elections (*Land*, local and European) and losses to the right-wing Republicans. Following these setbacks, there were moves in the CDU to find a successor.

In his fight for survival, Kohl resorted to a string of populist measures, the most notable of which was a government reshuffle that included the ditching of the defence minister whom he had appointed only a few months earlier. Through this move Kohl bowed to popular resentment against NATO military exercises; it signalled a change of tack on the government's previously strong support for nuclear deterrence. Kohl also scrapped plans to increase the period of obligatory military service. Above all, though, Kohl's survival stemmed from his ability to reassert his control over the CDU, marginalising Lothar Späth, his principal rival, and sacking the party's secretary-general, Heiner Geissler. The removal of the latter, an advocate of liberal-centrism in the CDU, was a deliberate shift to the right on Kohl's part in order to counter the threat from the right-wing Republicans.

It can be doubted whether these concessions and tactics would have proved sufficient for long without the rapid collapse of the GDR and the sequence of events leading to unification. In most respects, the 'first life' of Chancellor Kohl was quite unremarkable. Given the extreme weakness of the SPD and the consequent imbalance in the party system, the impression is that the CDU won by default and largely despite Chancellor Kohl.

In the course of securing German unification, Kohl's reputation underwent a remarkable transformation. From being regarded as a rather ordinary, if astute, politician he emerged as a statesman of international calibre. There are differing evaluations of this 'second life' – a short one of little more than a year, from late 1989 till the all-German election of December 1990. One interpretation is that early on, as the communist régime was losing its grip, Kohl was one of the first to believe that the vision of a unified Germany could be brought to reality. Throughout the complex process of securing international agreement to bring the two states together, Kohl showed himself to be a determined and decisive leader. According to this viewpoint, he could even be counted as a chancellor comparable with Adenauer. A second, less favourable evaluation, however, is that Kohl's role was little more than instrumental to a process which had its own momentum and whose outcome was inevitable. According to this interpretation, the chancellor was an opportunist who saw that by playing the national card he could free himself from electoral and party pressures which a few months before had threatened to oust him. There is truth in both these conflicting explanations, but the overwhelming effect of the events of 1989–90 was to boost Kohl's popularity to an all-time high.

By the time of the all-German elections of December 1990, the euphoria of national unity had died away. Even though Kohl's coalition was returned with a comfortable majority, the CDU vote stagnated, at a time when circumstances could hardly have been more favourable: Kohl was the master-builder of a united Germany, and the SPD was quite unable to present itself as a credible alternative. The growing vulnerability of the chancellor and the CDU was shown in subsequent *Land* elections during 1991 and 1992, when there were heavy losses to the radical right. Kohl's newly enhanced international stature did little to help him in domestic politics. The rise of the radical right was symptomatic of a general discontent, in both eastern and western Germany, with the economic costs and social disruption of unification. Thus Kohl's 'third life' began to take on some of the characteristic features of the first one.

Unification as Strategic Change?

Does the third, post-unification 'life' of Chancellor Kohl mark a return in most essentials to the first one – or for that matter to the somewhat similar mould of SPD chancellors before him? This raises a second question about how the impact and consequences of German unification are to be assessed in the context of the development of the Federal Republic since 1949. Is the new Federal Republic fundamentally different from the old one?

At one extreme, unification can be treated as a fairly straightforward process of transition. Although uneven in many respects – since adjustments in the political system, society and economy occur at different speeds – the transition might be expected to lead to harmonisation on the basis of continuity with the existing order in western Germany. Taken literally, the outcome is simply the enlargement of the old Federal Republic. The transition itself could be prolonged; for instance, post-unification forecasts of how long it will take for the east German economy to catch up with the west tend to be pitched around the year 2020.[8] The difficulty with this

---

8. It would be misleading to take the year 2020 as an average forecast, since some scenarios take a more pessimistic view – for instance, seeing eastern Germany as

approach is that it takes insufficient account of the enormity of the changes signified by unification. Moreover, Kohl is associated with a 'soft' version of the transition that assumed a quick and trouble-free adjustment, a scenario which is now discredited.

At another extreme, unification may be regarded as involving a number of strategic changes. However, in this context, the idea of a 'strategy' as part of a 'grand design' is unsustainable. The manner in which unification came about, with Kohl reacting to the tide of events, precludes any notion of a pre-conceived plan. Rather, the 'strategic change model' rests upon the fact that one of the basic postulates of West German foreign policy, the absolute requirement of identification with the Western powers, simply became redundant with unification and the subsequent collapse of the Soviet Union. The fact that it is no longer operative means that Germany's foreign policy and security options have become varied and flexible. This new freedom, and the greater strength of a united Germany, places a far greater responsibility on the chancellor in determining and if necessary altering the guidelines of foreign policy.

Yet in other respects the irreversibility of the primary decisions made for the Federal Republic has not been undermined by unification. First, the entire structure and mechanisms of the Basic Law remained intact. This was a logical consequence of effecting unification by means of Article 23 rather than Article 146, which could have required the adoption of an entirely new constitution. Secondly, the social-market economy was transplanted wholesale and immediately on to eastern Germany, even though many observers at the time warned of the harmful consequences. Kohl was intent on safeguarding both pillars of the Federal Republic, and in this he was helped by two factors. One was the clamour of popular movements in the east which hastened unification and made it impossible to give careful consideration to alternative approaches. The second factor was the dominance of the international dimension in securing unification: the negotiations with the four Allied powers, and the close liaison and treaty-making with the authorities in the GDR. The international nature of policy-making during 1990 inevitably centred on the chancellor and his advisers, precluding wider participation. With the significant exception of the Federal Republic's increased international prominence and the added status accruing

---

a 'northern Mezzogiorno', or (even more drastic) picturing the west German economy being dragged down by the burden of financing the east. On the scenarios, see Jan Priewe, 'Wirtschaftswunder – Deindustrialisierung – Rückschlag für Westdeutschland? Zur politischen Ökonomie der deutsche Vereinigung', in B. Muszynski (ed.), *Deutsche Vereinigung. Probleme der Integration und Identifikation*, Opladen: Leske and Budrich, 1991.

to the chancellor, unification has not altered the established features of the Federal Republic. Does this mean that Kohl 'Mark 3' is really a reversion to Kohl 'Mark 1'? Much must depend on how the Federal Republic develops over the next few years, on whether the new Federal Republic is significantly different from the old one. However, there are already several indications that the tasks facing the chancellor and the role he may have to adopt are different from those of pre-unification Germany.

Chancellors in Post-Unification Germany

Chancellor Kohl's prediction that any economic difficulties of unification would be quickly overcome were soon proved false, and it was no surprise that disappointment with the outcome was widely expressed in both east and west Germany. The government faced a whole range of problems requiring a new style of political leadership. There are *four* areas, domestic and international, where the role of the chancellor appears to be principally affected. First, the strength of the party system has been eroded, weakening the supportive infrastructure on which the chancellor depends. Secondly, an intensification of distributional conflict makes 'the politics of allocation' harder to manage. Thirdly, pressures on the federal system add complexity to the policy-making environment in which the chancellor is the pivot. Finally, Germany's new foreign policy responsibilities place a heavy burden upon the chancellor.

The chancellor and the party system. One of the most striking features of unification was the way in which the existing west German party system was successfully grafted on to the east, thus avoiding fragmentation, unstable coalitions and the need to deal with different party systems in the two parts of Germany. In these respects it seems that the chancellor faces no greater difficulties in asserting his position in managing the coalition and in dealing with his own party than he did in the past. However, although the problems are largely the same, they have intensified. The apparently secular decline of the *Volkspartei* as an agent of social and political integration, evident since the mid-1970s, continued during the 1990 federal elections. If this tendency were to become more pronounced, it would make coalition formation and maintenance far more difficult. In the early years of the Federal Republic, Adenauer also had to contend with a multi-party system, but then the CDU was on a sharply rising electoral trend and consequently Adenauer secured an easy dominance over the party. Kohl's supremacy over the CDU is of a different character, arising more from astute management than from an ability to hold the party's electorate together. There is, too, an endemic tension between the more liberal, modernising wing of the party and its conservative-national elements. Kohl's centrality in the unification process placed him in a position to keep a grip on these two tendencies in the CDU. However, this style of leadership carries inevitable risks:

Success on these terms made the CDU more dependent than ever on Kohl himself and the image of his government, threatening to start the old cycle: electoral stagnation for the CDU, elite level debate over the party's identity, and thus to further problems in holding voter support.[9]

An SPD chancellor could hardly expect to be in any stronger position, since the decline in the party's electoral base has been far more serious than any fall in support for the CDU. Moreover, although in opposition the problem of reconciling the new and old left tendencies within the SPD have receded, they would be certain to return if an SPD-led government had to fashion policies to deal with the economic problems of post-unification Germany.

Chancellors from both major parties have almost always had to work within the constraints set by coalition government. Since unification there is also the added restriction of having to pay attention to the requirements of the 'constitutional coalition': the need for a special two-thirds parliamentary majority in order to amend the Basic Law. On the one hand, the circumstances of present-day Germany necessitate fairly radical decisions; on the other, the government is increasingly reliant on a broad cross-party consensus. Attempts by the chancellor to put his policy-making authority into practice are susceptible to the veto of the junior coalition partner. Thus, the FDP was able to frustrate Kohl's attempts to implement constitutional changes concerning political asylum and German participation in UN peace-keeping operations, arguing that a broad inter-party consensus – the constitutional coalition – should be formed. In some circumstances the drive to reach a consensus can lead to policy immobilism, and this frustration was given as the prime reason for the resignation of one CDU cabinet minister in 1992:

The government's incapacity is programmed in advance because party conference resolutions are treated as imperative mandates that have to be respected in coalition deliberations. The wearing down of the large, majority coalition party, the CDU, and the constraints imposed on the chancellor

9. C. Clemens, 'Helmut Kohl's CDU and German Unification: The Price of Success', *German Politics and Society*, no. 22, Spring 1991, pp. 33–41.

make quick decision-making impossible. Yet at the present time that is what is needed and what others expect from Germany.[10]

It is difficult to avoid the conclusion that the coalition constraint is a far greater check on a chancellor now than it was in the past, and grounds for divisions in the government on matters of principle or interest will multiply. In these conditions, it is perhaps insufficient for a chancellor to be a consensus-seeking coordinator. It may be argued that it is necessary for him to reassert his prime responsibility for government policy and the composition of government. The FDP – continuously in office since 1969 – takes for granted its own presence in government and insists upon its 'right' of appointment to key ministerial positions. It did so over the appointment of Klaus Kinkel to replace Hans-Dietrich Genscher as Foreign Minister in 1992. A more glaring example occurred in 1993 with the replacement of the Economics Minister Jurgen Möllemann by Gunter Rexrodt. Much to Kohl's annoyance, the latter let it be known that it was only a matter of form for the chancellor actually to appoint him. This is a good illustration of the extent to which 'coalition dependence' has become the dominant mode, at the expense of a chancellor-led governmental system.

The new 'politics of allocation'. In an analysis of the 1990 federal elections, Herbert Kitschelt distinguished three themes that parties use as a focus of their electoral appeal: politics as involving the principles of 'democratic procedures'; politics as the 'definition of citizenship'; and 'politics as allocation'.[11] The first theme became largely the property of the Greens in making 'the linkage between the *form* of democratic procedures and the *substance* of authoritative allocation in key policy areas'. In 1990 the CDU was able to exploit the national issue, while the SPD made the error of framing the issue in terms of allocative politics instead of following the CDU's line. Kitschelt commented:

In some ways, voters witnessed a unique inversion of political front-lines. For once, the Social Democrats appeared to be less eager to engage in economic redistribution, whereas the Christian Democrats and Liberals, based on a patriotic appeal, projected the image of being the more generous political parties.

Although largely accurate, this assessment requires some qualifi-

10. From the resignation statement made by Christian Schwarz-Schilling, federal Postal Minister, *Die Welt*, 15 Dec. 1992.
11. H. Kitschelt, 'The 1990 German Federal Election and the National Unification', *West European Politics*, vol. 14, no. 4, October 1991, pp. 121–48.

cation. It is unlikely that Kohl was aware of the extent of the 'generosity' that had to be contemplated. Moreover, he would certainly have been wary of possible conflict if the question of how to pay for unification had had to be answered by his own party.

In the aftermath of unification, the question, 'Who pays, and how much?' still has to be answered. According to Kitschelt, the 1960s and 1970s saw allocative politics reaching a peak, but without resulting in widespread conflict. This was a period of strong economic growth, in sharp contrast to the Federal Republic in the early 1990s. It is the combination of slow growth and rising public expenditure which provides the potential for political conflict. Many social and economic interests are likely to be adversely affected by the inescapable expenditure required to bring the economy and living conditions in the east up to a par with those in the west. On what terms, and with what possible effects on the chancellor's position, are the new politics of allocation likely to be resolved?

Kohl's solution was the wide-ranging 'solidarity pact' concluded in March 1993 as a means of financing recovery in the east, without placing even greater strain on public finances or risking high levels of inflation. In effect, the solidarity pact represented an ambitious attempt to forge a long-lasting 'super consensus', including the main opposition party, and could even be seen as a hidden, all-party coalition. It was designed to ensure that responsibility would be widely shared, but – as with the restrictive effects of the formal coalition – the result might be to curtail the chancellor's policy-making powers even further. However, a solidarity pact is unlikely to serve as a model for the future, since such all-encompassing arrangements tend to be fragile.

Pressures on the federal structure. Although German unification was accomplished with the minimum of change to the constitutional structure, the effects on the balances of the federal system have been significant, partly because of the increase in the number of *Länder*, but mainly because of the economic weakness of the new states. Contrary to the attempt of the Basic Law to create a strongly decentralised federal system, the trend during the 1970s and 1980s was towards increasing centralisation. That trend has been sharply reinforced by unification.[12] The financial weakness of the new

12. But see, for instance, H. Abromeit, *Der Verkappte Einheitsstaat*, Opladen: Leske and Budrich, 1992. Abromeit argues that the federal system was faultily designed in the first place, and that its problems have been worsened as a result of unification because the opportunity was not taken to engage in a fundamental review.

Länder has made them far more dependent on the federal government, and dependency has made the system much more complex. The contrast between the under-privileged east and the affluent west is reflected in the composition of the Bundesrat, creating a dividing line that cuts across existing political divisions. The Bundesrat in the new Germany can produce a variety of patterns of alliances, and the federal government faces different kinds of pressure which have to be reconciled in order to carry through its legislative programme and financial measures. How are these complications likely to affect the federal government, and in particular the chancellor?

In examining the implications of the changing federal balance, Manfred Schmidt takes Katzenstein's model of the Federal Republic as a 'semi-sovereign state'[13] as the point of reference: 'a central government Goliath tied down by checks and balances, powerful co-governing institutions, and centralised societal organisations'. Schmidt poses the question of whether the new Germany can be expected to conform to the characteristics of Katzenstein's model. He concludes that: 'Changes of this order are unprecedented for German federalism. . . . A higher level of centralisation and a larger weight of the parties are part of the price which West Germany must pay for unification.' Although Schmidt accepts that the outcome is a more 'complex process of consensus formation', his basic position is that the new situation 'provides the federal government and the incumbent parties with greater room for manoeuvre'.[14]

Although it can be agreed that greater centralisation is likely, the implications for the federal government of the greater complexity involved in reaching policy agreement are singularly unfavourable. It makes it much more difficult for the chancellor to define and maintain clear policy guidelines. Increased centralisation and more overt party influence can actually weaken the chancellor. He has to act as the ultimate arbitrator, mediating between competing interests, bargaining with the parties and making concessions in order to secure policy agreement. An alternative possibility is that a chancellor who finds that his ideas are continually frustrated by the *Länder* and the parties in the Bundesrat may try to by-pass the usual channels of decision-making. Yet that would be a risky course to take: for better or worse the chancellor has to work through the federal structure, not against it, since any other way invites confron-

13. P. Katzenstein, *Politics and Society in West Germany: The Growth of the Semi-Sovereign State*, Philadelphia: Temple University Press, 1987.
14. M. Schmidt, 'Political Consequences of German Unification', *West European Politics*, vol. 15, no. 2, April 1992, pp. 1–15.

tation with the *Länder* and stalemate in the government's dealings with the Bundesrat.

The chancellor and foreign policy. A leading preoccupation for the federal government's conduct of foreign policy prior to unification was to ensure the security of West Germany. This need, together with the dependent status of the Federal Republic in the Western alliance system, sharply defined the extent of a chancellor's foreign policy options. Subsequent to unification both these constraining factors have lost their force. Instead, a key emphasis is placed on the need for the Federal Republic to assume its full share of international responsibilities. However, whilst the definition of security in the old Federal Republic was clearly understood, the foreign policy responsibilities of the new Germany are not well defined. Three features help to define Germany's changing foreign policy perspective. First, the effect of unification and the collapse of the Soviet Union ended the dependence of the Federal Republic on the United States. Secondly, partly as a result of unification, Germany has emerged as the predominant force within the European Community, adding political weight to its economic ascendancy. Thirdly, Germany has become the single most important external influence on the development of the new democracies of Central and Eastern Europe.

All three features allow the Federal Republic greater freedom in its choice of policy, whether in security matters, EC priorities or relationships with Eastern Europe. Successive chancellors have been able to make the best of foreign policy opportunities, since constraints in this area are fewer than they are for domestic policy. In the new Germany, the use of the foreign policy resource by the chancellor is likely to become more pronounced. However, the new 'freedom' also entails obligations in taking initiatives and assuming a leadership role, especially with regard to European policy.

The problem here is that, in taking on responsibilities for the Federal Republic and launching initiatives, the chancellor may enter into commitments that are divisive within Germany, running ahead of public opinion and leading to attack from the opposition. Thus, Kohl's drive to greater European integration leading to the Maastricht Treaty subsequently attracted strong domestic criticism because of the possible threat to the stability of the currency. Moreover, Kohl's attempts to secure a larger measure of German participation in United Nations operations were regarded by the opposition as being in conflict with both the spirit and the letter of the Basic Law. In other words, although the Federal Republic is now a more independent actor on the international stage, the chancellor is unable to ignore public opinion or the political opposition, and there is no likelihood in these respects that he could make a return to Adenauer's style of autonomous foreign policy-making.

Chancellors in the Context of their Times

Only the normal person, not particularly good, not particularly bad – healthy, sane, moderate – has never set his stamp on German history.[15]

At least, in contrast with previous history, the Federal Republic has been fortunate in its choice of political leaders. The chancellors can all, on Taylor's criteria, be rated as thoroughly 'normal' people. Some have decidedly left their mark on Germany's modern development, and taken cumulatively their record has been impressive: successive chancellors have largely built upon the contributions made by their predecessors. It is naturally tempting to compare one with another, but the problem is that direct comparison of individuals has to take account of personal characteristics, and these are difficult to weigh up one against another. An alternative is to select some basis for generalisation, as with the idea of chancellor democracy, or to construct a kind of checklist of spheres of activity, for instance in looking at the resources available to a chancellor. A further possibility is to take a functional approach: what does a chancellor do, and/or what should he be doing? Answers to this question can, again, take a checklist form, but there may be one attribute selected as being of leading importance – integration or coordination, say, with the chancellor regarded as an 'integrator' or a 'coordinator' and rated accordingly. These models of evaluation and comparison all have their uses, but they are all necessarily time-bound. It is no doubt fascinating to speculate on how Adenauer, Brandt or Schmidt would have handled German unification. But we are unable to conclude whether one or the other would have performed rather better than Kohl. This is partly because of the difficulty of evaluating how appropriate their individual qualities would have been in any given situation. Moreover, the circumstances of the Federal Republic have changed so much over the years – Germany today is a country with problems quite different from those it faced even just a short time ago.

In the course of his 'three lives ', Kohl has had to cope with these fundamental changes. On one level, the first and third 'lives' have much in common, given the continuity of his political style, party

---

15. A.J.P. Taylor, *The Course of German History*, London: Hamish Hamilton, 1945, p. 1.

management and government administration. Indeed it might well be asked whether changes are at all necessary when Kohl's methods have served him and his party so well in the past. Yet, on another level it is clear that the leadership style which ensured Kohl's survival in the 1980s is scarcely a reliable guide for the 1990s. The challenges facing society and the economy in unified Germany are such that a new kind of leadership may be required. To look for some latter-day equivalent of 'chancellor democracy', that is, for the emergence of a powerfully integrative chancellor, is probably misconceived. Instead, it may be preferable to think in less personalised terms and to look at alternative means of securing integration. Most importantly, that would include rethinking the basis of coalition formation. The long-term decline of the *Volkspartei* as an integrative force casts doubt on whether the favoured pattern of coalition government, the alternation of the CDU and SPD in government, will – or even should – continue. If there are changes in the kind of party government we see in Germany, then they will determine the role of the chancellor and a fitting style of leadership.

INDEX

Abs, Hermann Joseph, 98, 160-1, 162, 164
Ackermann, Eduard, 124, 125
Adenauer, Konrad (chancellor, 1949-63): 2, 7, 8, 9, 11, 12, 13, 18, 36, 37, 39, 40, 53, 57, 76, 82, 89, 100, 144, 107-8, 133, 190, 196; and advisers, 158-63; and cabinet, 81-2, 83, 85-6, 91, 97, 98; era, 55, 93, 134-5, 171, 176, 180-1; and foreign policy, 128-32, 196; and leadership style, 79-80, 99, 100, 112-15, 116, 119, 121, 145, 158, 162-3, 167, 179-80; relations with party, 44-5, 46-8, 92; and Presidency, 27; and strategic change, 181-2; succession to, 48-52; and *Westpolitik*, 142-4
Agriculture, Minister of, 82, 85, 159, 164
Ahlers, Konrad, 56, 117
Albrecht, Ernst, 124
Allensbacher Institute, 114
Altmann, Rüdiger, 165
Apel, Hans, 66, 82, 90
Arendt, Walter, 168
Association of German Craft Industry and Trades, 161
Association of Refugees, 160
Atlanticism versus Gaullism, 144-5

Baden, Prince Max von, 107
Bahr, Egon, 119, 120, 125, 134-5, 147, 148, 150
Barschel affair, 91
Barzel, Rainer, 29, 53, 55
Basic Law (*Grundgesetz*): 5, 33, 34, 38, 40, 42, 78, 103, 106, 113, 140, 179, 180, 182, 189, 191, 193, 195; adoption of 23; amendments, 26; and armed forces, 25, 154; basic principles, 24, 189; and Bundestag dissolution, 30, 31; and chancellor, 26, 27, 39-41;

and chancellor's office 108; and civil service, 113; and collective security, 25; Deputy Federal chancellor, 37; federal system, 17, 24, 32, 33, 34, 35, 41, 44, 78, 96, 99, 100, 128, 129, 135, 139-41, 157, 175; and international relations, 28; jurisdiction of basic law, 41, 189; and *Länder* 24, 139-41; and legislation, 34; and federal government, 26, 31, 34-5, 78, 96, 129, 157; and ministerial appointments, 34-5; and parties, 33, 37; and protection of human dignity, 24; and presidential election, 27; and state of emergency, 31, 34; transfer to sovereignty, 26
Basic Treaty (*Grundlagenvertrag*), 147-8
Becker, Kurt, 124
Berg, Fritz, 161, 162, 164
Bergmann-Pohl, Sabine, 89
Berlin Agreement, 147-8
Berlin Wall, 127, 131, 138
Bismarck, Otto von, 106; and constitution, 21-2, 32
Blankenhorn, Herbert, 98, 130
Blücher, Franz, 38
Böckler, Hans, 158-9
Bölling, Klaus, 121, 122, 123, 124
Bracher, K., 182
Brandt, Willy (chancellor, 1969-74): 10-11, 66, 87, 90, 96, 98, 100, 117, 134-5, 145, 169, 196; and cabinet, 81-2, 85-6, 88, 92, 175; and chancellor's office, 118-21; and SPD, 57-62; leadership style, 166-9, 176, 183-5; and *Ostpolitik*, 2, 12, 28, 30, 40-1, 54, 56, 60, 125, 145-8, 168, 183; as party chairman, 65-6
Brauchitsch, Eberhard von, 172
Brentano, Heinrich von, 130, 132, 133, 134
Briefs, Götz, 165